Are You (Still) Ready For W.O.R.?: Without Reservations: Native Hip Hop and Identity in the Music of W.O.R.

Alan Lechusza

Published by Alan Lechusza, 2024.

Are You (Still) Ready For W.O.R.?: Without Reservations: Native Hip Hop and Identity in the Music of W.O.R.

Alan Lechusza Ph.D.

DEDICATION

"This is dedicated to those among us, who rose above us, because they chose to love us, and we didn't push ourselves, they were the first to shove us, sent from the sky and gave birth to the toughest"

– Tru Rez Crew

This work is dedicated to the women – and one man - in my life who have sacrificed their love and lives to support me through these endeavors. Without their strength, courage, wisdom, patience, and love, I could not have completed this work.

A-Ho, Mitak-wea-seh~

Grandma Mary Ann Hernandez/Guzman

Rosalie Blair

Sage Monet Lechusza Aquallo

Papa Robert Russell

EPIGRAPH

Lakota pey-key
    wanta womblie chiawo
    ahyahoo
    e-ho-ne-yeh kiapo
    oyate
    we-io-shkey
    e-yapi-ehielo
    ahyahoo
    (*"The People are excited*
    to see what you will do
    with your knowledge")

"The sense of family, the pride of heritage, the seriousness of the occasion, and the humor of the moment are the same as they have always been when Indians gather."

\- Scott Bradshaw
(Osage-Quapa)

Honde-tahon-da-konde
    Me-key eyohn-da
    kei-yon-beton-gwa
    hey-ya-tahon-da
    wei-eyaho
    (*"Students, take it to the finish..."*)

ACKNOWLEDGEMENTS

"This funky radical bomb track started as a sketch in my notebook, and now dope hooks make punks take another look, my mind ya hear and ya begin to fear, that ya card will get pulled if ya interfere..."

Rage Against the Machine (1993)

The path that has brought me to this point has been long and arduous. I could not have even imagined that this would have been possible except for the unwavering love, care, insight and strength and beauty offered by the numerous men and women, young and old, whom I have the privilege of calling family and friends.

It is first important to thank the Creator; for all that we have and all that we will have in this life and future. Thank you, Creator, for the many gifts that you have bestowed upon us. Thank you, Creator, for the medicine that you have blessed and offered for all the People. Ah-ho!

As a Native person we remember those who have come seven generations before us and seven generations to come. This work finds its place within a continuum of work from Native artists and scholars who have paved the way for me to arrive at this point. The nameless many of the Native Nations within this Nation who have sacrificed more than I can define are the grandmothers and grandfathers to whom this work is forever indebted. Mitak-wi-ase, Ah-ho, All My Relations!

Por mi familia; Lechusza y Aquallo. Nada es impossible! Nada! Gracias para mi vive.

I am honored to have a committee of men and women who have illustrated their care and patience with my work. These iconic figures in their respectful disciplines have earned the titles to which they have received and continue to support the growing research and creative artistry for the coming generations. I have been tested and challenged by these men and women well beyond the confines of the classroom. The echoes of their work and resilience of their care continues to be a mantra for me during my own professional engagements. Thank you for your generous offer to assist me through this work. This is not a closure to our collaborations, but merely another step in the life journey that will continue to bring our paths together. Respectful thanks to: Professor Anthony Davis, Dr. Ross Frank, Dr. Nancy Guy, Dr. Elizabeth Newsome and Professor Mark Dresser.

I am forever grateful to the members of WithOut Rezervation for their creative work that caught my attention and inspired me to invest, what is quickly becoming my life's work, into the arena of Native Hip Hop. The hours spent listening, sharing, and confiding with Chris LaMarr is time worth its weight in gold. I am humbled to know such a man who has endured and persevered through his own trials and tribulations. Inspiring is the word that continues to resound when I think of Chris LaMarr; inspiring.

"Shout outs" are certainly required to a few instrumental people who have continued to support me through the endless endeavors that have occupied my days and years. These people certainly have stood by and defined the terms "thick and thin": Craig Stone, The CSULB Drum Group, Master Vinny Golia, Master Bertram Turetzky, Dr. Edwin and Bonnie Harkins, Dr. Jason Stanyeck, Dr. Michael Dessen, Dr. Christopher Adler, Pandit Vikas Srivastava, Maestro James Newton, Professor George Lewis, Maestro Christopher Garcia, and Professor Robert Zelickman.

Likewise, it is important to acknowledge a few key Native Hip Hop artists who offered a spark of inspiration during the times when I thought that there was nothing left but defeat. Julian B., Shadowyze, One Nation, War Party; keep it "real", keep it proud, keep it sacred and keep it loud!

I shall not forget the many scholars, musicians/composers, multi-media artists and rare individuals who I have met, shared time (and tea!) with over the years. They are many and continue to fortify the ground upon which I walk. I wish them all blessings and generous gratitude for their individual work within their respective fields. Our world could not revolve without your discourse and sounds!

To the many students with whom I have had the pleasure and opportunity to share time and knowledge with throughout the years. Whether it was in an individual instrumental lesson, rehearsal, or classroom lecture context you all listened to the words and sounds that we shared with intensity and passion. You were equally my teachers regardless of the discipline, age, or location. Those hours together are not simply historical moments upon which to wax poetically. Those moments and times are the heirlooms that I continue to draw upon for guidance and wisdom as a new situation and context is presented before me. Thank you all for being so patient, honest, and passionate.

Never last, but always in mind, heart, and spirit. My stepfather Robert Blair-Russell who continues to give his life so that I may be able to strive for a better tomorrow. The selflessness and dedication that he offered to my mother is a pillar upon which to build a new generation. To a veteran who literally offered his life for my generation to be able to create, write and live, I offer you a humble debt of gratitude, family love and the promise to work to the fullest degree in honor of the sacrifices that you have offered.

In the wee small hours of the morning on August 29, 2003, Sage Monet Lechusza Aquallo came screaming into this world. Her first sounds were those of soft powwow music and Maurice Ravel. Her inquisitive sight has been a blessing as she continues to be an inspiration for me to strive to better myself to support her life.

On July 20, 2007, my mother, Rosalie, crossed into the next world. The day before she left this world, she asked how close I was to finishing this work. It was at that point that I realized she was holding onto the years to see me complete my writing. My highest level of embarrassment is that I did not finish nor publish this work for her to see and read with her own eyes. Yet, I know that she is still listening to what we say in the family and reading what scraps of thoughts I leave laying around in the hopes of pushing this work forward. She gave more than I could ever imagine for me to basically live. It is from this persistent attitude and grateful heart that I was "born at 18".

ABSTRACT

Are You (Still) Ready For W.O.R.?!
Native Hip Hop and Identity in the Music of W.O.R.
by
Alan Lechusza Ph.D.
2009/2024

"Its Bigger than Hip Hop" - Dead Prez[1]

This work focuses on how the Native Hip Hop group WithOut Rezervation (W.O.R.) incorporates Hip Hop both as genre and culture, to construct a contemporary sense of identity. Through a critical review of contemporary Native identity within Hip Hop culture, this critical analysis will illustrate that there exists a point of dialogue between the Native and non-Native communities. Considering the cultural and political histories of the forced diaspora of Native people into the urban centers, my work will examine the persistent identity and (mis-)representation of Native people within Hip Hop history through the integration of the sample Apache. A deconstruction and re-construction of the pluralities present within contemporary Native identity is articulated through the development of three identity formations, Tribal, Inter-Tribal and Multi-Tribal. This writing addresses how WOR re-presents and expresses the socio-political issues of stereotype, gender, oral traditions and contemporary identity negotiation in the lyrics, rhythm and Hip Hop techniques of sampling and scratchin'.

My critical analysis serves to the benefit of the large Native and non-Native intellectual communities by presenting a contemporary understanding of the expressive cultures present within the genre of Native Hip Hop. Further, this dissertation seeks to serve as a critical model that permits the expansion, development and further investigation of other Native musics.

Introduction

"I thank Creator for my Life, the strength to live and the wisdom to write"

-Julian B. (Muscogee Cree)[2]

"Our task is not to organize the revolution but to organize ourselves for the revolution; not to make the revolution but to take advantage of it"

-Karl Kautsky[3]

This chapter presents the histories, methodologies and theories used to construct a contemporary Native identity and its negotiation through the expressive cultural and musical agent Hip Hop. By focusing on the Multi-Tribal Hip Hop group WithOut Rezervation (WOR), this work serves to demonstrate the development and persistence of Native identity in Hip Hop.

Ontological Reason

In the late 20th/early 21st century, Native people must still work to educate a broad range of non-Native communities about the different Native histories, cultures and arts. By incorporating the artistic media of the times, in this case Hip Hop, Native artists engage in dialogue with the large non-Native communities locally, nationally and globally. However, this engagement is by no means fixed or stable.[4] As the Hip Hop community continues to grow, its tentacles that have reached into most, if not all major consumer markets on a global scale. These tentacles also find their way into the Native Hip Hop community (Kitwana 15, Basu and Werbner 237 – 259, Garofalo 319 - 351). Or, perhaps, the inverse is the case. The point here is that these very tentacles introduced the non-Native Hip Hop community to Hip Hop created by Native artists, poets, MCs, DJs, graffiti artist and break dancers. Currently, Davey D's on-line Hip Hop resource website credits six pages totaling forty-nine listings of articles and information referencing Native Americans in Hip Hop culture (DaveyD.com reviewed 9 Feb. 2009). The legendary Tupac (2Pac) Shakur offers a very telling quote about the primacy of Native people in Hip Hop: "On the other hand we as persons of color have to remember as was put by the great Indian warrior Geronimo 'the soldiers always had scouts!! You never saw the Calvary go out without a Native American in the Lead.'"[5]

Even with the "street cred" of Tupac, the Hip Hop community still requires a history lesson about Native people. This repeated history lesson has become a birth rite for contemporary Native people. Native Hip Hop artists convey their message with an eye on the education of the non-Native community. These messages speak in multiple voices from a dynamic location of culture within the U.S. and the global arena. Additionally, these messages challenge Native identity as it is constructed, deconstructed and re-constructed within Hip Hop. By placing a critical focus on the music of WOR, I demonstrate how this Native Hip Hop group navigates and constructs complex forms of Native identity.

While it is necessary to include some historical background on Hip Hop and the Native diaspora in the urban center, this will not be the central focus of this work. Instead, this work investigates the conjunction of Hip Hop and the Native migration to the urban center and how it is that contemporary Native Hip Hop artists, specifically WOR in this case, create a complex form of identity through this dynamic global medium, Hip Hop.

In the history of Hip Hop there are several examples that reveal the presence and persistence of Native identity. At the start of the 1960s, Jerry Lordon's song Apache was originally composed as a musical reflection of Western films about Indians. This selection has been sampled and reworked by numerous artists and serves as a living link between Hip Hop culture and the ongoing presence of Native people. Apache (mis)represents Native identity and ironically becomes a driving force in Hip Hop. The Village Voice article "Rap, Rage and REDvolution" by Cristina Verán cites a very telling point by Davey D. Cook (aka Davey D.): "There is an unwillingness to give Native American artists credit for expressing, really, what hip-hop is supposed to be about: the music and the heritage of the people who present it."[6] Davey D. continues further not realizing the historic landmark statement that he waxes poetically: "If an artist like Litefoot doesn't come out with a song that has a James Brown sample or an 'Apache' bassline, people aren't trying to hear it."[7] This statement is evidence of the (mis)representation of Native identity by the Hip Hop community. This dissertation seeks to contest the hegemonic (mis)representation of Native identity in Hip Hop by critically examining the song/sample Apache and four artists/authors through their varied representation of Native identity within this genre.

The Intercultural Expressive Exchange

Hip Hop is a multidisciplinary genre that has its origins in the urban post-industrial New York City community of the Bronx. Originating out of the block parties in the late 1970s South Bronx (Smallwood 172), Hip Hop grew as an expressive vehicle to counter socio-political conditions of oppression for the inner-city youth of New York City (Rivera 52 – 53). The two 1979 recordings, "King Tim III" by The Fatback Band and "Rappers Delight" by the Sugarhill Gang, solidified the arrival of Hip Hop (Conyers 181).[8] The culture of Hip Hop involves the art forms, or "Elements," (Rivera 50) originally beginning with four (DJ, MC, breakdancing, graffiti) that have escalated into the present Six Elements of Hip Hop with the addition of aesthetics/clothing and journalism (Watkins 55 – 84).[9] The collective energy harnessed from this on-going culture has continued to gain local, national and international attention. Hip Hop has been accessed by various cultures as a flexible political agent to debate and critique oppressive colonial strategies to establish self-identification and sovereignty.[10]

The history of Native people within the United States is highly dynamic and complex varying with each Native community. Two forms of historical representation generally emerge when discussing Native history: pre-contact (indigenous history) and post-contact (European history). Between the years 1930 – 1960, Native people were subject to a forced diaspora into the urban centers (Niels 1971). This movement led to the "spiritual and ideological battleground" (Niels 121) that began a struggle for self-identification and self-determination in the 1960s that reached a climatic point during the Red Power Movement of the 1970s (Nagel 1997, Cornell 1988). The ongoing political and ideological struggles between Natives and non-Natives (read: EuroAmerican) continue to play themselves out in the representation of Native people in the popular culture of non-Natives. The resistance to Native representation is based upon sustained cultural (mis)understandings and racist stereotypes. Hip Hop as a postmodern expressive art form allows contemporary Native people, post 1970s, to express a self-representative identity. This research seeks to view how Native artists, specifically WOR, engage the expressive agent of Hip

Hop to construct a complex Native identity that I note as Tribal, Inter-Tribal and Multi-Tribal identity. In doing so, this dissertation demonstrates a form of Native colonial resistance that seeks to advance creative and intellectual sovereignty for Native people.[11]

Methodology of Research

The primary research for this work was conducted from 2002 through 2008. The research for this critical analysis requires a multidisciplinary approach that reflects the cultural areas under examination. The research process included interviews (personal, phone and email correspondence), interdisciplinary scholarship review of Native and Hip Hop culture, on-line review and critique of Native Hip Hop events and videos, conference presentation including critical feedback from Native scholars, performers and composers, personal attendance to numerous Native cultural events (powwows, cultural days, political events) and audio/visual review and critique of Native artwork (recordings, posters, record art, clothing designs, et al).

Interviews played a significant role in the creation of this work. Numerous hours of personal and phone interviews as well as email correspondence (when other means were not available) offer direct and specific focus on issues and questions that help shape the research. Interviewees included Russell Means (activist, poet, actor), John Trudell (activist, poet, actor), Ernie Paniccioli (photographer, artist, author), Susan Lobo (author, educator) and the lead member of WithOut Rezervation (WOR) Chris LaMarr. The interdisciplinary and scholarly reviews of both Native American and Hip Hop literature offer insight and a critical base for this critical work. Film criticism, theoretical journals, aesthetic cultural articles, musicological studies and Native cultural, historical, political, artistic books and articles are just some of the sources that assist in formulating the theories that construct and provide the basis of this analysis.

The on-line review and critique of Native Hip Hop events and videos receive a similar level of attention. The use of the internet by Native Hip Hop artists, and specifically WOR, to communicate and re-construct their expressive identities comes as an added benefit to this research. This inter-active communication allows the conducted research to remain up to date with events and input from Native and Hip Hop communities.

Once I gathered enough research, it became useful to present this work to an inclusive academic community. Conference presentations of this and related work began in 2002 and have continued up to the present (2009). The information and critical feedback gained from these presentations assist in the formation and focus of this work on numerous levels. Colleagues offered a critique not only of the presentation and documentation, but also suggested areas of discourse and research for further review and possible integration into this primary work. Also, at these conferences networking provided new interview possibilities.

It was also necessary to attend regular powwow and cultural events within the Native community. This firsthand contact and primary research offered an unspoken verification that this dissertation fulfills a glaring need in the Native community. The hours of active listening, deconstructing and critiquing Native artworks (audio and visual) not only quenched the academic thirst, but also shed a revealing light on the importance of this subject area.

A working lexicon for Native Hip Hop

Throughout I use the term Native, Native American, Indian and American Indian in a consistent manner with those defined by Devon A. Mihesuah in Natives and Academics: Researching and Writing about American Indians (1 – 22).[12] Like Gerald Vizenor, Teresia K. Teaiwa and Linda Tuhiwai Smith, Mihesuah notes that these terms are inadequate in themselves because they are constructed on a hegemonic sliding scale based on politics and blood quantum (Mihesuah 12).[13] Smith lists numerous identifiers, and their problematic usage, in regard to indigenous people around the world including: First Peoples, Native Peoples, First Nations, People of the Land, Aboriginals, Fourth World Peoples (Smith 6 – 14). The use of the term indigenous "is a way of including the many diverse communities, language groups and nations, each with their own identification within a single grouping" (Smith 6). Though the use of indigenous would be a reasonable identifier for people within the limitations of the United States, I have rather elected to use Native as a qualifying term. This does not undermine the work of Smith, but rather, speaks about Native people who are specifically indigenous to the land within the present borders of the U.S. In doing so, I follow the lines of prescription recognized by Andrew Jolivétte and Teresia K. Teaiwa. Jolivétte recognizes the importance of popular Native culture as a means of actively re-narrating and rearticulating the images of Native people who have been historically exploited through (mis)representation within the U.S. (Jolivétte 6). Teaiwa acknowledges the "mobility and fluidity and a dynamism which confounds and resists colonial, nationalist and even post-colonial representations" (Teaiwa 19). Native, in my work, defines a postcolonial ambivalence articulated through a dynamic cultural, intellectual and political space realized within the internal diasporas of the U.S. This ambivalence affords a flexible re-presentation of identity constructed through the ideology of self-determination. Throughout this writing reference is made to a specific tribe whenever possible.

My use of the terms, Tribal, Inter-Tribal, Multi-Tribal as terms of identity representation should not be viewed as exclusive. The current tenor of indigenous studies, 2007-9, presents an argument based within postcoloniality[14] that strives to decolonize indigenous history and establish a political space and place for indigenous identity (Bruyneel xvii-xix). Electing to use the base-term "Tribal", I do not re-iterate the colonial and political connotations of this term. Rather, I employ this term as a point of departure from its limitations. This analysis articulates a release from structured notions of identity fixed within the dominant hegemony of the West. The term "Tribal" assists in re-presenting the fluidity of Native identity.[15] This re-presentation is a strategy designed to usurp and reverse the infused political implications of this term for indigenous people. By redefining this term "Tribal," I establish a flexible space and place for indigenous identity that may be defined further through self-determination.

My work contends with issues of representation. Frequently, I employ the inverse of representation, "(mis)representation." This offers an alternate reading of how a subject presents a distorted perspective. This reading demonstrates the parallel meanings, colonial and postcolonial, that are being negotiated within a single work.

The deconstructionist theory "signifyin'" used in this dissertation follows Henry Louis Gates Jr.'s definition. Signifyin':

> functions to redress an imbalance of power, to clear a space, rhetorically. To achieve occupancy in the desired space, the Monkey rewrites the received order by exploiting the Lion's hubris and his inability to read the figurative other other than as the literal. Writers Signify on each other's text by rewriting the received textual tradition. This sort of Signifyin(g) revision serves, if successful, to create a space for the revisiting text. It also alters fundamentally the way we read the tradition, by defining the relation of the text at had to the tradition (Gates 94).

Samuel Floyd describes Signifyin' as:

> a way of saying on thing and meaning another; it is a reinterpretation, a metaphor for the revision of previous texts and figures; it is tropological thought, repetition with difference, the obscuring of meaning – all to achieve or reverse power, to improve

situations, and to achieve pleasing results for the signifier (qtd in Perry 61).

From Gates and Floyd, signifyin', is noted as the ability to re-read a text for political gain allowing Native artists to re-present identity in a fluid fashion.[16]

Throughout I place "Hip Hop" with proper capitalization in order to signify that, at this point in history (2009), Hip Hop is understood as a global culture that includes a multiplicity of voices and perspectives. For the late 20th century, Hip Hop continues to be an active postmodern agent re-defined in its own terms. However, in Hip Hop scholarship and pedagogy, there still lacks codification regarding the use of capitalization (hip hop) or hyphen (hip-hop or Hip-Hop). The cultural significance of this codification is not the intent or focus of this present work.

Hip Hop terminology is consistent with its use in the field with such terms as: emcee (MC), disc jockey or deejay (DJ). I include the use of names, nicknames, taglines or other means of Hip Hop cultural reference to artists and authors. Though I have worked endlessly to find the actual names of artists who are more easily acknowledged by their Hip Hop surname, I use pseudonyms, when necessary, for ease in identification across the varied scholarship disciplines that encompass the arena of Hip Hop pedagogy.

Chapter Outlines

Chapter1 describes the diaspora of Native people because of the Relocation and Termination policy of the 1950/60s. This chapter explores the conjunction of this migration with the emergence of Hip Hop in the 1970s. The diaspora of Native people into the urban center assisted in the creation and development of Native Hip Hop. Hip Hop then became an active expressive agent for contemporary Native identity. The Hip Hop group WithOut Rezervation (WOR) engages their Native cultures with cross-cultural connections and influences from the growing body of Hip Hop in the 1980/90s. The chapter uses aural examples from WOR to define the points presented.

As stated earlier in this introduction, the Native presence in Hip Hop is a cornerstone of Hip Hop culture. Chapter 2 is largely a case study dealing with the (mis)representation and re-presentation of Native identity within Hip Hop. The chapter realizes the dialogical importance of Native identity within Hip Hop and relocates Native identity through interdisciplinary techniques that problematize the cultural hegemony and stratified stereotypes of history. As stated previously, this chapter deconstructs references to Native identity by four influential figures within the history of Hip Hop: Pow Wow, Professor Griff, Kevin Powell/Ernie Paniccioli and Cowboy. A deconstructive review of Apache presents both a racialized perspective of Native identity as well as a liberating device for resistance.

Chapter 3 tracks the development of three fluid forms of contemporary Native identity that I refer to as Tribal, Inter-Tribal, and Multi-Tribal. Here, I present how these identities are integrated and are useful in recognizing a fluid form of identity for contemporary Native people. This chapter investigates and deconstructs the work of Stephen Cornell, Joan Nagel, Donald Fixico, and others, who have advanced the scholarship within the area of identity construction for contemporary Native people. The intent here is not to diminish the work of these highly regarded scholars, but to illustrate how these three identity formations, Tribal/Inter-Tribal/Multi-Tribal, can be incorporated in this present body of scholarship to enhance the work of future generations. The chapter applies these identity formations to selected examples from WOR to illustrate their use and functionality.

Chapter 4 investigates how WOR signifies on Hip Hop culture through lyrics, technical devices and samples/scratching. An analysis of selected lyrics and their literary forms explores how issues of stereotyping, gender issues, sexual politics, oral tradition, and the construction of personal/tribal histories are re-presented. The chapter explores the varied technical devices from Hip Hop culture (Sermonizing, Flow/Rupture, Cut/Mix, Layering) and how each are incorporated within the work of WOR.

The final chapter of this dissertation, Chapter 5, summarizes the important points articulated in this dissertation along with examining some of the shortcomings within the current work of WOR. Possible directions and proposed future research is presented as a method of composing a critical field of Native Hip Hop.

In one respect, this work is a large case study of WOR, demonstrating how this Native Hip Hop group examines their Native identity within the genre of Hip Hop. Questions arise such as: "is there Indian Hip Hop?", "what does it sound like?", "why would Indians want to get into Hip Hop?", "what are they trying to say?", "isn't all Indian music drum and singing?", and the list can continue from there. These questions of authenticity and identity construction are confronted just as the undercurrent of racism and segregation is brought into light for critical examination. The transposing energy that affords a drum to (break)beat and a jingle dress to shimmy while listening to Public Enemy is the same signifyin' energy that Chris LaMarr captures when he states, "Are You Ready For W.O.R.?"[17]

BONUS TRACK

This is a slightly edited version of the original Introduction. Only minor changes were made to clarify the language and flow of this updated version.

In the following chapters the included BONUS TRACKS are designed to provide further insight, research analysis, and the development of epistemologies steaming from this initial work.

Chapter 1. Raps to Re-present

"The Earth is breathing through the streets."

Linda Hogan (Chickasaw)[18]

This chapter will present a working outline of how the Diaspora of Native people to the urban centers in the mid 20th century helped establish a cross-cultural dialogue that fostered the development of Native Hip Hop. Examples from WithOut Rezervation (WOR) will assist in defining these points.

An Outline of the Native Diaspora into the Urban centers (1934 – 1971)

Movement for Native people is not uncommon. In the history of the U.S.-Native relations, there have been two major Diasporas of Native people. The policies that led to the construction of these two Diasporas maintained an undercurrent of assimilation campaigns designed to eradicate and eventually terminate Native people (Churchill 147 - 161). The reservation system for Native people in the United States begins to be formalized in 1778 – 1780 after the Second Continental Congress established an agency to deal with Indian affairs in 1775. After 1778, Congress established federal Indian reservations by federal treaty or statute, conferring to the occupying tribe(s) recognized title over lands and the resources within their boundaries.[19]

In 1830 Congress passed the Indian Removal Act thus setting in motion the first forced Diaspora of Native people within these United States (Fixico a. ix - xiv). Native people were then removed from their original homelands to the "Indian Territory" west of the Mississippi into Oklahoma. During the tenure of the Bureau of Indian Affairs (BIA) Commissioner John Collier (1933 – 45) the "Indian New Deal" was constructed to progressively urge and support Native people to reorganize tribal governments, to become more self-sustaining, and to develop the confidence to integrate and assimilate into mainstream America.

However positive and encouraging this appeared on paper, the actual results of the legislation led to the psychological, economic, spiritual, and cultural devastation of Native people. Stephen Cornell points out that the large-scale economic conditions in the post-WWII era assisted in the urban migration of Native people. (Cornell 129 - 132) This included job placement and expanded opportunities through BIA placement programs, including the adoption of the Indian Vocational Training Act (1956), that relocated Native men off of the reservation and into the urban centers such as Los Angeles, Oakland/San Francisco, San Jose, Minneapolis, Oklahoma, Seattle, Dallas, Cleveland, Salt Lake City, Denver et al. (Fixico xiii – xiv, 25 – 26, Churchill 140 - 147, Nagel187 – 205, Cornell 130).

The inception of the Howard-Wheeler or Indian Relocation Act (IRA) in 1934 assisted in the political restructuring of the Native political system that would then encourage the other components of the Indian New Deal. (Neils 7 – 9) This primary level of work not only assisted in the establishment of a retribalization of Native politics, and ultimately Native identity, but also put in motion the Termination Policy set to remove Native people from their traditional lands and/or assimilate them into mainstream America. This act of displacement moved Native people from the reservation into the urban centers and echoed a sentiment that was noted throughout the Eisenhower years that, "[t]he sooner we can get the Indians into cities the sooner the government can get out of the Indian business." (Cornell 131).

Following these political and economic situations, the establishment in 1946 of the Indian Claims Commission (ICC) with the Termination Policies, which included Public Law 280 and the Indian Relocation Program of 1954, to forced Native people to migrate into urban centers and helped to extinguish the reservation system. (Neils 7) In August of 1953 President Eisenhower signed into law Public-Law 280 (P.L.-280) which confirmed the transfer of jurisdiction over tribal lands to state governments in California, Oregon (except for Warm Springs Reservation), Nebraska, Minnesota (except for Red Lake Reservation), and Wisconsin (except for Menominee Reservation) (Fixico 111 – 133)[20].

This transference of power to state from federal jurisdiction of Indian affairs was seen as a method to spur Indian self-determination, but as stated prior, was in reality one of the political strategies designed during this era to terminate Native people. The post-WWII Native population and economic growth, the Indian New Deal policies, the IRA, ICC and P.L.-208 together ideologically recognized as the Termination Policies, together effect the relocation of Native people for the sole desire of eventual Indian termination. Donald Fixico confirms that, "Relocation took its place beside termination as the second goal of federal Indian policy in the 1950s." (Fixico 135).

In the urban centers Native people came face-to-face with loneliness, isolation, depression, and substandard living conditions with the evolution of Native ghettos. Substance abuse and alcoholism became methods of coping with the stress and struggle that came through this disenfranchisement from reservation and family contact. From this point of devastation, Native people found solace in what has become coined as the "Indian Bars". These locations offered more than a mere alcoholic fix for Native people. It was in these locations that Native people could gather, share stories and culture, and, ultimately, find a sense of place within a complex urban society.

Importantly, in these bars Native people were first introduced to non-Native popular music (Lechusza 2002). As an act of resistance to the bar scene, and the possible complete annihilation of Native people who had relocated to the urban center, Indian Cultural Centers were formed, and a revival of the powwow was witnessed in urban centers. (Fixico 156, Lobo 74 – 80, Lowrey 277 – 290). Coupled with these two active cultural centers came the creation of the American Indian Movement in 1968 (http://www.aimovement.org/index.html reviewed 6 Feb. 2009) and the Red Power Movement in the early 1970s (Johnson 86 – 90). As Johnson notes, the Red Power Movement emerged after the success of the Black Power Movement and the Chicano Movement of the 1960s (Johnson 86).

A critical juncture in Native history occurred on November 20, 1969, that would help secure Native inter-tribal (multi-tribal)[21] relationships and visibility and serve as a launching pad for future Native agency, the Occupation of Alcatraz Island. In the 18 months of the Occupation of Alcatraz Island (November 20, 1969 – June 11, 1971) Native people throughout the U.S. were able to come together and foster relationships that previously were severed due to the Termination policies enacted by the Federal Government. Although this movement began as an urban Indian movement the focus was not limited to urban Indian conditions, but rather drew national and international attention to Native issues in general.[22]

Through this activism the urban centers became the location for a dynamic exchange of Native cultures within the growing Native population (Fixico 123 - 189, Nagel 114) thereby leading to a resurgence and re-presentation of Native traditions and cultures (Johnson 96 - 150). Though upon their first arrival to the urban centers Native people were exposed to other forms of creative expressions from cultures both Native and non-Native, it was not until this period in Native history that the appropriation of these expressive styles for their own campaigns became abundantly visible.

The irony for the federal government was that the process of relocation was designed to terminate Native people on every account: political, cultural, historical and, literally, personal. Joan Nagel aptly defines this point when speaking about how relocation enabled this ethnic and cultural resurgence with the application of assimilation as a strategy that was, "...the very processes thought to reduce or destroy ethnic distinctiveness can, ironically, become the means by which ethnicity is regenerated and renewed." (Nagel 114) From this historical point Native visibility and activism were firmly rooted in the San Francisco Bay Area.

Though other locations were visible considering Native activism (i.e. Minneapolis, Chicago, Detroit, Denver, Albuquerque, Phoenix, and Seattle), it was the San Francisco Bay area that would eventually play an important part in the evolution of Native Hip Hop to come from a post-Alcatraz sense of activism and Native pride. In the early 1970s Native people were taking active control of this urban space where cultural connections were situated. These Native cultural exchanges, or Inter-Tribal[23] connections, expanded through the cultural influence of the (large) surrounding non-Native communities. To understand the expansion of space within the urban center which Native people occupied, we are assisted by Henri Lefebvre who notes three theoretical definitions of space: spatial practice, representations of space and representational space (Lefebvre 38 – 39).

Simply stated, the spatial practice within a particular society's perceived space can be a method through which social spaces are formed. Spatial practice, then, is the daily routine of individuals and the networks created within a society. Representations of space recognize the symbiotic correlation between "what is lived and what is perceived with what is conceived" (Lefebvre 38). "[W]hen we create representations of space" Lefebvre notes, "we do this through the conceptualized arts of scientist, planners, urbanist, technocratic subdividers and social engineers in the production of scale models and the plans used to bring these models into actual operation." (Lefebvre 38). Representational space occurs because of cultural and subcultural groups. The spatial practice of these "inhabitants" and "users" seeks only to symbolize their shared social life.

Lefebvre states, "[t]hus representational spaces may be said…to tend towards more or less coherent systems of non-verbal symbols and signs" (Lefebvre 39). Taking this into account, we can discuss how Native people actively took possession of their space as articulated by all three of these theories. Spatial practice was, and continues to be, articulated through daily interaction with one's Native culture. As we will see in chapter three, the dynamic fluid way this space is defined can be along three identity formations of Tribal, Inter-Tribal and Multi-Tribal. An example of the representations of space is within the political activism and dynamism of the Red Power Movement. This form of political representation of space continues to exist as a post-Red Power Movement (post 1970s) affording an influence upon the younger generations. WithOut Rezervation identifies this through their conscious integration of elder Native activists and performers on the recording "Are You Ready for W.O.R.?" who themselves were part of the Red Power Movement, namely John Trudell, Nilak Butler and Russell Means.[24]

Finally, representational space results from the cross-cultural connection between the Native and non-Native communities. It is within this rhizome of cultural fabric that Native transposition of non-Native cultural artifacts become visible and function as an agent for expression. The dynamic intersection, dialogue, negotiation, and cross-cultural connection between culture (Native and non-Native) and music (popular, namely Hip Hop) affords the agency of following Native generations to embrace American popular culture, transposing pop cultural signifiers through an active Native identity. In her work with the indigenous Mapuche people of South America Andrea Avaria Saavedra reminds us of this importance, "that spatial mobility comes from a holistic vision integrating all kinds of different cultural traits that are part of cultural/social/political particularities of what it means to be Mapuche (Native). Spatial mobility creates fundamental changes in existing relationship and work." (Saavedra 56- 57)

Through the application of these concepts, space (cultural, social, and political) is re-contextualized. Centering these theories in line with the Native/non-Native communities, we begin to see how Native people expressively and creatively transpose non-Native expressive culture to survive and to ensure self-determination within urban centers. Following the era of Native activism in the 1970s, the late 1980s gave rise to the nascent genre of Hip Hop that became a vehicle for creative and critical Native investigation.

Cross-cultural connections in Hip Hop

In discussing the blending of expressive traditions, Joy Harjo recounts the important connections between Native and African cultures at the earliest developmental stage of Jazz history when she states, "the Native people were there too when everything was going down in Congo Square," (Harjo 2007). In this section we will see how Native Hip Hop converges with African American Hip Hop and grows into a strong musical movement in the late 1980s. This section will also examine how Native Hip Hop transposes the signifiers of Hip Hop culture into Native representations that reflect cultural issues that are ongoing and in flux within the Native communities. Finally, we will see how WOR constructs a complex form of Native identity that extends through the transformation of Hip Hop.

An outline of the History of Hip Hop: Bronx to Los Angeles (1970 – 1988)

Hip Hop culture has a complex historical origination. Though it is not the intent of this document to outline the entire evolution of Hip Hop, it is necessary to identify the origins of this genre and culture to see how it has influenced, and has become influenced by, Native artists.

Most Hip Hop scholars point to the work by the Watts Prophets (Los Angeles), The Last Poets (New York), Gil Scott-Heron (New York) and Nikki Giovanni at the start of the 1970s as being a precursor to the creation of Hip Hop (Perkins 1996, George 1998, Toop 2000, Fricke and Aherarn 2002, Keyes 2002, Rivera 2003, Cepeda 2004,). Their street conscious jive, even paced rhymes, toasting, and boasting poems, Afrocentric rhetoric and socio-political awareness laced with bongo, conga, funk, and soul underpinnings captured a literary tradition derived from Amiri Buraka, Langston Hughes, Cab Calloway and the Black Church. These early precursors of Hip-Hop transposed themes and forms from a post-Blues genre. The Watts Prophets and the Last Poets both embraced the free-jazz and musical experimentations of the early 1970s by John Coltrane, Miles Davis, Archie Shepp, Max Roach, et al. seeking to move their own literary works into new territories of personal and cultural expression.

The year 1979 gave birth to two origins of Hip Hop; The Fatback Band "King Tim III" and the Sugarhill Gang's popularly successful "Rapper's Delight" (Toop 81, Watkins 15). "King Tim III" by the Fatback Band was a B-side work that referenced a disc jockey personality. Common for the era, many disc jockeys began using some form of rhyming and rapping to bridge musical selections on the radio. This created excitement and interest in their programs and promoted interest in their respective radio stations. This technique is what caught the attention of the public but was not interesting enough to hear repeatedly on a record selection. Rahiem (Guy Williams) is quoted as stating,

> "'No! Nobody wants to hear this suff on a record'. Then the first record that we all heard was "King Tim III". It was rap, but it

wasn't anyone who was known to us. As far as we knew, we (GrandMaster Flash and the Furioius Five) were the best doing it at the time, and we felt like this "King Tim III" guy, he's kinda wack. He's not a real MC." (Fricke and Ahearn 201)

For this, and the fact that it was a B-side selection, this innovative work by the Fatback Band took a backseat to the ever-popular work by the Sugarhill Gang. The Sugarhill Gang was the creative product of Sylvia and Joe Robinson in 1979. "Rapper's Delight" was a success from the start. Using live musicians to record sampled bits from Chic's "Good Times" and the never-tireless promotional skills and work of the Robinson's, "Rappers' Delight" found its way from the hands of radio DJs to the ears of the late 70s youth. This established rap as a pop culture genre in the making.

In 1982 after acknowledging the success of "Rapper's Delight", Sylvia Robinson approached GrandMaster Flash and the Furious Five to produce and release their now infamous "The Message". "The Message" may not have been most successful recording for Sugarhill Records (it only reached sixty-two on the pop charts and four on the R&B charts), but this work signaled the foundation of Conscious Rap, or Conscious Hip Hop, between 1987 and 1994. (Watkins 21) This selection sparked Africa Bambaataa's call-to-action to establish his Zulu Nation.

Africa Bambaataa (Kevin Donovan) was no stranger to the streets of New York. He was a member of the Black Spades street gang and entertained a life of crime and punishment throughout his youth. During his mid youth Bambaataa had the idea to use the popular music of the time to help his gang brothers break the endless cycle of violence. Bambaataa borrowed the name "Zulu" from the movie that he saw and began to work toward anti-violence and unification of the youth through education and community involvement. Bambaataa originally identified his movement as the "warriors for the community" that began to take shape in 1974 and provided a secure foundation for Hip Hop by 1979. (Watkins 23). Bambaataa was a powerful DJ who found his niche in weaving tracks together rather than developing scratch techniques like Grand Master Flash (Joseph Saddler) or Grand Wizard Theodore (Theodore Livingston). Bambaataa was known for his large, powerful sound system that was only equaled to the Herculords (speakers) of Kool DJ Herc (Clive Campbell) and the Wheels of Steel (turntables) of GrandMaster Flash. "Planet Rock" (Tommy Boy Productions 1984) secured Bambaataa's strength within the Hip Hop community.

Around 1971 Graffiti was starting to take hold as an art form for youth expression in New York. It is widely held that Graffiti was part of the culture during the Parties and street events that took place around the Bronx starting as early as 1966.[25] Pistol, an early Hip Hop graffiti artist recalls, "graffiti...it was like a virus. They (New York Police Department) had no way of controlling it; every subway line was completely covered. We had our way with it. We just saw it as art and a way to get recognition." (Fricke and Ahearn 13) It was not uncommon for groups of young graffiti artists to gather at the Writer's Corner (149th Street Grand Concourse) and share works with those master artists of this genre: Blade, Bom5 (Ray Abrahante), Comet, Phase 2 and Taki 183 (Demitrius)[26] (Fricke and Ahearn 275 – 283)[27]

In this same period, c. 1969, Breakdancing became a notable component of Hip Hop culture. Like graffiti, breakdancing can be traced back through the dance/gang culture of the mid-1960s and took a strong hold at the start of the 1970s. Chiefly highly by the Puerto Rican community in New York City, breakdancing emerged in 1975 – 1976 as gang violence was noticeably fading out. The foundational B-Boy (break-boy/girl, boogie-boy/girl, Bronx-boy/girl) Crew was the Rock Steady Crew whose members included: Jimmy D, JoJo (Santiago Torres), Kevin Swift, Jorge "Pop Master Fabel" Pabon, Frosty Freeze (Wayne Frost) and Crazy Legs (Richard Colon). (Rivera 50 – 58) Beginning in 1982 the Rock Steady Crew gained notoriety as breakdancing had a revival in the public sector via the films Wild Style (1982), Style Wars (1984), Beat Street (1984), Breakin' (1984), Breakin' II: Electric Boogaloo (1984) and Flash Dance (1984) (Rivera 72).

By 1974 the art of scratching, beat juggling, punch phrasing and break spinning had been developed and were starting to be used with more eloquence and technical skill. The Master DJ's who pioneered this genre are: Grand Master Flash (Joseph Saddler), Grand Wizard Theodore (Theodore Livingston), Kook DJ Herc (Clive Campbell). (George 16 – 21, Fricke and Ahearn 56 – 67)

The 1980s brought the development of Conscious Hip Hop. In 1987 KRS-One (Kris Parker) released his first recording, "Criminal Minded"

(Boogie Down Productions, 1986). This selection featured a polished use of beats, samples, and rhetoric of the streets for the time that spoke to performers and a developing audience. KRS-One (Knowledge Reigns Supreme Over Nearly Everyone) (Watkins 241) was pushed into the limelight along with another heavy hitting rapper of the time, Chuck D.

Chuck D (Carlton Douglas Ridenhour) began the eminently important conscious rap group Public Enemy in 1987. The Long Island group released their debut recording that same year, "Yo! Bum Rush the Show" (Def Jam Records, 1987). The music and the message of this song is like the first release. Criminal Minded by KRS-One, with its use of hard-hitting rhetoric and fast paced samples, created music that was much more developed and complex. Public Enemy's following release, "It Takes A Nation of Millions To Hold Us Back" (Def Jam Records, 1988) found equal success with their creative use of musical genres like funk, avant-garde and noise coupled with abrasive and socially charged lyrics. From this recording Public Enemy created the bedrock of socially conscious Hip Hop that would spark the flames of intelligent rap for the next wave of Hip Hop.

On the West Coast, the Bay area developed a very important style of Hip Hop called Mobb Music. This Oakland based style is known for its use of synthesizers, low bass grooves and digital drum machines. Different from the looping and sample-based music by this time on the East Coast, Mobb Music did maintain a recurring theme noted throughout Hip Hop culture; a focus on the "reality" of the day and the necessity to express this perspective through the vehicle of Hip Hop. (Murray 15) Too Short (Todd Anthony Shaw), aka 2Short, Too $hort, is noted for this style in his releases on the 75 Girls label (1983/85) and Jive Records (1987). It was this style that brought about the early incorporation of the blues and funk that would then inspire the Southern California Gangsta Style (G-Funk) a few years later. (Toop 185)

Chicano Hip Hop had already begun in the 1980s. The seminal Kid Frost (Arturo Molina Jr.) began his career coming out of East Los Angeles with selections such as "Mexican Border" (Ruthless Records, 1984 promo), "Commando Rock" (Baja Records, 1984) but really caught national attention with his 1990 release "La Raza" (Virgin Records, 1990). Kid Frost, who by 1990 was known only as Frost, was accompanied in 1991 by

Skatemaster Tate (who also crossed over into the subgenre of Skate Hip Hop inspiring the forthcoming Beastie Boys), Mellow Man Ace (Ulpiano Sergio Reyes) (1992) and Proper Dos (Ernie Gonzalez)(1992). (Toop 187) What distinguished these artists was the use of salsa, Cuban rhythms, reggae, jazz samples along with Spanish and English text/slang that layered, like their musical cousins to the East, the rhetoric of the street. It was in this same Los Angeles area a little further north in Compton and South Central that things began to shake even more.

South Central Los Angeles is recognized as the birthplace of Gangster Rap (Kelly 118 – 158). Noting KRS-One's "Criminal Minded" and the Philadelphia centered Schooly D's "P.S.K." (Park Side Killers) (Boggie Down Records 1985), "Smoke Some Kill" (Jive Records, 1987), Ice-T released his debut "Rhyme Pays" (Sire Record Company, 1987). Ice-T (Tracy Marrow) used his debut work to speak about conditions in South Central Los Angeles and presented the sheer hard facts about life as a gangster. The work of Ice-T inspired the infamous gangster (gangsta) rap group was N.W.A. (Niggaz with Attitude) that included members: Easy-E (Eric Wright), MC Ren (Lorenzo Patterson), Ice Cube (O'Shea Jackson), DJ Yella (Antoine Carraby) and Dr. Dre (Andrew Young). N.W.A. took the energy and fury expressed by Ice-T and expanded on this with their ground shattering "Straight Outta Compton" (Priority Records, 1988). It was this recording that helped establish gangsta rap form and placed Los Angeles on the Hip Hop map. The rage, furry filled lyrics were backed by hard thumping bass lines and funk samples that borrowed from the best; James Brown, George Clinton, Sly and the Family Stone, Rick James, Ohio Players, et al, borrowed the Mobb Music use of synthesizers and low bass which then lead to it being coined G-Funk (Gangsta Funk). This genre was known for its autobiographical lyrics that attempted to dispel myths about the street. Ironically, it was this same level of "O.G." (Original Gangsta) style of rap that caught the attention of youth who would by the 1990s flood the commercial and mass market making the O.G. style another Hip Hop genre for sale.

By 1988, the origins of Native Hip Hop began to be recognized through the active integration, influence, and inspiration of Hip Hop culture. The act, and art, of transposing Hip Hop signifiers required the Native Hip Hop artist to be involved in a process of transformation and re-presentation.

In a similar fashion Janet Berlo notes that contemporary Inuit artists have been successful in asserting cultural recognition that bypassed the formation and articulation of a static identity by the (larger) governing body through artistic creativity, balance of self-determination and traditional functions of culture and a sense of the Western art market.[28] This new art exemplified the dynamic, and sometimes extreme view of Inuit culture through active appropriation of modern art styles and techniques including sculpture, drawing and graphic art. These artistic works "transformed in both discourse and practice [are able] to express their active [rather than passive] relations..." to the larger non-Inuit community (Graburn 150). This similar process of traditional through contemporary transformation is seen in multiple fashions throughout Native artists including Southwestern pottery (Wade 1986) and Pacific Northwest transformation masks (Holm and Reid 1975).

This method of creative expression allowed these contemporary Native artists the ability to control their social and cultural relationships internally (Tribal) as well as externally (Inter-/Multi-Tribal)[29]. Difference in cultural signifiers offered a means of discourse and a creative entry, not limitation, within the expressive arts. For these Native artists, then, the space and method of identity representation, and eventual re-presentation, were self-defined, establishing an active point of cultural agency. Graburn confirms this method of identity re-presentation and transposition through artist expression when he stated, "[o]bjects, with their multivalent potentials, seem uniquely able to carry out such symbolic projects." (Graburn 150)[30] This is akin to the process WOR established, and continues to undertake, as they shape their creative work using the genre of Hip Hop.

WOR takes active possession of the spatial dialectic present within Hip Hop transposing these internal/external relationships to construct a complex form of Tribal identity. Through this process, WOR is also able to communicate current relevant issues to the (large) non-Native community in a manner like those African American artists who have come through the rank and file of Hip Hop. WOR supercedes historical limitations prescribed to Native people through the dynamic integration of Hip Hop from the1980s.

Toward the formation of Native Hip Hop
(1988 – 1994)

Building upon the inter-cultural connections between the African American and Native communities in the urban centers Native Hip Hop begins to develop within the late 1980s, capitalizing upon the energy and activism of the Red Power Movement from the 1970s. As stated previously, Hip Hop began to be developed as a complete artistic movement in 1979 and led to full-scale popular recognition by 1982 (Watkins 9 – 33). Native Hip Hop, around 1988, has similar origins in both Los Angeles/Long Beach and the San Francisco Bay Area in California. The literary and musical works of the Native poets, musicians and performers like John Trudell, Floyd "Red Crow" Westerman, Charlie Hill et al, in these multi-cultural cities inspired a generation of Native youth in the post-Alcatraz Island Occupation era (post-1971) (Lechusza 2002).

Historically Los Angeles and Orange County have been important cultural references in contemporary Native history (Lobo and Peters 2001). Likewise, the San Francisco Bay Area continued to remain involved with Native activism, arts and culture particularly stemming from the post-Alcatraz era of the 1970s. (Carocci 263 – 282). Grey Paul Davis, aka Litefoot, acknowledges Los Angeles and Long Beach as being centrally important locations for his development as a Hip Hop artist beginning around 1988. The original members of the Native Hip Hop group WithOut Rezervation (Kevin Nez, Corey Aranaydo, Mike Marin and Chris LaMarr) all originate from the San Francisco Bay area and continue to recognize this location as an important genesis of their work within the Hip Hop community that eventually extended into the Native community[31]. WOR first begins to form around the mid 1980s in the Intertribal Friendship House in Oakland, California. It was here in this Indian cultural center that they began to share thoughts, music, and individual interest in Hip Hop. Just as Grey Paul Davis referenced the origin of Native Hip Hop in Southern California in 1988, Chris LaMarr of WOR references the development of Native Hip Hop in the Bay area in this same year with the complete formation of WOR as an underground Hip Hop group (LaMarr phone interview 14 Dec 2008).

Both WOR and Litefoot produced their first Hip Hop works in October/November 1988. However, it is not until 1992 that these artists find larger success. Ironically it is this same year, 1992, that is recognized by the non-Native community as the 500th anniversary of Christopher Columbus' arrival and discovery of the "New World". Taking a lead from the political energy and critical response to the national celebrations that are visible at this time, WOR begins to gain regional and national attention through concerts and radio airtime particularly of their selection "Was He a Fool? (Columbus)" (LaMarr phone interview 2008). In a similar gesture during this year, Litefoot formed his Red Vinyl Records and began releasing his own work through this record label. 1992 is the year in which Litefoot self-identified his Hip Hop style as "maturing", affording him national distribution of his recordings with commercial success with a steady increase through 1994. (Winter 2003) In 1992, WOR was approached by Canyon Records to produce a recording that would within two years become the now infamous national debut recording Are You Ready For W.O.R.?. This 1994 recording acknowledges WOR as the first Native Hip Hop group to release a work on a major label.

From this timeline and representation within the forming genre of Native Hip Hop, it is plausible to argue that Litefoot can be attributed was one of, if not the first Native Hip Hop solo artist, while WOR can be recognized, without a doubt, as the first Native Hip Hop group. One can follow the origins of Native Hip Hop as a genre beginning in 1988 with underground formations in Los Angeles/Long Beach and the San Francisco Bay area, with the full arrival of this genre in 1992 reaching major success in 1994. What divides these artists is the repeated insistence by Litefoot that he is "the only one (Native Hip Hop artist) of his kind" (Winter 2003). What complicates this statement is that Lisa Mitten entered WOR into the Native American music databases on October 16, 1998, whereas Litefoot was added on later February 9, 1999, through his Red Vinyl Records label (www. nativeculturelinks.com/music.html reviewed 13 Feb. 2009). Contrary to this listing, the NAMMY's (Native American Music Awards), which were launched in January 1998 (Prinzing 20), note Litefoot as consistently receiving either Best Rap artist or Best Rap and Hip Hop recording/song since 1998 until the present (2008) with the only exception coming in 2001.[32] WOR, it appears, did not make this listing while other more highly vocal Native Hip Hop performers who glorify a gangster lifestyle in Hip Hop (i.e. Night Shield, Shadowyze) continue to be present.

In 1988 Litefoot speaks of his work as Native Hip Hop only after he and fellow music producer Willie Fresh (aka Big Will) coined the phrase "tribalistic funk" which is a style that he maintains has a very strong street ethic and 'hood authenticity via the African-American gangsta Hip Hop style which originated in Los Angeles/Compton in 1987/88 (Easy-E, Ice-T, Snoop Dogg, et al).[33] Litefoot presently, 2009, continues to perform in a solo context with the emphasis being placed upon himself.

In contrast, WOR presents Hip Hop that is performed and created by Native men that negotiates a group ethic that is consistent with the lineage of Hip Hop crews (Wu-Tang Clan, Public Enemy, et al). WOR further defines their style as being influenced by funk, post-Soul, and R&B popular music forms in a very striking and similar manner to how the early Hip Hop rappers used the vitality and literary insight of the early Rap Masters: The Watts Prophets, The Last Poets, Gil Scott-Heron, et al. Mobb Music was in the Hip Hop sonic landscape of the Oakland that would have a placed an influence upon WOR through the use of their samples and bass lines.[34] Their further adaptation to these musical styles is influenced through powwow singing and drum styles. The distinctions made here suggest that Litefoot strives to formalize Native Hip Hop along the lines of (solo) gangsta rap, where WOR appears to be more interested in the use of Hip Hop as a device that can communicate to Native/non-Native community about current issues facing Native people.

Putting all of this together, we can see that Litefoot works to construct an authentic representation of Native Hip Hop through his own glorified self-image that is itself a caricature and stereotype of gangsta rap. Litefoot's selection "My Chick" (Red Vinyl Records 2008) illustrates this point through the incorporation of commercialized gangsta fashion and aesthetics, urban language and lyrics, predictable musical components (simple rhythm, distorted timbre, limited harmony) and misogynistic representations of women.[35] Litefoot demonstrates a restricted Native identity that is marginalized and frozen in a specific point of time. The flexibility of self-representation is removed and the necessity to restructure and re-present identity is limited to a static form of DuBois' double-consciousness that is defined by the non-Native community. For Litefoot to have authenticity in Hip Hop he must create, for himself, an Indian Hip Hop identity that relies upon a fixed stereotype of Indian ethnicity. Litefoot requires the stoic Native male persona and deceased Indian heritage to persist thereby leaving him as the sole Native Hip Hop survivor. Litefoot's reliance upon a stereotype of Native ethnicity for authenticity is the reason why he is adamant about being the "only one (read: Indian)". If there are other Native Hip Hop artists/ performers, then he runs the risk of being either an inauthentic Indian or an inauthentic Indian Hip Hop artist. However, given how Litefoot elects to construct Native identity, both are void of substance. The gangsta image that Litefoot embraces is translated into an "Indian warrior" image that he romanticizes as a lost, historic Indian culture[36]. "The warriors of simulations, then and now, uncover the absence of the real and undermine the comparative poses of tribal traditions." (Vizenor 12) Given this understanding, Litefoot's use of a gangsta image a la "Indian warrior" is a constructed simulation of Native identity. Litefoot conforms to the stereotype of Indian identity constructed through a non-Native pop culture image of the Native that must function within the limited space and place defined by a non-Native community. "Indians, in this sense, must be the simulations of the 'absolute fakes' in the ruins of representation, or the victims in literary annihilation." (Vizenor 9) Hip Hop defined by a pop culture gangsta image becomes, for Litefoot, a limited space of context. The vacant simulation of the indian[37] that Litefoot strives to perpetuate is defined by Gerald Vizenor as "the absence of the tribal real." (Vizenor 4)

By contrast, WOR seeks to construct Native identity through Trickster hermeneutics. (Vizenor 15) "Trickster hermeneutics is survivance, not closure, and the discernment of tragic wisdom in tribal experiences." (Vizenor 15) WOR's active involvement within the multiplicities of culture(s), albeit Native (Tribal, Inter-Tribal) or non-Native (collectively Multi-Tribal)[38], assist in their reconfiguration of space (social, political, historical) in order to find a balance of culture that is re-presented through Hip Hop as a vehicle of cross-cultural connection. By shifting the emphasis from authenticity to historical socio-political transformation, WOR constructs a Hip Hop Native identity that uses the elements of Hip Hop culture to formalize and continually negotiate a space and place for the complexity of Native identity (Forman xxx).

Xavier Albo defines this cultural shifting for the indigenous people of Bolivia, particularly artists, as a methodology for defining identity through art as the "return of the Native" (qtd. in Bigenho 4 – 5). Taking this concept and applying it to the work of WOR, we can see how this Native Hip Hop group transcribes and re-presents contemporary Native identity through the dynamic cultural agent of Hip Hop. Authenticity then is not based on an essentialist paradigm or a hybrid cultural model. Rather, WOR constructs a notion of authenticity that is in under constant cultural scrutiny at the intersection of their tribal identity (Tribal, Inter-Tribal, Multi-Tribal)[39] and Hip Hop culture. This ontological framework affords WOR a mobility of identity formation that enables improvisation within the form of Hip Hop. As Taiwo recounts in his work on the Orishas, "[r]ather than seeing our existential experience as "definitive', with closed, unified structures, it becomes 'relative', with open unified ones." (Taiwo 118) Hip Hop then, is the site where Native artists can "redefine their intellectual identity, one that allows these various worldviews to tell, form their perspective, their own 'lived', 'perceived' and 'conceived' spaces." (Taiwo 118).

The ongoing question about which Native Hip Hop group/performer came first ultimately leads to a dead end. Multiple and simultaneous origin is the most likely reason that these two perspectives of Hip Hop begin at nearly the same time. Though the focus here is not on the work of Litefoot, his contribution to the conversation is necessary to see how the development of Native Hip Hop is, like any other cultural form, not without its persistent controversies. What continues to be of interest is that Native artists, specifically WOR, represent multiple views of tribal identity within their work that are constructed using Hip Hop to transpose this genre and re-present a fluidly complex form of Multi-Tribal Native identity. WOR begins this journey by taking the lead from several socially conscious Hip Hop artists and activists. In Chapter 3 the application of the Native identity formations and how they are re-presented by WOR will be discussed.

A Brief Musical History of WOR (1992 – 1994)

As mentioned above, WOR formed as a Hip Hop group in 1988 through interactions within the Intertribal Friendship House. The gentlemen who first created WOR settled on this name as a conscious effort to draw attention to Native issues, historic and contemporary. WOR retains the double entendre implication of the name itself. Some examples would be, Native people living without a reservation system, Native people obtaining complete sovereignty, self-representation, and self-determination without overarching political devices controlling, dictating, or defining their socio-political existence, Native artists who may present their socio-political opinions without a fear of recourse, and Native artists who work without legal restrictions placed upon them and their work. These examples are all realized within the present Indian Arts and Crafts Law that was signed into law on November 29, 1990.[40] Since the drafting of this law in 1988/89, that builds itself upon the Indian Arts and Crafts Act of 1935, the Indian Arts and Craft Law continues to question Native identity as an "Indian" artist, certification of Native authenticity within a given art or craft, production and sale of Native arts and crafts as well as the sovereignty of Native artists to define their work(s) traditionally and contemporaneously.[41]

WOR recognized the importance of a name for their group that expressed multiple meanings (Native/non-Native, generational, historical, socio-political) and highlighted the importance of Native issues on a national and local level, instilling a sense of pride and empowerment for a Native audience. A similar manner of identification and representation of Native identity can also be seen in the Aboriginal pop band Yothu-Yindi (mother-child): "Social solidarity is reflected in the name of the pop group Yothu-Yindi who have directly adopted the yothu-yindi [mother-child] concept as evidence of a unified Aboriginal identity through the organization of the band and the meaning of the song texts." (Magowan 147).

The level of consciousness evident in the selection of a name, illustrates a complex form of resistance through an indigenous identity that brings into focus issues of politics, culture, and history. In this manner, any past or previous accommodation, within a non-indigenous or non-Native structure, becomes obsolete. The focus is now placed on issues presented by the performers that re-present a critical (re-)reading of history and culture.

In 1992 the indigenous communities throughout the Western hemisphere were active in replacing the historic mantra of Columbus' "discovery" of the "New World" replacing the "500 years of contact" with "500 years of resistance". (Bigenho 5). As Bigenho writes, "[t]he quincentennial moment brought a symbolic return to the cataclysmic moment of conquest, and indigenous peoples throughout Latin America (and the Western Hemisphere) forced their reading of this event into public light." (Bigenho 5). This was the same year that Canyon Records approached WOR about the possibility of producing and releasing a national record. Canyon Records made a conscious decision in the late 1980s/early 1990s to record more contemporary Native music on their label. WOR took advantage of two opportune moments, Native political energy via 500 years of resistance, and a national record contract, both helping to launch WOR into national recognition as a Native Hip Hop group. By this time WOR has assumed a level of importance among Native youth in both the San Francisco Bay Area Hip Hop scene and the surrounding Native reservation systems. This allowed WOR to balance their work both in the Native and non-Native communities. Embracing support from Native elders in the International Friendship House, WOR set out to "inspire the next generation"[42] of Native people who, by the 1960s, connected with the sounds, aesthetics, and culture of Hip Hop. This form of support and recognition of their Hip Hop work from the older generation, those who came through the political activism of the Red Power Movement and the Occupation of Alcatraz Island, fueled the passionate fire that WOR continues to express in all their work.

On April 23, 1993, the selected tracks for the recording Are You Ready for W.O.R.?[43] (AYRFW) were mixed and produced. The included tracks on this recording came from the large body of work that WOR had accumulated since they each began working within Hip Hop in the late 1980s. In selecting the works for the recording AYRFW, WOR realized their position as a vehicle for Native activism, positive social change, and a place for dynamic multi-tribal connection with the Native community. WOR compiled selections that engage gender issues ("Born at 18"), stereotypes and racism ("To The Sell Outs," "Guilty 'til Proven Innocent," "Mascot", "Red, White, And Blue," "502 years," "Was He A Fool?" (Columbus)) and Native empowerment ("Are You Ready For WOR?", "Skin I'm In", "Time For Some Action").

On September 1, 1994, AYRFW was released, arriving in a climactic year for WOR. Chris LaMarr completed his Law School studies at Colorado University within a few months following this release. From this point forward, WOR now found themselves performing, speaking, and presenting an alternative way for Native people to illustrate and voice concerns that they have in their own Native community. WithOut Rezervation Productions (WORP) was established in 1995 by Chris LaMarr and his wife Heather. WORP focused mainly on Native Hip Hop and sports team clothing, although recently they have been producing decals and other Native and sport focused items. WOR released their second recording, World WOR II in 1999 through WORP records with lower total sales than AYRFW. As of the winter season 2008 there has been preliminary discussion amongst the members of WOR to begin work on a new recording.[44] Chris LaMarr remains the central person in WOR who is active as a Native attorney and educator. Until early in 2009, LaMarr maintained administrative and teaching duties as the Director of the Native American Studies Program at Lassen College. He currently is performing similar duties at UC Davis.

The Cross-Cultural connections of WOR

In composing their "BAND THANX"[45] WOR acknowledged cross-cultural musical influences that, as will be seen, favored a similar political perspective. The selection of people/groups to acknowledge and their placement within this section was, as LaMarr noted, intermixed and in no specific order (LaMarr email correspondence 2 Jan 2009). Following this lead, the BAND THANX will be examined as a whole, rather than attempting to isolate "who named who", which would be an inconsistent reading from WOR's democratic standpoint. Still, for the purposes of understanding how WOR capitalized upon their diverse musical influences the BAND THANX will be grouped according to musical styles/genres.

Within the Native community, WOR referenced John Trudell and Quiltman, along with the Young Eagle Singers and Dancers and R. Carlos Nakai. As noted previously, WOR arose from a post-Alcatraz Island Occupation manifestation of Native activism where Trudell was a central figure. Quiltman was the back-up band for Trudell. Trudell encountered Quiltman after he left the Bay Area and arrived in Santa Monica (Trudell interview 14 December 2008). The Young Eagle Singers and Dancers illustrated WOR's active involvement with the local powwow scene in the Bay Area and their importance in the contemporary powwow arena.[46] WOR expressed their group appreciation and acknowledged the influence of a number of hard rock and heavy metal artists like: Made by Hatred, Blackfire, Culture of Rage, B.S.A. NIRVANA, Pearl Jam, Siren, Rage Against the Machine, METALLICA, Fungo Mungo, Siren, Nine Inch Nails, Tool, Slayer, and Vio-lence. In this listing we can see that WOR was signifyin' on the genre of aggression attributed to these bands. The lineage of punk, hard rock and heavy metal spoke to a contemporary sub-cultural aesthetic present in the late 1980s through 1990s that helped define a post-punk era of music. As with Hip Hop, most of these groups were also quite vocal in their concern for public opinion regarding issues of mass media, commercialization, and the recording industry. (Connell and Gibson 251 - 269)

The Latino influence on WOR came through in the listing of: Los Lobos, Latin Poets, DJ Beto, Cisco, Quiz One and Santana. The range of Latin American styles here stretched from Puerto Rican Hip Hop, ala DJ Beto, to traditional Mexican chorros placed in a pop culture context by Los Lobos. WOR did not suppress the involvement of Latino styles within the history of Hip Hop and their inclusion in this list reflected this sentiment.

The Hip Hop, Ska and Reggae were the most obvious influences on WOR. It was no surprise to find the names Culture Hype Crew, Burning Sky, Rarebreed Tribe, Public Enemy, Ice-T & Body Count, ICE CUBE, Tribe Called Question, Blacksheep, Primus, Deftones, KOAS, Too Short, E-40, Del, Souls of Mischief, Skankin Pickle, Paris, KRS-1, The Organization, Puzzlefish, MCM & the Monster, Run-DMC, Cypress Hill, Fishbone and Quiz One. From this list we can see the influences of what has been coined Old School Hip Hop (Tribe Called Questi and Run-DMC, et al), Gangsta/West Coast Hip Hop (Ice Cube and Ice-T & Body Count, et al), post-Ska (the Deftones and Skankin Pickle, et al) and Reggae (Burning Sky). This list demonstrated WOR's knowledge of African diasporic music that came to signify mainstream American and global popular culture.

Reflecting these influences through a Native creative lens that is aligned with Hip Hop, we see more than the mere theoretical cultural leakage of styles. LaMarr noted, as will be discussed in more detail in the following chapters, that WOR recognized three different musical genres/styles that were central to their Hip Hop foundation: powwow music, ceremonial music, and popular music. This relationship will be discussed in more detail in Chapter 3. WOR illuminated musical roots in late 20th century popular music that is intermixed with contemporary Native music styles that functioned, for the post-modern Native, as both traditional and ceremonial music. By not placing a hierarchy on these styles or artists, WOR outline a conscious binding of expressive cultures, Native and non-Native, in a fluid connection between genres. WOR took inspiration from these genres to re-present a Native identity as well as an identity local to the urban San Francisco Bay Area. What more eloquent a way to call subtle attention to this concept than in WOR's quick fourty-four second selection "Defend the Territory". WOR transposes the "territory" from a limited location of physical urban space to a location of complex Native culture and identity.

Involving brief supporting samples of police sirens and car chases behind an echoing voice that repeats, "Defend the Territory", WOR signals their conscious understanding that Native identity is constantly under political surveillance and requires defending. The second echoing phrase repeats, "the world's only" followed immediately by Chris LaMarr stating "WithOut Rezervation". This affirms WOR's commitment to their level of socio-political activism that is rooted in the mechanics of Hip Hop. Along this same line of thinking, Magowan quotes Stephen Yunupingu, the singer of the Aboriginal Soft Sands band, who stated, "[w]e have to protect the background and be strong because our ancestors fought for their rights. Through words and feelings in the songs we show our political history. We claim the rivers and the land through song. You can change the song but not the land. The land is our marr (essence) – it stays forever." (Magowan 147)

This powerful statement summarizes many of the points discussed by WOR on the recording AYRFW: a political connection to the land, the strength of the ancestors/elders, the importance of spirituality and ritual that is transposed contemporaneously, and cultural preservation and sustainability that functions along multiple tribal levels. Briefly, WOR defined these as: articulation, understanding and individual dynamic connection to the reservation vis-à-vis a tribal cultural exchange within the urban center, cultural knowledge and support foundation from the elders, spirituality and ritual reflected in contemporary ceremonial tradition transposed through powwow culture, and contemporary cultural re-presentation through Hip Hop.

As stated earlier, Public Enemy arrived on the Hip Hop stage in 1986/7 with the recording, Yo! Bum Rush The Show!. In 1988 Public Enemy released their now infamous recording It Takes A Nation Of Millions To Hold Us Back. It is this recording that WOR attributed as one of their main influences in becoming involved with Hip Hop. Chris LaMarr also referenced early funk (Parliament, P-Funk All-Stars) and R&B (Barry White, Marvin Gaye) as important to WOR's development and movement into Hip Hop. This artist and stylistic recognition, along with the before analyzed listing of BAND THANX, helped to align WOR in the lineage of Hip Hop that is rooted in California by way of the New York Hip Hop scene in the early 1970s. WOR took a cue from the critical, conscious and activist nature that has come to define the work of Public Enemy, by addressing the Native political history of the area in which they were residing, the San Francisco Bay Area. Chuck D, of Public Enemy fame, reciprocated WOR's attributes to Public Enemy on a recording by Urban Renewal (April 2000) where, "Chuck D is featured on this bold jam about Native Americans. Entitled 'At Least The American Indians Know Exactly How They've Been Fucked Around' is a reggae flavored song that features a montage of voices and excerpts from speeches from Malcolm X and Chuck D." (eLine Productions Review 2008, reviewed 22 Dec 2008)

Although this political statement did not specifically mention WOR, the sentiment, content and its location within Hip Hop history recognized the importance of Native people. As we will see in the following chapter, for many of Hip Hop's most shining stars, this basic level of recognition was not easy to come by.

Conclusion

By understanding the Diaspora that led to the arrival of Native to the urban centers in the mid 20th century we can recognize the inter-cultural connections between Native and the surrounding non-Native communities. With the arrival of Hip Hop near the close of the 20th century minority communities were offered an opportunity to speak from a personal and cultural position that continually questioned and reshaped an understanding of cultural authenticity. The 1980s gave birth not only to the sub-genre of Hip Hop now recognized as West Coast Hip Hop or Gangsta Rap, but also to the formation of Native Hip Hop. WOR captured the energy and spirit of West Coast Hip Hop transposing this sub-genre through multiple tribal influences. As a result, Native Hip Hop arrived as a presence within the dynamic national and global Hip Hop culture. As we will see in the following chapters, WOR continues to investigate and re-present their multiple tribal influences within Hip Hop gaining energy and attention through the repetitive articulation of Native identity. The following chapter will discuss how Hip Hop affords a fluid cultural and political position for Native identity.

Bonus Track

In the time since this chapter was written there have been developments, changes, and other Native centered points that have escalated the necessary attention to Native Hip Hop. The magnitude of the developed Native Hip Hop canon has bred a younger generation – a second Native Hip Hop generation (1990s – 2000s) – that has positioned their collective voices to speak out for tribal issues, against inaccuracies and atrocities that still continue to plague Native identity and representation. Their collective artistic conscious has operated as a unified pan-Indian progression for the security of tribal communities, advancement of Indian welfare policies, and, fair, equitable, and tribally centered support. The second generation of Native Hip Hop artists have harnessed the implicit energy and contemporary visibility of Hip Hop culture to rescript socio-political agendas as tribal agency. Not succumbing to a token Indian fallacy, essentialized racist referential image/icon, or a sub-dominant marginalized participant, the second generation of Native Hip Hop artists extended the reach and expanded the voice(s) of tribal sovereignty as imposed by W.O.R., et al. who were at the forefront of Native Hip Hop.

Even with the advancement of Hip Hop's global visibility and cultural relevance there has not been enough attention projected toward Native Hip Hop. Those deep within the mechanical system of the modern-day Hip-Hop artistic industry complex still read Native Hip Hop as being an afterthought or a catchy selling item. The inclusive proper tribal identity signifiers and expressed tribal artistic posture for Native Hip Hop artists is overrun by a market sensibility seeking to sell an Indian artistic commodity for economic purposes. To obfuscate this racialized biased essentialist operation, Native Hip Hop artists have had to build their own infrastructure to sustain an artistic platform. This repeated discipline, underscored, and supported by the scaffolding of tribal sovereignty and Indian self-determination, has been a recent echo across time from the O.N. (Original Native) artists. It is this specific call to action that sparked the formation of Indian Hip Hop. The lack of progress in reception to Native Hip Hop is not the fault of the second generation of Native Hip Hop artists. This lack of currency and depth of inclusion for Native Hip Hop is the fault and fracture of the ongoing Hip Hop artistic industry complex and economic capitol. Maintaining a biased profile and marginalized understanding of Native/Indigenous/ Indian Hip Hop, the Hip Hop artistic industry complex itself reverses the principles of socio-political struggle and civic resistance that stands at the core of Hip Hop's origin. At this advanced and socially accepted point in time for Hip Hop culture, Native/Indigenous/ Indian Hip Hop should not have to struggle for relevance or acceptance. Yet, this limited position remains a norm rather than an equitable expansion of tribal self-determined expressive sovereignty.

Embarking on a path to establish their own location of tribal culture(s), Native Hip Hop has progressed into a thriving canon. Earlier in this chapter, Native Hip Hop is identified as a "sub-genre" of Hip Hop. Considering the advancement of Native socio-political activism, legal struggles for sovereignty and self-determination, and accurate media representations, Native creative expressions poised a counterpoint reference that can be read from the Native news sources (i.e., Indian Country Today, Native American

Times, Native America Calling, Native National News, Native News Online, Indianz.com). The struggles for critical Native voices within the Diversity, Equity, Inclusivity (DEI/DEIAA) and BIPOC (Black, Indigenous, People of Color) academic rhetoric, has become another avenue for socio-political tribal struggle. Native Hip Hop has become a vehicle through which a younger Indian generation has been able to capture and construct by, for, and through their own stable references.

The acquisition of Hip Hop's organic nature and roots of resistance have spoken to the younger Native generations, those Indian artists who follow in the well-worn footsteps of W.O.R., et al. The second generation of Native Hip Hop artists (1990s – 2000s) has not come to rest on the laurels of the Native Hip Hop elders. What has manifest in the years following the foundational release of *AYRFW* by W.O.R. is not a new frontier of Hip Hop. The second generation of Native Hip Hop artists have come to form, develop, express, and contribute their own tribal voices.

In the generations since the forced Relocation and Termination Policies, the urban Indian population has continued to advance, in numbers and in/visibility. The Native population in 2023 surpassed 700,000 (757,628 in California, 523,360 in Oklahoma, 391,625 in Arizona). Given these numbers, it's still worth noting that the visibility of Native Peoples can be limited, neglected, and even discounted. This process of erasure – identity, sovereignty, representation, cultural expressions – is not new to Native Peoples in North America. Earlier in this chapter there were outlines of this process leading toward the development of the urban Indian identity - an unexpected outcome vis-à-vis the Indian diaspora across North America.

Still, in this assumed-to-be advanced age and time, the 21st century, Native Peoples must continue to find ways of articulating their tribal identity, sovereignty, culture, customs, traditions, knowledge, and expressions.

The contemporary urban and reservation Indian populations have come to script the vernacular, signifiers, and Elements of Hip Hop to serve as agency in codifying tribal perspectives. The variation that the second generation of Native Hip Hop artists denote is that they have been able to avoid stereotypes, racist ideologies, socio-political unjust agendas, and marginalized institutionalized identity by way of using Hip Hop's vernacular, signifiers, and the core Elements. The expressive energy of Hip Hop stands as a point of departure from artistic atrocities inspired and fueled by resistance action-meaning-content/context. Taking active possession of the socio-political language, media visibility, growing cultural acceptance of Hip Hop, and the global expansion of the Four Elements of Hip Hop, Native Hip Hop artists replace resistance with critical voices speaking toward tribal issues, identity representation, and tribally centered, sovereign self-determined ideology.

#Native Hip Hop artists have an uphill battle to describe and re-present a tribal hermeneutic. The new generation of Native Hip Hop artists install tribal issues within Hip Hop's artistic elements. It can be argued that this manner of operation is one that most Hip Hop artists at some point come to embrace throughout their career. To contest an essentialist reductive view, Native Hip Hop artists are poised to produce strategic creative tribal manifestos within their use of Hip Hop language, culture, and art. It is these articulated tribal realities that forces up against non-Native assumptions of contemporary Indian culture(s). Rebuking limited, neglected, discounted, and, marginalized Indian culture, customs, knowledge, sovereignty, and expressions is a firm core witnessed in the growing Native Hip Hop canon.

Dj-ing, breakdancing, media, graffiti, clothing, writing, or rap, the younger Native Hip Hop artists continue to challenge racist references of Indian identity by way of tribally magnifying and centering Hip Hop upon the areas of tribal culture, customs, knowledge, sovereignty, and expressions. What W.O.R., et al. codified was a tribal lingua franca expressed, as agency of a Tribal/Inter-tribal/Multi-tribal identity. The Indian diaspora formed a point of post-modern/post-Indian identity that possession of non-Native expressions to re-present their own contemporary realities. This revolutionary process continues to fuel the artistic manifestations of current urban/reservation Indian artists.

By couching tribal issues within the non-Native musical landscape the early Indian activist during the 1970s/1980s set in motion the ability for an affordable Native voice(s) to be heard and understood by multiple audiences. No longer was the Indian experience limited to tribal urban or reservation centers. The threshold for positioning attention to tribal issues has expanded. Native voices discovered a mechanism to speak to, and against colonizer rhetoric and structures. The following Native generations followed this pattern. Native artists continue to infuse tribal elements within non-Native artistic expressions. Native Peoples find it necessary to re-script the vehicles of contemporary artistic expression by their own standards. It is this cyclic process expanding the dialectic from Tribal (culturally specific), into Inter-tribal (creating an ebb-and-flow exchange between Native and non-Native expressions), toward a Multi-tribal (a fluid dynamic of non-Native expressions incapsulated with a sovereign tribal identity) creative advantage, the second generation of Native Hip Hop artists have managed to bring into focus proper tribal posture utilizing the Elements of Hip Hop culture.

With the unfolding of time, and the repeated creative developments of the second generation of Native Hip Hop artists, fallacies, defeated historical references, racist ideologies, educational denials, and disenfranchised socio-political agendas are challenged by trial artistic expressions. This is the point of tribal sovereign inclusion and Indian self-determination that the second generation of Native Hip Hop artist face, pivot from, and direct their Native/Indigenous/Indian identities, realities, cultures, customs, expressions, and sovereignty toward as they embrace Hip Hop's flexible artistic Elements.

References:

Sanchez-Rivera, Ana I., Paul Jacobs, Cody Spence. *A Look at the Largest American Indian and Alaska Native Tribes and Villages in the Nation, Tribal Areas and States,* 3 October 2023. Census.gov.

Chapter 2. A Deconstructive survey of Native representation in Hip Hop

"When they hear the drum and the song...they want to live."[47]

Leonard Cozad, Sr.

This chapter will outline the integral importance of Native identity present within Hip Hop culture. An overview of four Hip Hop artists and authors within the Hip Hop community will assist in articulating this discussion. Additionally, a case study of the sample *Apache* will further highlight the (mis)representation of Native identity in Hip Hop culture. The conclusion will present a theoretical strategy that fluidly re-presents Native identity, refocusing its position within Hip Hop. This strategy circumvents historical stereotypes and a racist approach to Native identity.

The African-American and Native Intercultural connections

As we have seen in Chapter 1, the history of Hip Hop is quite complex involving cultures on a global scale. Hip Hop culture exists through the Six Elements (DJ, MC/Rap, Breakdancing, Graffiti, Fashion, Journalism)[48] and they continue to transform on a local/global level. An interesting connection in this history is the use of and reference to Native culture by Hip Hop artists. As will be discussed in this chapter, Native identity is an ongoing presence within Hip Hop culture that has been stereotyped and romanticized. Figures of prominence within Hip Hop culture confine Native identity within a colonialist perspective. This chapter addresses the understanding and recognition of Native culture in Hip Hop by those who have assisted in sculpting this culture. By now, in the early 21st century it is no mystery that African and Native American people interacted for issues of personal and cultural survival. Though these connections may be deeply rooted in history, ongoing struggles for identity recognition and representation on an individual or tribal level persist. The purpose in this chapter is not to restate the well-documented and individually complex cultural connections between African and Native Americans. Such notable scholars as Bennett (1961), Debo (1970), Katz (1986), Forbes (1988, 1993), Weatherford (1988), hooks (1992), Vaughn (1995), Brooks (2002), Perdue (2003) and P. Deloria (2004) have achieved this work. Additionally, the Smithsonian Institute Libraries offer a comprehensive and current listing of books pertaining to African-American Indian studies.[49] This chapter will build upon the work of these scholars and integrate this research with other Hip Hop scholars and artists to demonstrate how Native people are recognized, realized and represented by non-Native, mainly African-American, artists within Hip Hop culture. Melville J. Herskovits states, "American blacks have mingled with the American Indians on a scale hitherto unrealized" (qtd. in Bennett 321). Herskovits continues, "[t]he Indian has not disappeared from the land but is now a part of the Negro population of the United States" (qtd. in Bennett 321). This demonstrates the importance of the Black-Indian, or as Forbes prefers "Red-Black", a relationship historically important in the early development of the United States. As Philip Deloria points out, Black American music came to dominate the popular musical landscape of the U.S., eclipsing Native music (P. Deloria 238). As we will see later in this chapter, this eclipsing does not extinguish Native identity or the inter-connected relationship between these two cultures. In Hip Hop, the relationship between these cultures built upon this historic precedent becomes transparent. This transparency does not erase Native culture and identity. Rather, the transparency indicates the depth of the Native identity's integration into Black expressive culture. The expressive inclusivity of African and Native American artists establishes a continuum of improvisational communication and re-presentation.

Two areas of Native representation appear in Hip Hop: one that acknowledges the historic relationship between Black-Indian cultures and the other that racializes Native culture. This first area acknowledges Native culture and identity within the arch of Hip Hop's history. In this perspective, Native culture is defined as part of the history and heredity of Hip Hop and is limited to only this position. The second area of representation appropriates Native identity through stereotypes producing a negative image consistent with the colonial dominance of Native identity. This area (mis)represents Native identity and/or culture. "(Mis)representation" considers the different modalities of reference, representation, and re-presentation in viewing Native identity and/or culture in Hip Hop, with an essentialist or racialized reading of
Native culture.

The Intercultural exchange in Hip Hop

Adam Krims notes that the "origins of hip-hop [are] reconstructed...and changed" in present global-local contexts by cultures to establish a form of identity (Krims 154 - 155). For Krims, this allows Hip Hop to be created, mutated, and mediated from a local origin through a global representation that expresses identity (Krims 155). As will be noted later in this chapter, this level of cultural exchange and transposition of Hip Hop by Native people constructs a position of post-colonial resistance. Venida Chenault states that an identity paradigm shift is important for "Indigenous Peoples [in order to] reclaim their right to say their own word, reclaim their identities, and name the [Hip Hop] world according to their understanding" (qtd. in Yellow Bird 6). The original four elements (Rap, DJ, breakdancing, graffiti), aesthetics and ideology of Hip Hop may have originated within the diasporic African-American urban community, but, as Andrew Sluyter points out, their transformation, for Native people, are the result of social consequences and conditions that arise in opposition to a colonial Eurocentric mental and physical landscape (Sluyter 413).[50]

Jacqueline C. Simpson incorporates the work of Pierre Bourdieu to define transformed cultural resources as "cultural capitol." These are the culturally familiar experiences that are adjusted to the dynamics of social interaction (Simpson 67). This opposes Max Weber's position that cultural capital is based upon "privilege" (Simpson 67). This flexible definition was gathered by Paul DiMaggio and re-presented as a "fluidity of cultural experiences" that are accessible as cultural tools for identity construction (Simpson 67 – 68). In her socio-political research of Black and Native people in the southern U.S., Tiya Miles recounts the fluency of values and cultural practices that belonged to the "dual and overlapping tribal/racial communities" (Miles 145).[51] James Brooks expands this point in the concept of "situational multi-ethnicity" that he defines as:

[o]ur own intellectual framework [is that] remain slow to admit complexity beyond the discovery and analyses of 'biracial' or 'triethnic' communities, to engage carefully with the cross-

cutting tensions and ambiguities of dynamic cultural hybridity and to do so as much as possible from the standpoint of those mixed-andmultiple-descended peoples themselves – to confound the color line... in ways as yet beyond imagination. (Brooks 6)

The foundational cross-relation between African and Native American cultures, or Black-Indian (Forbes 1988), Red-Black (hooks 180 – 182), makes cultural exchange possible. This allows identity formation to expand across cultural boundaries as it retains a locus within the original culture. This cultural exchange places a mobile dynamic in motion.

An example of this mobility is found within each of the four characteristics of Hip Hop culture as defined by Perry Imani: "(1) the primary language is African American Vernacular English (AAVE); (2) it has a political location in society distinctly ascribed to black people; (3) music and cultural forms [are] derived from black American oral culture and; (4) it is derived from black American musical traditions" (Perry 10).[52] Perry Afro-centric definitions verge on essentialism. On the other hand, a cultural exchange re-reading of these characteristics with a Native perspective would be: (1) the primary language is Inter-Tribal using black American vernacular within Native signifiers; (2) it has a political location in society distinctly associated with Native people, music and cultural forms that include black American popular culture; (3) it is derived from Native oral culture and; (4) it is derived from Native musical traditions that inclusively involve black American musical traditions. This re-reading sheds further light on the inter-connected relationship between Native and, as Perry states, black American popular culture. This refocuses the discussion on the development of culture essentialist and not on Perry's essentialist argument that limits and binds culture.[7]

Davey D draws the connection between Black, Latino/Puerto Rican and Native cultures in a 1999 interview by Necro entitled "Is Hip Hop Black Culture?".[8] Davey D. says:

Hip Hop [is] multi-cultural in the sense that there were Black and Puerto Ricans who put this whole thing down. We lived next to each other and for the most part experienced the same urban problems and in many ways we shared same culture legacy of exploitation, oppression and colonization. Puerto Ricans are really the native Taino Indians who inhabited the island of Boriken. Columbus came with other Spanish settlers from Europe came on over and discovered them. He also discovered the island had gold. He pillaged the island and depleted its gold resources and since Columbus and his boyz didn't bring any women they started raping the native women of the island. Not long afterwards African slaves were brought over. That's how things

7. A similar analysis and expansion could be made between the relationship of Native cultures to Mexican American, Spanish, Puerto Rican and other global cultures within Hip Hop.

8 FNV: Nov. 1999. Reviewed 22 Dec 2008.

got ethnically mixed up in Puerto Rico. Blacks as you know have Native Americans and European blood. Again the European blood was the result of slavery where African women were raped.

Adding to this point of reference, Raquel Rivera cites the inclusion of Native identity as a "popular strategy – which extends beyond hip hop – of defining Puerto Rican culture history in terms of Native American ancestry, particularly to distinguish Puerto Ricans from the U.S. African American experience" (Rivera 158). Rivera recognizes the "shared indigenous American connections" present in these different cultures, African, Puerto Rican and Native American, as a "bond to the 'ghetto' connection they share with each other" (Rivera 158). Rivera identifies the urban industrial complex that has historically challenged Native, Puerto Rican and African American communities.[53]

These perspectives suggest that Hip Hop artists have an historical involvement with Native identity that connects culture. These inter-cultural connections recognize the fluidity of Native identity that becomes a nexus point of cultural exchange. Jorge "Pop Master Fabel" Pabon, of the legendary Rock Steady Crew and Universal Zulu Nation, notes the cross cultural and intercultural connection between Afro-diasporic and Native music and dance when he wrote his 1999 article "Physical Graffiti, The History of Hip-Hop Dance", "[s]ome of the earliest dancing by b-boy pioneers was done upright, a form which became known as "top rockin'". The structure and form of top rockin' has infused dance forms and influences from Brooklyn uprocking, tap, lindi hop, James Brown's "good foot," salsa, Afro-Cuban and various African and Native American dances" (Pabon 18 - 19).

This statement recognizes the same lineage and cultural connection that DeFrantz reveals in his research into the diaspora of African dance

(DeFrantz, *The Black Beat Made Visible: Hip Hop Dance and Body Power*, 2004). Pabon's recount of the borrowing of Native dance confirms the Native contribution to Hip Hop culture. Pabon identifies the Native influence within the multi-focal reality of Hip Hop culture. Further, Pabon recognizes that this borrowing is not limited to an African-Native binary but is inclusive of many cultures, and expressive forms, that exist within the continuum of the African diaspora.

Popular music historians Kip Lornell and Charles Stephenson provide another example of the liberal exchange between African diasporic music and Native culture. Lornell and Stephenson outline ten basic characteristics of gogo music, a musical genre that predates the funk movement of the late1970s and is linked to Hip Hop. These ten basic characteristics are: 1. African- American, 2. Washington, D.C. – based, 3. Contemporary and popular among its audience, 4. Rooted within and for Funk and Hip-Hop, 5. Male dominated, 6. Highly syncopated, 7. Driven by a variety of percussion instruments, 8. Thrives in live performances, 9. Utilizes call and response, 10. Features extended performances, sometimes grouped in suites.[54]

This listing is not an essentialist structure designed to neglect the dynamic influences of go-go music in the formation of Hip Hop. Rather, these basic characteristics assist in understanding the evolution of Hip Hop as it dislocated from its center and progressed creating its own diaspora through club culture, mix tape exchanges, digital file sharing and word-of-mouth inspiration.

This listing can be reduced into three political areas: space, time, and identity (Bruyneel xix). Kevin Bruyneel defines political space as "the lived and envisioned territorial, institutional, and cultural location through which a people situate its past, present, and future as a political identity." Political time is defined as "the narratives of struggle, development, and transformation through which a people historically position itself or is positioned by others as some form of coherent collective identity." Lastly, political identity is defined as "that which binds a group together both through its relationship to discernible power inequities...and through its collective vision of how to generate, sustain, or expand the group's capacity to determine its future" (Bruyneel xix). Collectively, for Glen Coulthard, these three spaces become the "transformative praxis." Coulthard bases his theoretical work on an expanded reading of Hegel and Fanon, defining the transformative praxis, through reference to James Tully, as the "critical self-affirmative process [that] must be consciously directed away from the assimilative lure of the statist politics of recognition and instead be fashioned toward our own on-the-ground strategies of freedom" (Tully qtd. in Coulthard 17). From this post-colonial position[55] that moves to identify "tribal self-determination" and contest the "repressive practices and consequences of the persistent American effort to impose colonial rule" (Bruyneel xviii), it becomes possible to navigate the areas of space, time, and identity as they are realized and mediated in Hip Hop's intercultural exchange.

This process of intercultural exchange between African-American and Native expressive culture forms the basis of my hypothesis for the evolution of Native Hip Hop. In this hypothesis Hip Hop serves as an agent for identity construction. For the purposes of this dissertation, the spatial arena is the art form of Hip Hop, realized within the African-American community that is transposed by Native Hip Hop artists, here namely WOR. The signifiers of Hip Hop (i.e., language, sampling, scratching, beat, et al) are transposed through Native engagement and will be discussed in the examples, "Tribal Shouts" and "To The Sellouts" in Chapter 3 and the four critical elements of Hip Hop

(sermonizing, cut/mix, rupture/flow, layering) in Chapter 4. The temporal space, for the purposes of this dissertation, is limited to the origin of Native Hip Hop, c. 1988, until the release of *Are You Ready For W.O.R.?* in

1994. This has already been discussed in Chapter 1, through the evolution of Native Hip Hop, and will be revisited in expanded form in Chapters 3 and 4.

The arena of identity occupies the greatest portion of this critical investigation. Identity will be discussed later in this chapter with an analysis of three (mis)representations of Native identity, in Chapter 3 with the construction of three identity formations and, in Chapter 4 with socio-linguistic techniques.[56] In each subsequent chapter, the hypothesis that I pose will be challenged and applied to audio and text examples from WOR to demonstrate the complexity of this exchange. Throughout this process the articulation of the Native identity formations (Tribal, Inter-Tribal, Multi-Tribal13) will be recognized, considering the fluid manifestations that arise from the interaction of these formations.

To begin re-reading Lornell and Stephenson's list it will be useful to see how the Lumbee have sustained and re-presented their musical style. In 1714, John Lawson identified a distinct democratic vocal style that that is "formed with…Equality and Exactness that [is] admirable how they should continue these Songs without once missing to agree" (Maynor 324).[14] Lawson also identifies the extensive use of rattles, gourds, sticks and drums in traditional Lumbee ceremonial music (Maynor 324). In 1930, John Swatson concurred the same results as Lawson noting that the music expanded and is now embedded in both ceremonial and social contexts. Lawson further noted the favoring of syncopation and vocal melodic complexity as dominant musical characteristics (Maynor 323 - 324). Charles Hudson notes in <u>The Southeastern Indians</u> the expanded length of musical forms, the complexity and tension present in vocal melodies and timbre, the use of repetition (antiphonal, responsorial and phrases) and the development of call-and response in Southern Indian music (Maynor 325).[57] Malinda Maynor echoes the points identified previously and notes the expansion of Lumbee ceremonial/social musical network to include gender balance, solidification of call-and-response, and the use of extended suites that thrive in the current (2009) religious community (Maynor 324 - 325).

Lumbee musical history (c. 1700 – 2002) contains a transformed "musical mixture" of African and European styles (Maynor 328 - 329).

African slavery imported to North/South Carolina established a cultural connection between the Lumbee (Native) and African (Black). These connections established "core influences" that included singing and rhythmic styles (Maynor 330). European contact brought the influence of notated music, expanded forms, and musical pedagogy to the Lumbee in the 1800s as shape note tune books (Sutton 1982). To preserve their musical traditions from European colonialism, cultural resistance took the form of transformation in Black traditions and isolation. Eileen Southern recounts that [c]ircumstances seemed to necessitate this [transformational] shift in survival strategy...we were ready to embrace change as a means of survival, [as] shifting racial attitudes and growing local hostilities toward Indians caused us to retreat further into our swamplands. (qtd. in Brooks 336).

Brett Sutton confirms that "[s]ince contact with Europeans and Africans, Lumbees have perpetuated and enriched [their] traditions through... use and adaptation" (qtd. in Brooks 339). The Lumbee initiated a postcolonial strategy by the adaptation and transformation their musical tradition in response to the colonization of the South.

Mike Cummings recognizes the adaptation and transformation of Lumbee music that is performatively expressed in non-Lumbee musical styles including "classic country/gospel...karaoke-style singing...and Top 40 hits" (Maylor 328 – 329). Electronic instruments were introduced after 1940 that further transformed the Lumbee (Native) musical characteristics within non-Lumbee (African-American) musical styles. Finally, Maynor states that contemporary Powwow music is the current (2002) musical form that embraces the ceremonial/social music characteristics of the Lumbee. Though Powwow music is not indigenous to the Lumbee, this genre has, for Maynor, absorbed the ceremonial/social characteristics of Lumbee musical expression (Maynor 325). Contemporary Lumbee music is the result of a historic process of exchange, between Black, European and Lumbee cultures, which transform and reinterpret expressive styles to construct a complex identity (Maynor 340). The agency of transformation, in contemporary Lumbee music, operates along the postcolonial lines of Multi-Tribal identity construction. This outline should not be taken as a pan-Indian representation. Rather, this is one example of how Native music can be transformed through non-Native intercultural exchange to construct a complex Native identity.[58] The Lumbee example is consistent with my reading of the Lornell and Stephenson list and the intercultural exchange available through Powwow music.

Analyzing the nexus of African diasporic music and Native culture, we find a similarity first to contemporary Native Powwow culture and music that then signifies on Hip Hop culture and music that finally transposes these signifiers on Native Hip Hop. With the transposition of these ten basic characteristics on Powwow culture and music, we find the following:

1. Native (American), 2. North American – based,[59] 3. Contemporary and quite popular among Native audience(s) – particularly as an inter-tribal form, 4. Rooted in traditional Native based music(s), 5. Balanced gender roles, originating from a male-dominated performing style, [18] 6. Highly syncopated – both Northern and Southern Powwow drum styles, 7. Driven by a variety of percussion instruments (i.e., Gourd Rattle in Southern California, Rattle and Shakers in the Kiowa based Gourd Dance Society, Frame/Hand Drum viewed throughout the North Eastern U.S. and the Powwow Drum), 8. Thrives in live performances (which is the Powwow itself!), 9. Utilizes call and response[19] – literal representation in Northern/Southern Powwow drum/singing styles, 10. Features extended performances, sometimes grouped in suites (i.e., grouping of songs performed in Southern Powwow style like the Gourd Dance and Northern Powwow style as the "penny songs" and honoring songs).[20]

This reading and exchange of an African-American based musical genre, go-go music, that is a sonic cousin to Hip Hop, with contemporary Native Powwow music, begins to identify the close similarity between these two genres. This exchange is the critical transformative praxis that will be outlined, as stated earlier, throughout the following chapters. In summary, the principle of exchange that I define recognizes that Hip Hop and Powwow music both occupy an intermediate space between African and Native American cultures. Following the work by Kevin Bruyneel, this intermediate space is constructed as a negotiation operating beyond dominant views of space, place, and identity.[60] Cultural exchange between the musical genres Hip Hop and Powwow is the politically liberal transformative location of a dynamic culture. Native Hip Hop is the result of this cultural exchange. This exchange brings to light multiple sonic realities and identities (read: MultiTribal)[61] that dynamically co-exist. As we will see in the following chapters, this fluid exchange of identity establishes Native Hip Hop as a Multi-Tribal identity.

For Ann Axtmann the power of "performative action" in Powwow music is also visible in Hip Hop:

> Resistance to oppression and great ingenuity and strength in the face of horror is part of the story. As people live and remember through the flesh, blood, mind, and soul, moving bodies express and communicate the intensity of these experiences. (qtd. in Lawlor 131)

The resistance to oppression in Hip Hop is expressed through the ingenuity of its artists. The "flesh, blood, mind, and soul" become real (read: lived) and metaphorical (read: imagined) through the application of Hip Hop's Six Elements.[62] Axtmann's reading brings the physicality of Powwow music into the ideology of Hip Hop yielding a "positive embodiment of what it means 'to be Indian'" [read: Native Hip Hop] (Axtmann qtd. in Lawlor 131). The integration here follows Stuart Hall's concept of cultural identity that is "constantly producing and reproducing themselves anew, through transformation and difference" (Hall qtd. in Pulitano 134). Taiaiake Alfred adds to Axtmann and Hall his term "independency" (Alfred 92). Independency, Alfred defines, is the "coexistence [and] social balance between...peoples, and a political relationship founded on an ethic of pluralism in a framework of respect" (Alfred 92). For this action to exist, Alfred notes that it requires the dual principles of respect and honor of difference ("independency") as well as the "organization of one's mind and attitudes around the idea of the sharing of space ("interdependence")" (Alfred 93).[63] Axtmann, Hall and Alfred outline a postcolonial identity that challenges colonial stasis and representation by transforming cultural space and differences in a self-determined fashion. The transformation of Powwow music and Hip Hop, because of their cultural exchange, is the transformative praxis.

Mary Lawlor presents the "third race" (Native) in contrast to the biracial world of White-Black racial constructions. The "third race" is like Homi Bhabha's "Third Space"[25] where the space between two points of reference becomes the departure point for critical discourse. Limiting the discussion as Lawlor does to race, an essentialized culture forms that is defined by its opposition to an "Other." Both Lawlor and Bhabha seek to define a poststructuralist space that is articulated outside of Western hegemony and essentialism to recognize "the possibilities of new revelations" (Maylor qtd. in Brooks 14). However, they continue to situate their work within the limited boundaries articulated by binaries of the imperial West (Bruyneel 7 – 8). Lawlor and Bhabha attempt to create new "networks of associations between objects and ideas, cueing and channeling interpretations without closing down alternative readings" (Thompon qtd. in Da Vasques 163). These networks only become visible through an expressive agent that, for this dissertation, is Hip Hop.

Once contemporary urban Natives appropriated Hip Hop culture they influenced this expressive culture with their own complex form of expression informed by Native cultures (traditional and contemporary). The "objects and ideas" prevalent in the urban center became the dynamic foundation of cultural expression for the newly relocated Native people. The fluid structure of Hip Hop culture offered urban Native people the ability to "cue and channel interpretations" of their own culture(s) "without closing down alternative readings". This complex representation of Native culture established in the urban center through the creative force of Hip Hop assisted in the formation of

Native Hip Hop. However, there are tropes in Hip Hop's history that exclude a

Native perspective or identity. These tropes repeat and reinforce the

(mis)representation of Native identity within Hip Hop.

(Mis)Represented Native identity in Hip Hop

The intercultural connection between African and Native Americans in the contemporary era is not a new phenomenon. The exchange of culture that arises out of these intercultural connections creates a complexity of issues related to identity. Hip Hop has been defined through an African-American diaspora that includes the influence of Brazil (Stanyeck 2004), England (Hebdidge 1979/1998), the Trans-Black Atlantic (Gilroy 1993) and Jamaica (Hebdidge 1987, Toop 2000, Krims 2000). Additionally, Hip Hop historians have noted the global tranformation of regional Hip Hop styles (Perkins 1996, Rahn 2002, Rivera 2003, Perry 2005, Chang 2006).

Four key figures at the onset of Hip Hop culture helped formalize the intercultural connection between African-American and Native culture: Pow Wow, Professor Griff, Kevin Powell/Ernie Paniccioli. And Cowboy.[64] These performers/authors all have contributed to the formation of Hip Hop culture. With their importance and visibility within the global arena, they either consciously or unconsciously neglect to acknowledge the Native presence identity in the music and culture.

Pow Wow[65] (Robert Darrell Allen)

Pow Wow (Robert Darrell Allen) is an original member of the MC group

Soul Sonic Force that included G.L.O.B.E., Mr. Biggs and Africa Bambaataa.

Robert Allen boldly introduces the name "Powwow" which, as noted by Lassiter (1998), Browner (2000/2002), Ellis (2003), Lawlor (2006) et al, is an inter-tribal cultural event that has multiple functions as ritual, ceremony, rejuvenation and the revival of culture, social interaction, and competition. By appropriating this name, is the artist Pow Wow stating that he represents physical manifestation of all these characteristics? Is Robert Allen exercising an authority over the representation of this Native cultural form by use, definition, and repetition? Or rather, is Pow Wow lessening the dynamic impact that this cultural signifier has established for contemporary Native people through mis-appropriation? Within the scope of Hip Hop's history, it could be argued that Pow Wow constructs an active space and place for Native people within Hip Hop culture by the very use of the signifier "powwow".

Given that Pow Wow is a founding member of the Soul Sonic Force, it would be logical to conclude that Pow Wow assisted in placing Native identity at Hip Hop's table. By the very presence of his DJ name, Pow Wow recalls the complexity of history, meaning and representation of Native people within the U.S. As a result, Pow Wow functions as an agent for cultural change for Native people within Hip Hop culture. This is evident in Pow Wow's raps.

In the selection "Renegades of Funk",[66] Pow Wow refers to Chief Sitting

Bull:

Prehistoric ages and the days of ancient Greece
On down through the Middle Ages

> When the earth kept going through changes
> There's a business going on, cars continue to change
> Nothing stays the same, there were always renegades
> Like Chief Sitting Bull, Tom Payne
> Like Martin Luther King, Malcolm X
> They were renegades of the atomic age So many renegades (Planet Rock 1984)

Situating the prominent Hunkpapa, Lakota Native figure Sitting Bull (who was born Hoka-Psice (Jumping Badger) and later took his father's name of 'Sitting Bull') within this now classic Hip Hop selection, Pow Wow draws attention to the influence and cross-cultural connection between the African and Native American communities. In this selection, Pow Wow, Bambaataa and the entire Soul Sonic Force connect these key figures (American, AfricanAmerican, Native) in American history who stood up for the civil rights of their communities, despite the official opposition to their campaigns within the U.S., Pow Wow recognizes Sitting Bull's influence on activism today.

In contrast to this sense of empowerment drawn from the inclusion of such a highly visible Native figure as Sitting Bull is the stereotypic use of Native regalia by the Soul Sonic Force. Pow Wow consistently wears a stereotypical Plains Indian headdress along with other Afro-Centric regalia. This is seen not only on the album cover to "Planet Rock" but also on the video for "Renegades of Funk."[67] Why would a seemingly politically conscious rap group present a stereotypical Indian image in their performance space? One plausible answer would be that Pow Wow is signifying on the Mardi Gras Indian tradition of New Orleans; a tradition that respects Native American traditions even to the point of considering the costumes to be traditional and "ritual" in nature.[31] Henry Durrell is mentioned by Smith as noticing the dress of the Mardi Gras Indians as being, *"well dressed"*[32] (Smith 55).

David Penny, who is supported by Lipsitz, Van Spankeren, Draper and Smith through their respective work in this field, most clearly articulates the integration and "natural synthesis" of the Black American culture, via the

"Old World African culture" and Native culture both in song, dance, dress and culture (Penny 39 – 40). Furthermore, Smith notes regarding the history of the Mardi Gras Indian:

> The largely underclass black Indian gangs remain outlaws. They remain tribal and anonymous, perform their own music, and march through the city on the back streets, where they come and go as they please...the black Indians refuse to subject themselves to the humiliation of being monitored and controlled by hostile authorities. To do so would betray the function and historical meaning of their independent spirit. (Smith 48)

Pow Wow's use of Native costume is directly in line with the Mardi Gras Indian tradition. Further, this Mardi Gras tradition connects directly with the attitude and ideology of the Zulu Nation, that included Pow Wow as a member. Resistance to outside surveillance and authority is a prevalent theme in the Zulu Nation that reflects the post-colonial ideology inherent in Hip Hop culture. There is little argument that Africa Bambaataa is one of the two dominant forces in the evolution of Hip Hop culture (Toop 2000). However, Africa Bambaataa exercises his self- proclaimed dominance over

31
A useful ethnography of the Mardi Gras Indians can be found in Draper, David E. The Mardi Gras Indians: The Ethnomusicology of Black Associations in New Orleans. Unpublished Ph.D. dissertation. New Orleans: Tulane

University,1973., Smith, Michael P. Behind the Lines: The Black Mardi Gras Indians and the

New Orleans Second Line., VanSpanckeren, Kathryn. The Mardi Gras Indian Song Cycle: A Heroic Tradition and Lipsitz, George. Mardi Gras Indians: Carnival and Counter-Narrative in Black New Orleans.

32 Emphasis in the original.

Hip Hop culture even to the point of being quoted as stating that his approval is "factology."[68] Bambaataa extends his hegemonic ideology through the Zulu Nation.[69] Pow Wow, therefore, does not consider his (mis)representation of Native culture as being stereotypical, but respectful of Native culture.

Africa Bambaataa is also photographed elsewhere donning a stereotypical Plains Indian headdress emphasizing the primary colors of the American flag: red, white and blue. By maintaining the presence of the headdress in performance and publications (video, audio and print) Pow Wow, Africa Bambaataa along with the other members of the Soul Sonic Force, recontextualize the use of Native regalia in Hip Hop in order to draw attention to the history and issues of Native people for non-Native communities. This then, is the Soul Sonic Force's attempt to construct a pan-Indian identity. This respect is undermined by the misuse of Plains style headdress. The repeated misuse of the flamboyantly colored headdress situates Native culture in a homogenous category defined by a displaced, commercialized representation of Plains Natives. This aligns the Soul Sonic Force's use of the headdress as an "Object hobbyist" representation defined by Philip Deloria (129 – 135). The "Object hobbyist favored the replication of old Indian artifacts and costumes" (P. Deloria129). Joanne Barker continues this thought when she notes that hobbyists "prefer[ed to] retreat into nostalgia and transcendence from a modern, impersonal society through Indian beliefs that they believed connected them to a more authentic, natural truth" (Barker 58).[70]

The headdress becomes a vacant racialized stereotype that (mis)represents

Native identity in Hip Hop culture.

Pow Wow, along with Bambaataa, could have used their artistic platform to discuss, present and illuminate the important inter-cultural connections between Black and Native cultures. Rather than offering an opinion about Native issues, Pow Wow makes these points loud and clear through his consistent (mis)representation of Native regalia. Pow Wow's (mis)representations enable a dialogue about Native culture originating at the nexus of traditional and popular culture.

Given the importance of the Soul Sonic Force in the history of Hip

Hop, one would hope to believe that the appropriation of Native regalia by Pow Wow would be more than a token gesture. This would make a political statement about Native representation within the Hip Hop lexicon. Rather, what remains is a negative trope of Native identity that is commercially reproduced and transmitted. Pow Wow's stoic silence about the use and incorporation of Native regalia leaves his actions subject to critical analysis. The romantic image of the Indian that is embodied within the commercialized artifact of the (mis)represented headdress remains a co-opted signifier of Native identity in Hip Hop culture.

Professor Griff (Richard Griffin)

Professor Griff is an original and founding member of Public Enemy who was dismissed in 1989 by Chuck D, Flavor Flav, DJ Lord and Terminator X due to his overly anti-Semitic raps stemming from his militant Afro-Centric rhetoric. The popularity of the movie *Do The Right Thing* offered Public Enemy a voice in the mainstream Professor Griff took advantage of this exposure when he spoke out against the Jewish community. He was removed from Public Enemy and the group reformed without him in 1990 (Toop 187).

Professor Griff is half Blackfoot and, despite his continued access and ability to communicate with activist circles and post-secondary students, he does not recognize his Native heritage. This is inconsistent for this controversial figure who lectures about issues of Afro-centrism, politics, and Hip Hop. One would imagine that Professor Griff would acknowledge the politically charged history and politics of Native people, even his own Blackfoot nation. These issues could fuel for fire for his presentations and creative work that speak against the U.S. government. However, Professor Griff continues to neglect his Native heritage and chooses not to speak about the importance of Native issues. Could it be that Professor Griff is overwhelmed by the complexity of issues that surround Native people? Does Professor Griff feel that the acknowledgement of his mixed-blood Native heritage would be weakening his militant Afro-centric position, even though he is repeatedly referred to as a "warrior."[71] How is it that such a focused, educated, and visible figure in the Hip Hop community could miss an opportunity to embrace a platform that others in Hip Hop have not entertained?[72]

Ron Welburn in his article "A Most Secret Identity, Native America Assimilation and Identity Resistance in African America" (292 – 320)[73] may be able to shed some light on the issues facing Professor Griff. This article presents a historical ethnological reading of social politics that is essentially autobiographical. This article helps us to understand why Professor Griff does not readily acknowledge his Native heritage.

"

Throughout the article Welburn outlines some of the complexities facing issues of historic and real identity loss, variations of resistance to Indian identity articulated through Black generational differences, and Black-Red White racial consciousness as they pertain to mixed Black-Indian contemporary identity construction (294 – 304).

The issue of cultural support leads the discussion by Welburn to view Native identity inclusion in a positive light within Black identity. This is central to Welburn's understanding of identity (297). The Civil Rights movement of the 1960s created a positive Black experience and offered a location of sociopolitical support for the Black community. Welburn redefines Afro-centrism, noting that this ideology not only essentialized the historical necessity of Africa as the center of humanity (304) but, further operates to close off the acceptance of any other identity or culture other than an outwardly recognizable African heritage. This then reifies the hypodecent, "one-droprule" or "one-drop-of-African-blood-rule" (304) that limits cultural interaction and rejects the complex identity of a mixed Black-Indian person.

As a result, the "Black first" perspective constructs a singular identity, thereby assimilating the Native heritage present within an individual. At the core of his creative work, Professor Griff allies himself to Afro-centrism. Professor Griff's Blackfoot heritage is always present, but it is assimilated into a form of Black urban culture, as a means of securing a rhetorical voice that does not require further explanation. Further, Welburn discusses the use of hairstyles and dress as a method of transmitting one's preferred identity. He mentions the use of the Afro, "freedom hair" (314) in the 1960/70s, the integration of Black language "'ebonics' to reinforce their Blackness", (314) and the specific inclusion of urban aesthetics/dress, foods, and black popular music (314 – 315) as examples that affirm a Black, Afro-centric heritage.[74] Professor Griff embodies these characteristics in his performances.

Without attempting to resolve this complex issue of Black-Indian biracial identity, Welburn concludes that each mixed, Black-Indian, racial person needs to:

> set for themselves [the level of] Indianness and who is an Indian – whether they are reservation, off-reservation, community enclave,

or urban-exurban-rural "lost birds" – will need to respond to and be measured by the unique destructive legacies...Native peoples have experienced. (316)

This rationale gives Professor Griff the license to accept his inter-cultural identity and embrace his Blackfoot heritage. The unique relationship between these two cultures, African and Native American, transforms identity from a singular location to one of dynamic complexity. This methodology offers Professor Griff the agency to elude the essentialist or assimiliationist tenor of his work by recognizing his mixed Native heritage. Yet, presented with questions along these lines Professor Griff refuses to reply. His silence confirms that his Black defined, Afro-centric focus has consumed, through assimilation, his Blackfoot heritage.

Kevin Powell and Ernie Paniccioli

A Native artist, legendary photographer, graffiti artist and author, Ernie Paniccioli (Cree) collaborated with the African-American editor Kevin Powell on a collection of photos for the book <u>Who Shot Ya?: Three Decades of Hip Hop Photography</u> (2002).[75] In his introduction titled, "Notes of a Hip Hop Head," Kevin Powell discusses the socio-political developments in the urban center in the mid-1970s that led to the development of Hip Hop culture. It is interesting to note where the Native is represented in Powell's musical outline of Hip Hop:

> [a]dd these factors together, multiply by, um, field hollers, work songs, the blues, Cab Calloway, zoot suiters, bebop, jitter buggers, low-riders, doo-wop harmonizers, jump-rope rhymers, lyrical assassins like the Last Poets and Muhammad Ali, Nuyorican salsa and soul, Jamaican dub poetry, Afro-Southern sonic calls and responses in the form of James Brown, the wall carvings and murals of Africans, Latinos, Native Americans, and the drum, the conga, the pots and pans, being beat beat beaten here there everywhere and it all equals hip hop.

(Paniccioli x - xiv)

Powell continues using the words "magical, spiritual" in reference to Native people (and Paniccioli presumably, though he is not named) furthering a ghetto commodification that is itself a marginalized racist perspective of African-Americans. Powell writes, "a miracle sprung from the heavy bags and hand-me-down rags of those deferred dreams Langston Hughes had sung about years before" (Paniccioli xi). Statements like this riddle the opening pages of this historic Hip Hop photo documentary by a Native person who, as Powell and Africa Bambaataa both state, is centrally important to the evolution of Hip Hop culture (Paniccioli x).

This diatribe by Powell deflates the importance of Paniccioli's photographic artwork by situating it within a dominant African-American perspective. Powell does appear to be aware of this strategy as he returns toward the end of his essay to reinsert Paniccioli's Cree heritage. However, this is mentioned only for the sake of representing the "lost" Indian identity within popular culture.

Through a left-handed compliment equating Paniccioli's artistic work within Hip Hop with the Native American photographs by Edward Curtis, Powell reinserts the Native and celebrates its loss. Powell casts Paniccioli's work in a romantic light that glorifies the ghetto ethic that he proudly promotes in his essay. Comparing the work of Paniccioli to Curtis is a recipe for cultural disaster. Curtis focused on a reified, stereotypical, essentialized, wordlessly romantic view of Native people that was unapologetically colonialistic. As David Lewis notes:

> By the beginning of the twentieth century they [Native people] were the disappearing Indians, fit for 'Wild West" pageants or, like Ishi, last of the Yahi, exhibition in the California Museum of Anthropology. They were Edward S. Curtis's 'Vanishing Race,' and James Fraser's "End of the Trail." After that Indians were forgotten, moved to the periphery of public place and attention. They became the subjects of salvage anthropologists who were more interested in their past than their future. Yet their symbolic value persisted, and images emerged as needed. (Lewis 220)

Quite like Curtis' Native American images, Powell limits the character, depth, space, place, identity, and content of the work that Paniccioli has produced. Powell had the opportunity to critically unravel the singular, limited view of Native people and their historic relationship to the foundation of American expressive culture. Paniccioli placed trust in an author who is more than capable of reading between the lines of stereotypes and compartmentalization. Powell elected to present a re-packaged perspective of Native identity that is centered within a historically inaccurate, commodified stereotype. Powell did not speak about the intercultural connections between the African diaspora and Native cultures. Little recognition is given to Ernie Paniccioli, a contemporary Native male who documented, through photos, the evolution of Hip Hop culture. For

Powell, the Native American "vanishes" adding another stratum of suppression and cultural assimilation that favors an African American position. Powell erases the Native influence within Hip Hop by neglecting its presence in an act of colonial control. This establishes a (mis)representation of the cultural evolution of this art form that was not the premise of this photo essay.

What Powell may not have anticipated was a rebuttal by Paniccioli to his colonial reading of the photos. Unlike the other examples of Native (mis)representation that have, and will be reviewed, Paniccioli positions himself within the work under examination. Paniccioli re-presents Native identity within the evolution of Hip Hop. To begin, Paniccioli reviews the intercultural connections between Blacks, Natives, Puerto Ricans and Latino at the epicenter of Hip Hop: the South Bronx, New York (Paniccioli 177 – 183). Powell and Paniccioli do concur on this birthplace. Though this positions a location for the inception of Hip Hop, Paniccioli does not prescribe a starting date for the genre. Powell found it necessary to trace the genealogy of Hip Hop, from the 1940s through the present, and prescribe a starting date for Hip Hop history, "with Sugarhill Gang's 'Rapper's Delight' in 1979" (Paniccioli xi).

Paniccioli realizes Hip Hop as an on-going art form that has evolved through collective cultural histories and socio-political experiences.[76] Electing not to prescribe a starting date for Hip Hop releases the genre from colonial transcriptions of time. Angela Cavender Wilson defines Paniccioli's postcolonial action as a "means [of] defying the disciplinary boundaries that dissect and categorize our [read: Hip Hop] traditions, as these boundaries simply do not exist in Indigenous ways in which the physical, spiritual, emotional, and intellectual are inseparable" (Wilson 73). Wilson places importance on Indigenous knowledge ("ways")[77] that allows for multiple readings of Hip Hop history that can be culturally defined.

Paniccioli addresses the racist brutality that he endured as a young Native man in New York.

> Here I am looking like Cochise in the neighborhood with kids
> who look like they came from *The Sopranos* on one corner; kids

who look like they're from Guyana or Africa on another corner; kids who look like they're from the Caribbean or Puerto Rico on another...And the brothers [African American males] just looked at me and didn't really care; every time they saw me get into a fight they were there on my side (Paniccioli 179).[78]

Paniccioli is clear about noting his Cree[79] heritage but does not attempt to replace this with an Afro-centric perspective. Rather, as this quote expresses, Paniccioli realizes an intercultural connection between

Natives and African Americans at the crossroads of resistance.

Toward the end of his essay, Paniccioli states that the current form of Hip Hop culture is a "second colonization" working to eliminate the combined efforts of African-Americans and Natives in Hip Hop (Paniccioli 196) through commercialization. For Paniccioli, this "second colonization" is an extension of the first colonization of Native people within the U.S. (Paniccioli 178). He acknowledges this colonial struggle as a shared site of intercultural resistance for Natives and African-Americans within Hip Hop. He lists the techniques of this second colonization[80] - "bootlegging", "overselling", "overproduction", "erasure" - coming through the vehicles of White racism, capitalism, police brutality and drug marketing, Paniccioli notes these techniques "articulated the root cause of *our* anger" (Paniccioli 195 - 196).[81] By identifying the colonial struggle as "*our*," Paniccioli does not limit the cultural importance of a postcolonial resistance in Hip Hop to either African-American or Native. Instead, he seeks to contest this colonial operation to represent an intercultural resistance. Taking this perspective, if Hip Hop is colonized, then African-American and Native people who participate in Hip Hop are ultimately colonized. Paniccioli performs his expressive anti-colonial maneuver through the combined theories of the "pictorial turn" and "transformational praxis." The "pictorial turn," as described in Foucault's Picture Theory and expanded by W.J.T. Mitchell, affords the object being viewed to reverse its position and reflect its perception upon the external environment (Paulitano 182). The "transformational praxis, as stated earlier, is the "critical self-affirmative process [that] must be consciously directed away from the assimilative lure of the statist politics of recognition and instead be fashioned toward our own onthe-ground strategies of freedom" (Tully qtd. in Coulthard 17). Applying first the "pictorial turn," followed immediately by the "transformational praxis," Paniccioli can reverse the embedded and external colonial power, gaining the liberty of self-determination and expression within an intercultural expressive agent, namely Hip Hop.

From this reading, one can conclude that Paniccioli is not only aware of the (mis)representations in the introduction to <u>Who Shot Ya?</u>, but sought further to challenge Powell's racialized colonial perspective. Paniccioli therefore re-presents and supports his Native identity through the agent of Hip Hop.

Through Paniccioli's documentation, Hip Hop was able to recounts its ongoing intercultural history. Paniccioli's reading of Hip Hop history stems from an understanding that he is "marginalized and an outsider in his own country."[82] As a result of this perspective, Paniccioli's photo essay of Hip Hop history can be read as a Native history of Hip Hop. This understanding recalls a quote from the legendary jazz drummer, Max Roach, who profoundly stated that, *"all American music is Native American"* (Gehr 2007).[83] From this statement, Roach points to three possible meanings: origin, cultural exchange, and musical identity. This identifies a third space of sovereignty, a location that affords Native people self-determination beyond the political limitations of space, location, and identity.[84] Jazz, like Hip Hop, is an expressive border- crossing agent (Murray 1976, Gabbard 1995, Monson 1996, Jones 1999/2002, Taylor 2002). Though established within the borders of the United States, jazz can co-exist with, and within, multiple musics, cultures and identities to persist as a dynamic cultural art form (Levine 1989). Jazz balances music "indigenous" (Native) to America and outside of the United States (Levine 8). Virginia Giglio notes that there is a "contemporary generation of Native American composers [who are] active in jazz and blues as well as the powwow drum" (Giglio 157). Cultural exchange, as we have seen earlier in this example, is present as an anti-colonialistic strategy that allows the possibility of self-determination regarding identity. Identity then establishes a fluid interactive space that is malleable by the invested actor. The pictorial turn-transformational praxis technique expands the engagement of expressive culture, beyond imposed colonial limitations. Both Paniccioli and Roach perform this function within their respective art forms (visual and audio) that are, at its core, influenced by a Native perspective.

Cowboy (Keith Wiggins)

Keith Wiggins (aka Cowboy) is an original MC who worked with GrandMaster Flash (Joseph Saddler), Melle Mel (Melvin Glover), Kid Creole

(Nathaniel Glover) in the 3MC's from 1973 - 78 (Fricke and Ahearn 70 – 74).

Scorpio (Eddie Morris) and Raheim (Guy Todd Williams) later joined to form Grand Master Flash and the Furious Five. This was the group who produced "The Message" (1982) that continues to be a legendary Hip Hop classic.

Cowboy is also the one who coined the phrase that is mistakenly assigned to Lovebug Starski, "Throw you hands in the air and wave 'em like you just don't care!" (Fricke and Ahearn 71) Cowboy, along with other MC's of the time, used a selection by the Incredible Bongo Band that reworked the song *Apache* to start their raps. *Apache* is a song composed around 1960 by a non-Native musician to represent Native Americans in music. As will be discussed later in this chapter, *Apache* spearheaded the Native influence in Hip Hop from its inception to today. The appropriation of the name

Cowboy, influenced by American history and the use of the song/sample *Apache* create a colonial dominance over Native (sonic) identity. Cowboy, who inherited this nickname because of his tall posture and bow-legged walk, took advantage of *Apache's* crowd shaking effect capturing the attention of the audience through his charismatic raps. The interplay between the master of ceremony, Cowboy, and the sonic sub cultural artifact, *Apache* (read: Indian) helped shape these early years of Hip Hop. Did the audience take note of this inter-cultural connection? Was it ever acknowledged that a pop culture conjunction was happening on Bronx streets? Was the technique of playing Cowboy and *Apache* (read: Indians) merely left to be a coincidence in the annals of Hip Hop history? David Rich Lewis recounts, "[f]rom the late 1930s when John Ford and Hollywood discovered…Navajos…Apaches and …Comanche Indians… became our cinematic projection of a savage West" (Lewis 212). In reference to the "cowboy and Indian" television shows of the 1930s, author T.V. Reed states an obvious point about the text, storyline/narrative, misuse, and historic stereotype of Native identity in television. He states that the writers, "wrote good cowboy and Indian stories because that was what they thought the public wanted" (Reed 79). Cowboy's use of the *Apache* sample situates his raps in a romanticized history consistent with the Western television/film programs of the 1930s era. Cowboy appropriates a hyper-reality constructed through a mass media stereotype and representation of Native identity. The "projection of [a] savage West" is articulated using the sample *Apache* and the hierarchy suggested by his DJ name. Together these factors express a "playing Indian" identity.[85]

Cowboy constructs an authoritative colonial image with the integration of a dominant physical posture expressed through body language (stance), a gross (mis)representative musical underscore (*Apache*) and the iconic use of name/language (Master of Ceremony, Cowboy). By co-opting this literal space, through the active engagement of these characteristics, Cowboy self-centers his raps within the growing territory (dare it be referenced as frontier!) of Hip Hop that exists not only in a regional location, New York City and the Bronx, but also through repetitive radio play and commercial recording. David Lewis again describes a fictitious and stereotyped Native identity.

> In twentieth-century American history, literature, art, movies, and advertising - in the images we create for ourselves and for export - mythic cowboys and Indians continue to symbolize the frontier experience, the romantic images that recall a simpler though nonexistent American West. (Lewis 220)[86]

The constructed persona of Cowboy creates an undercurrent of fantasy and myth that refortifies nostalgia for the colonial west.

Due to a laundry list of circumstances following the success of "The Message", the members of the Fabulous Five departed on less than hospitable terms. Although there were some collaborations among the members in later years, they never fully returned to their collective work. Unfortunately, in

1989 Cowboy passed away at the age of twenty-eight after spending two years fighting a crack cocaine addiction.[87] However, like the rap name that he appropriated, the legacy of Cowboy continues to live on as part myth and part reality in the pioneering history of Hip Hop.

The diaspora of the sample Apache

In a phone interview with Chris LaMarr he spoke about the influence of funk and R&B on the work of WOR (phone interview 14 Dec 2008). When asked if this illustrated the influence of the African diaspora in the music of WOR, LaMarr noted that the music, "Hip Hop and powwow music," are not stable, but continue to be used "again and again" (phone interview 18 Dec 2008). Combining the previously outlined concept of transformative expression with this idea of repetition and fluidity, LaMarr recognizes the importance of music in motion. Elsewhere Hip Hop scholars discuss the importance of mobility in Hip Hop as a method of "glocalization" in order to broaden the sphere(s) of Hip Hop culture that communicate, and perform, between various local areas and on a global level (Androutsopoulos 44 – 45).

Bakari Kitwana's states that, "Hip Hop as a culture indisputably emerged in the South Bronx in the late 1970s...before branching out around the country in the early 1980s" (Kitwana 201). Kitwana, a noted author, and journalist in Hip Hop, was the Executive Editor of <u>The Source</u>, the Editorial Director at <u>Third World Press</u> and the music reviewer for the National Public Radio program "All Things Considered". Additionally, his works were published in the <u>Village Voice</u> and <u>The Progressive Magazine</u>.

With these literary credentials one would suspect that this journalist would be well informed about the numerous global and cross-cultural contributions within Hip Hop. Kitwana acknowledges Native people as being "to a lesser extent" influenced by Hip Hop culture. However, he locates the Native influence from Hip Hop as following, in order, Blacks, Latinos and Asians (Kitwana 200). Again, the Native perspective is marginalized in popular culture nearly to the point of erasure by a constructed (mis)representation from the dominant society. Kitwana consciously constructs a position of cultural authority for Hip Hop comfortably within an African-American perspective and more aptly within the perspective of "Black youth" (Kitwana xii).

As we have seen earlier in this chapter, there are many other African-American scholars and artists who recognize and understand the cultural dialogue that Hip Hop affords. However, in defining a cultural hierarchy within Hip Hop, Kitwana substantiates not only an Afro-centric perspective, but also illustrates the depth of mis-understanding that prevails in Hip Hop.

Native Hip Hop artists have not rested on their proverbial laurels, but their exclusion in the documented history fuels inspiration for artists throughout the evolution of Hip Hop. This example moves the discussion of cultural contact from a cross-cultural setting to the intercultural.

As defined by Jason Stanyek in his work on the intercultural connections within the African diaspora (Stanyek 2 – 12) "interculturalism" Stanyek writes, "seems to subsist on the simultaneous maintenance and transcendence of the spatial formations that play a role in the creation of distinct identities" (Stanyek 11). A critical reading of the example *Apache* helps to illuminate the intercultural connections in Hip Hop between Native/African American communities.[88]

Briefly surmised, *Apache* is an instrumental composition that was created by a non-Native performer/composer who attempted to reference Native American music. The result became one of Hip Hop's most treasured devices, a sample. This sample has served as a creative source for many artists. Most importantly, this sample emphasizes the importance of Native identity in Hip Hop. The sample defines what Stuart Hall has coined, "a still point in a turning world" (qtd. in Lawlor 38). Composed by a non-Native individual, this song, and later sample, was never intended to be a specific Native American musical representation. Instead, this work produces a critical discussion of authenticity, cultural authority, and mimesis. This sample continues to be masked and reworked by artists since the 1970s, recollecting a Native identity that supports a post-industrial urban African-American identity.

The creation of an Apache

The 1950s brought a new attitude in film toward Native people. Film director John Ford attempted to portray Native people in a more sympathetic and realistic light in his films (Price 158 – 161). Although other films related to Apache culture were already visible during this period, it is the 1954 film *Apache* that firmly established Native representation within popular music.

Apache was developed by the integration and borrowing of two very important elements of musical evolution: melody and rhythm. The melodic evolution of *Apache* was originally composed as an instrumental work by British guitarist Jerry Lordon. Lordon was inspired in 1959 by viewing of the film *Apache* (1954).[89] In a 1993 interview Lordon explained, "I wanted something noble and dramatic, reflecting the courage and savagery of the Indian" (Lordon/Matos, 1993/2005). Lordon's recording of the original *Apache* was completed in forty-five minutes, and he expected the release "to be a B-side" (Lordon, 1993). Instead, this composition became a hit that has inspired the beat and (Native) spirit of Hip Hop culture.

Since its arrival on July 21, 1960, on the British pop charts this selection has been re-recorded and remixed by many artists. The first released version was recorded by British group The Shadows in June 1960 and released the following month. One week later on July 28, 1960, Bert Weedon released his version of *Apache* that reached number forty-four on the British singles chart only to resurface on August 11, 1960, where it found its place at number twenty-four.[90] After this two-week listing the Shadows' version of *Apache* returned on August 25, 1960, to the British singles chart and remained at the top of the charts for five weeks through the end of September of that same year.[91]

In the United States, The Shadows' original 1960s version remained unknown. However, *Apache* was introduced in 1961 by a jazz guitarist from Denmark, Jorgen Ingmann. Ingmann produced a cover version that was entitled "Jorgen Ingmann and His Guitar;" that arrived at number two on the US pop charts and number one on Canada's CHUM Radio Chart.[92]

In his article "Images of the American West in Rock" Richard Aquila recollected:

> Jorgen Ingmann had a hit with an instrumental entitled "Apache". Ingmann used guitar riffs to imitate the sound of arrows whizzing through the air. The trick sound worked, and thousands of Americans purchased the record, which capitalized on the exotic image of the Indian. (Aquila 419)

Apache gained popularity through a sonic presentation of "playing Indian" that, by the early 1960s, was already located within the mental landscape of the dominant (read: white) American mainstream. This representation and fictional "play" does not empower Native identity but further establishes the limits of Native identity to colonialist control (Deloria 7 – 8).

The rhythmic development of *Apache* has a similar twisted lineage. A reworked version of *Apache* by the Incredible Bongo Band surfaced in 1972, and is noted by Africa Bambaataa and DJ Kool Herc as "hip-hop's National anthem" (Toop 60). Although this version was not a hit upon its release, the long percussion break in the middle has been sampled countless times on Hip Hop recordings from the 1980s onward. The version to which Bambaataa referred was not the earlier productions by The Shadows, Ingmann or Weedon. The 1972 studio project version by Michael Viner and an ad hoc group of percussionists from Los Angeles, known as the Incredible Bongo Band, produced this recording for MGM Pride in 1973. The Incredible Bongo

Band disbanded shortly thereafter in 1974. Michel Viner borrowed the track *Apache* from Preston Epps's funky, Latin work "Bongo Rock". This selection by Epps was attractive to Viner because of the extended bongo break in the middle of the song. Viner added more percussion to Epps' already exciting musical creation and lengthened the mid-section bongo break. "Bongo Rock" via the Incredible Bongo Band, became *Apache* and remained a staple throughout the 1970s in the DJ repertoire featured at parties and B-Boy/B-Girl battles. Hip Hop historian Jeff Cheng notes that these battles were appropriately mislabeled as war dances (Cheng 21).

The *Apache* sample continues to be revisited and re-mixed in contemporary electronica, techno, drum and bass, funk, DJ/party collections and, of course, Hip Hop. A quick listing of some important recordings that use this sample from 1960 – 2003 is: Bert Weedon: *Apache* (1960), Cliff Richard and the Shadows: *Apache* (1960), Jorgen Ingmann: *Apache* (1961), The Ventures: *Apache* (1963), Davie Allan and the Arrows: *Apache* (1965), Incredible Bongo Band: *Apache* (1973), West Street Mob: *Break Dance*

(Electric Boogie) (1973), The Sugarhill Gang: *Apache, Jump On It!* (1981),

Goldie: *Inner City Life* (1995), Future Sound of London: *We Have Explosives*

(1996), Moby: *Machete* (1999), The Roots: *Thought @ Work* (2002), Nas:

Made You Look (2003).

At the core of these recordings and productions is the (mis)representation of Native identity.[93] If that were only the point to be made, the concept of Native identity in Hip Hop would be a mere residue on the vinyl of history. However, there is more at stake than just a simple reworked track and break-beat.

The glocalization of Native identity from the original song is constructed by an Englishman, which is then brought to the U.S. by a Dutch guitarist and exposed to the Hip Hop Nation (Alim 1- 19) by two African-American DJ's who are of Jamaican heritage. Though created as a romantic stereotypical reference to Native identity, the song/sample itself transposes this meaning into a stable signifier of Native identity. The song/sample produces a semantic inversion or "flips the script" (Smitherman 279 – 282) on the non-Native author of this work to become a firm representation of Native identity within Hip Hop culture. Once the song *Apache* is reduced to a sample, the work is not limited or bound. Rather, the work is elevated to the location of a pliable and repeatable sample. Yet, within each of the repetitive re-versions of this sample through the many subgenres of Hip Hop, as stated above,

Apache continues to be defined by its multiple lines of cultural identification.

Imani Perry reminds us of the cipha that is the "conceptual space in which heightened consciousness exists" (Perry 107). The cipha defines a space for the sample to converge sonically with a Native reading and application. The conceptual space is the repetition of the sample. The heightened consciousness is the realization of the Native reference within the sample. These references, either positive or negative, of the Native identity within the sample are then transposed through the space provided by the cipha. The identified Native representation within the sample engages the cipha through Thomas Turino's "trans-state cultural formations" (Turino 58 – 63). The trans-state cultural formations are three categories of glocal interaction (immigrant, diaspora, cosmopolitan) that afford the represented identity the ability to transform and function outside of predisposed colonial binaries. The trans-state cultural process of a Native sample produces a Native cipha for Hip Hop that has the potential to re-contextualize the genre through a Native perspective. As a result, for Native artists, the Euroamerican musical hegemony over Native identity is sonically disrupted by a glocal transposition of identity. For non-Native artists, the sample engages the distortion-for-protection hypothesis.[94] As defined, the distortion-for-protection hypothesis allows the object, in this case the sample, to counter forms of colonial oppression in a self-determined fashion, while retaining a core identity. The distortion (rhythmic variation, melodic adjustment, word/title substitution) is the application of the sample. The protection is the Native identity. A sample that contains a Native representation, utilized by a non-Native artist, can perform a dual function of creative application for the non-Native artist and cultural retention for the Native identity. Within Hip Hop, *Apache* reclaims and re-presents Native identity, for both Native and non-Native artists.

The attempted sonic assimilation of this sample finds an ironic parallel to the IRA, Termination Policies, and economic push/pull factors of the post-WWII era. If we examine the place and origin of *Apache* considering the U.S. political landscape of the time (c. 1954- 60s), Native identity is articulated both visible and invisible in Native and non-Native communities.

As discussed in Chapter 1 of this dissertation, the Termination Policy for Native people has been reinforced in many ways throughout U.S. history: 1953 – 1968 (Public Law 280.67 Stat. 588), 1934 – 1953 (Indian Reorganization Act), 1887 (General Allotment Act), 1831 (*Cherokee Nation v. Georgia*), 1823 (*Johnson v. McIntosh*), 1790 (Trade and Intercourse Acts) (Canby 11 – 33). If we look closely and connect these laws designed to "terminate the Indian problem" (Canby 26) within the U.S., the song/ sample, *Apache*, came at a time when the hallmark of this policy, the Indian Reorganization Act, the Indian Relocation Acts and PL-280, were enacted. As Native people have endured these political strategies of termination, so too does the sample *Apache* persist in the groove of Hip Hop. Recognizing the impact and importance of this sample throughout the course of Hip Hop history, and the transgressive theoretical concepts that offer the sample the ability to transform and re-present a negotiate space, it becomes quite evident that Native identity is the internal thread, the bloodline that has persisted from the vinyl to the digital age.

More Apache: The Apache Walk and Film

Another (mis)representation of Apache in Hip Hop culture is the *Apache Walk* (Fricke and Ahearn 5). This is the line that a person seeking to be a gang inductee walks between other inducted members of the gang, thereby subjecting himself/herself to physical attacks and beatings. A survivor of this "ritual" is awarded with acceptance into the gang and would be allowed to wear colors, insignias, and other visible markers of gang culture (Davis 11-17). The name's origin can be attributed to the South Bronx (41st Precinct area) and to the aforementioned music selection "Apache" that was popular during this period. BOM5 of the Rock Steady Crew recalls, "Even when I was in a gang, we played 'Apache'…on a phonograph hooked up to a lamppost outside….Gangs were already doing it, man" (qtd. in Fricke and Ahearn 9).

The walk itself symbolized a racialized reading and mis-appropriation of Native culture. Rituals of becoming a man/woman are held in high regard and considered sacred rights-of-passage into adulthood (Deloria 39 – 43). It should be noted that break dancing was an outgrowth of gang culture where fighting, dance "battles" and, as mentioned previously, "war dances", began to overtake physical violence.

Thomas DeFrantz remarks that social power, physical identity, and authority of space is affirmed through this performative art. DeFrantz traces the physicality of this dance style from the evolution of capoeira, a Brazilian martial art dance form that was "disguised as dance." Breaking developed as a style of movement when break dancers – B Boys-filled the musical breaks between records mixed by disc jockeys at parties and discotheques" (DeFrantz 83 – 84). Noting the use of the circle as a means of building community, the dance was performed in a circular formation, or ring-shout. The ring-shout has been evident throughout the African diaspora evolving from capoeira and into break dancing (DeFrantz xv – xvii).

If the concept of the circle was used to define space and community physically within the performative arena of dance, the use of the parallel lines for the *Apache Walk* can be seen as a repositioning of this inclusive attitude into a trajectory that is defined by the compression and architecture of the modern urban landscape. A potential gang member, performing the *Apache Walk* does not only physically state that he/she is willing, and effectively able, to support the community of the gang, that is prescribed by the surrounding linear structures (economics, education, employment, et al), but is also in agreement with the ideology of the gang itself. This attitude of resistance is epitomized by Fort Apache.

Fort Apache: The Bronx was another appropriation of the Apache image that appeared on film when it was released on February 6, 1981 (Rivera 54 – 55). This 1981 film borrowed its name from the 1948 film simply titled, *Fort Apache*. Since the first showing of this post-WWII film on March 9, 1948, by film director John Ford, which included the iconic actor John Wayne, myths and romantic images of the Apache continued to reign. Though viewed as more sympathetic to Native people, the Western romantic myths of Native identity remained. As John Price noted following John Ford's 1950 classic film *Broken Arrow*, by 1967 there was a popularization of films that included Apache themes and made use of this tribe's name including: *Apache Drums*

(1951), *Apache War Smoke* (1952), *Apache Country* (1952), *Battle at Apache Pass* (1952), *Apache* (1954), *Apache Ambush* (1955), *Apache Warrior* (1957),

Apache Territory (1958) and Geronimo (1962).

The Fort Apache in this 1981 film is the 41st Precinct in the South Bronx. George Hankins simply stated, "[i]t was bad..." (Fisher 1), referencing this Precinct in a 1993 New York Times article. Mr. Hankins further discussed the names of the gangs who were visible during this time and place (Savage Skulls, Savage Nomads, Ghetto Brothers, Black Spades, Spanish Mafia, Seven Immortals, Seven Crowns) and the "cowboy nicknames" (Fisher 1) that were in frequent use (Wyatt Earp, Billy the Kid, Jesse James).[95] The police station Fort Apache opened in 1914, but was not prescribed the nickname until the early 1970s by Lieutenant Clitter during a protest at the precinct (Walker 2).

The retired police officers that worked in this precinct consistently spoke of the poor and inhumane conditions of the area. The police felt that a growing immigrant population was surrounding them and that they were constantly "under siege" (Kappstatter 1). Walker suggested that this population has "171,000 [policing area] – 92,000 Puerto Ricans, 73,000 blacks, and 6,000 designated as others" (Walker 7). Walker took liberty to compare this dense non-Anglo community to "the grassy plains of Custer's last stand...this historic and tiny outpost [known] as 'Fort Apache'" (Walker x). As a reaction to the perceived growing unstable conditions in the area, the police there developed a sense of pride and camaraderie. "Serving there was a badge of honor" stated Officer Manuel Galarza (Fisher 2).

The inhumane conditions of the area (i.e., a reservation system), the growing surrounding immigrant community and the romantic projection that the 41st precinct is the "tiny outpost" on the urban landscape that is an updated version of General Custer's "last stand" reveals, a telling racist undercurrent directed at Native people. This example perfectly draws together the phenomenological issues at stake with the evolution of gang-police interaction and Hip Hop's (mis)representation of Native identity.

By juxtaposing Fort Apache with the Bronx, we see the militarization of the post-industrial center that is New York City, and more aptly the Bronx itself, become linked to the historic warfare between the U.S. government and members of the Apache Nation. Though not stated directly, the repetition of this signifier enabled the officers to believe, consciously or unconsciously, that they will ultimately prevail. The precinct functioned like Wild West literature, and later Wild West shows, television, and film, where the police (frontiers men, cowboys) struggled against the inarticulate savage Indians (Price 156). Like Custer's prophetic last stand with the 7th Calvary that would result in an epic battle between Native people and the U.S military, the police precinct is surrounded. This becomes a point of signification for the police officers as they assume suitably prescribed roles.

Geronimo's resistant efforts (Goyathlay) toward the U.S. government define a Native identity. Once the Apache Nation, and Geronimo specifically, were (mis)labeled as rebels, due to their resistance toward the U.S. government, numerous campaigns were launched to arrest Geronimo. This appeared to be the modus operandi for the 41st Precinct. Each arrest attempted to control the increased presence of the surrounding immigrant community; a community represented by Hip Hop culture. This helped solidify the simulation cum simulacra historical myths that originated from pop culture (mis)representations. The police, therefore, played and performed "cowboys and Indians" in their daily professional lives.[64] This possessive investment of power and authority defined the maintenance of a localized hegemonic structure that allowed little or no room from opposing (minority culture) points of view. To conclude, Geronimo was eventually arrested on September 4, 1886, by General Nelson Miles, was first moved to Fort Marion, FL, then moved to Mt. Vernon, AL in 1887, and finally to Fort Sill, OK where he eventually died on February 17, 1909 (Debo 1986). With this ending to the story, the repetition of the name, Fort Apache, rang loud across the grand divide that the precinct, in the end, always does get their (Native) man.

Repositioning and Analysis of Native Identity in Hip Hop

The title of the musical work by Lordon, *Apache*, represented a direct racial stereotype of Native culture. As stated earlier, Lordon was seeking to create, "something noble and dramatic, reflecting the courage and savagery of the Indian." This cultural (mis)representation of an entire Native culture was nothing less than sonic racism. Lordon took active possession of Native identity and distorted its image creating (mis)representations that have remained through today. Native identity became colonized and marginalized not only through British (Lordon, The Shadows, et al), but also Danish (Jorgen Ingmann) sonic control.

Ingmann exercised his authoritative privilege on the meaning and representation of Native identity through a fictitious image that was created by historic stereotypes from the Wild West Shows of television and film (Price 167). In this photo, we can see that Ingmann defined an Apache culture in a Plains-style headdress ripe with commercially produced colored feathers as he donned an aggressive grimace.

These two artists, Lordon and Ingmann, objectify Native identity that is consistent with George Lipsitz's concept of the "Possessive Investment in Whiteness". In this revealing work, Lipsitz traced the racialized power play that exists between minority communities (African-American, Latino American,

Asian American and Native Americans) and "white" communities.

As a result of this historic racism "white" communities found themselves in a position of privilege that is embedded within the psychological landscape of the U.S. social climate at the end of the 20th century (Lipsitz 1 – 23). "The possessive investment in whiteness is not a simple matter of black and white; all racialized minority groups have suffered from it, albeit to different degrees and in different ways." (Lipsitz 2) Specifically addressing the Native communities, Lipsitz writes:

Although reproduced in a new form in every era, the possessive investment in whiteness has always been influenced by its origins in the racialized history of the United States – by its legacy of slavery and segregation, of "Indian" extermination and immigrant restrictions, of conquest and colonialism. (Lipsitz 3)

The new form to which Lipsitz referred in this era is the recording of the 1960s that gave birth to the sample in the 1970s.

John Connell and Chris Gibson discussed the cross-cultural manifestations that breed intercultural relationships through the mobility of recordings via tapes, CDs, MP3s and, presently, internet file sharing (Connell and Gibson 160 – 191). The transition from home to regional, regional to national, national to international (i.e. glocal) yields a complex transformation and active re-presentation that traverses each contact point or contact zone (Connell and Gibson 188 – 189). Identity then for the recording, or in this case the sample *Apache*, becomes dialogically transformed from cross-cultural to intercultural via the process of diaspora. Yet, the core identity is still present and fluidly re-articulated within the layers (Native and non-Native) of cultural interaction. The combined cross-cultural (borrowing, appropriation, influence, incorporation) and intercultural (corporeal) context for this work, *Apache*, illustrates the multiple dynamic levels of Tribal Native music/expressive culture.

What sets this sample in motion is the "exotic," (mis)representation of Native culture, identity, and music. Without this contact, Hip Hop culture would not have a "heartbeat" to sample and re-mix. *Apache's* continued (mis)representations "emphasize the song's coded Native American war-drum associations," that further stereotype Native identity in versions, for example, by The Sugarhill Gang (1981) who stated "Tonto, jump on it / Geronimo, jump on it" (Matos 2005). The influence of *Apache* does not stop there. As Matos stated in 2005, "Apache didn't die—it migrated into dance music. Drum and bass, which was created by speeding up hip-hop breakbeats, took to it instantly...Goldie and Digital utilized 'Apache' for 'Inner City Life' and 'Metro,' respectively" (Matos 2005). As discussed previously, the repeated (mis)representation of Native identity through the integration of the *Apache* sample in Hip Hop challenges sonic assimilation and termination. The sustainability of Native identity and its re-presentation through rhythmic variation (i.e., Incredible Bongo Band, The Adventures of Grand Master Flash on his Wheels of Steel), melodic adjustment (i.e., Future Sounds of London, Moby, The Roots, Nas) and word substitution (i.e., *Apache, Jump On It!, Inner City Life, We Have Explosives, Machete, Thought @ Work, Made You Look*) is an example of the hypothesis that I posed in Chapter 1 of distortion-for-protection. Native identity was forced into a position that flirted with near termination by transparency but found a strategy to contest this erasure by active re-presentation through a lineage of Hip Hop works produced in the years following the 1960s.

The Native identity at the philosophical core of this sample applies W.J.T.

Mitchell's "pictorial turn," a liberating form of agency offered to Native identity. By making this "pictorial turn," the sample engages the entire range of meaning and complexity regardless of year, location, or artistic technique. The Native identity at the core of this sample re-presents its position from within, constructing an improvisational position of resistance. From the philosophical perspective of Michel de Certeau, Native identity within this sample can:

> produce behaviors that obey their own logic, a logic that crisscrosses technocratic and functionalized space. Despite drawing on established vocabularies, these actions trace counter interests. They are embodied in bricolage, in artisan-like inventiveness. Accordingly, alongside the monolithic homogeneity of disciplined practices lie heterogeneous, scattered practices, multiform practices that elude yet reside with discipline. (qtd. in Michael and Still 880 – 881)

Through the established vocabulary and disciplined practices established here as the performative lexicon of Hip Hop, Native identity fluidly re-creates itself.

Gibson's analysis offers one final step toward a subversive re-presentation of Native identity in *Apache*. Gibson outlines a philosophy of resistance that capitalizes on the agency between the individual (a member of a particular group) and the external environment (surfaces, reflectance, opacities, and transparencies) (Michael and Still 881). Central to Gibson's view is that the: constitutive interlocking of physical environment and organism [individual], and the transgressive act [are] grounded in the affordances that are intrinsic to the relation of organism [individual] and environment. Resistance is thus drawn from beyond the symbolic: it balances on the dynamic border of subject and object, in the affordances that are rooted in ecology. Where discipline imparts a sort of tunnel vision and delineates an impoverished repertoire of practices, affordance opens the horizon to draw upon the full potential combinations of physical organism and physical environment. (qtd. in Michael and Still 881)

With all three of these perspectives acting in concert, Mitchell's pictorial turn, de Certeau's multi-formed improvisational inventiveness and Gibson's transgressive resistance between individual and environment, the Native identity at the core of *Apache* is released from its assimilated position. The appropriated *Apache* sample usurpes cross-cultural essentialization by interculturally articulating its own identity in dialogue with the surrounding artistic practice in which it finds itself.

We can see the important impact of Native identity (text based, recorded, sampled, re-mixed, re-presented) on American popular culture. The urbanization of the (mis)represented Native became the location of a dynamic youth culture where, in the *Apache* sample, Native people were present in the many tributaries that Hip Hop fostered in succeeding decades. Applying Vizenor's "trickster hermenutics" (Vizenor 15), *Apache* can be read as a metaphor for Hip Hop. The "trickster hermenutics" balance the integral relationship and foundation of Native identity in Hip Hop. Vizenor observes the trajectory of the *Apache* sample and describes how this sample defies historical (mis)representation for Native identity to persist:

> Trickster hermeneutics is the interpretation of simulations in the literature of survivance, the ironies of descent and racialism, transmutation, third gender, and themes of transformation in oral tribal stories and written narratives. Trickster stories arise in silence, not scriptures, and are the *holotropes* of imagination; the manifold turns of scenes, the brush of natural reason, characters that liberate the mind and never reach a closure in stories.

(Vizenor 15)

Apache exemplifies the multiple Tribal realities and the intercultural necessity of dialogue with non-Native people to further construct a complex Native identity. Native identity is not lost but rather strengthened by each repetition and subsequent re-mix of this sample. Through this repetition, Native influence can be seen/heard beyond the sonic masks of (mis)representation.

Conclusion

Native identity was included throughout the evolutionary years of Hip Hop culture, through cross-cultural and intercultural connections. Fischer introduces a metaphorical and literal representation of repetition to deduce that "systemic patterns generate new social forms" and that "there is the analysis of change through intended repetitions that in fact work through misappropriation or distortion" (Fischer 207-08). From this statement we can clearly see that Native artists capitalize on the recycled elements and energy of Hip Hop.

These artists additionally fortify not only a sense of identity but also confront issues directly affecting contemporary urban and reservation Native people. Hip Hop offers an emotionally charged agent of expression and representation for Native people. The (mis)representation of Native identity discussed in this chapter is challenged on the grounds that it is constructed. Native identity within Hip Hop moves away from being invisibility, and assimilated object validated only through historical recollection. Limited simulations of Native identity found in literature, film, music, and art during this evolutionary period in Hip Hop's history, c. 1960 – 70s, informed popular culture. Native identity is revealed as a cornerstone of the house of Hip Hop.

In the following section we will begin to see how identity formation for Native people is an ongoing process that remains in flux negotiating Tribal, Inter-Tribal and Multi-Tribal identities (Chapter 3). Lornell and Stephenson note that the expressive quality of Hip Hop offers identity to the audience and performer alike as it serves as a persistent sounding board for the community.

> Lornell and Stephenson state, "I'm black, I'm creative, I'm proud, and I'm representing" as the undercurrent 'shout-outs' present in Hip Hop culture (Lornell and Stephenson 45).

With their Multi-Tribal identity, WOR culturally transcribes the meaning of these statements to be, "I'm Native, I'm creative, I'm proud, and I'm re-presenting."

BONUS TRACK

This chapter elected to outline several theoretical perspectives and critical Native epistemologies that are at the core of this reading and Native scripting of Hip Hop. It's worth noting that the closing quote by Lornell and Stephenson, transcribed through the Native agency of W.O.R., remains stable and has even had the needle moved toward prominence by the new generation, the second Native Hip Hop generation. "I'm Native, I'm creative, I'm proud, and I'm re-presenting." Harnessing the socio-political energy and local/national/global visibility of the current civil rights demonstrations (i.e., Black Lives Matter, Me Too Movement, Idle No More, Dakota Access Pipeline) the younger second generation of Native Hip Hop artists continue to firm this articulated theme.

The opening of this chapter identifies the critical theoretical trajectory that is central to this work. The before mentioned "theoretical strategy" outlined within this work has been tried and tested since the writing of this work, 2009. Native Hip Hop artists – regardless of the Hip Hop genre these artists elect to employ – has sufficed the "[fluid] re-present[ion of] Native identity, [that is refocused and]...[repositions tribal identity] within Hip Hop." This development of Native Hip Hop further articulates that the interconnected points of space, place, and identity have been used as the "strategy [to circumvent] historical stereotypes and a racist approach to Native identity." No longer do Native Hip Hop artists have to rely upon intercultural connections, or an invested possession of ownership recognized by the early African-American Hip Hop communities.

As Hip Hop has matured into its 50th year of cultural, artistic, and social expression, those who came to be known as the O.G. (Original Gangster) or the founding artists and media influencers at the core of the Hip Hop lexicon no longer hold a firm grip on the dynamic glocal expressions of Hip Hop. Extending this dialectic, the younger Native Hip Hop generation has re-presented Androutsopoulos' glocal theory. Applying the trickster hermeneutics of Vizenor, Native Hip Hop has ascertained each of the

Elements of Hip Hop. Native Hip Hop applied a pivot from the assumed direction of acculturation and artistic appropriation to embrace an intercultural dialectic. Native Hip Hop narrates a dialogue through the fluid multiplicities of tribal identity formation, Tribal/ Inter-Tribal/Multi-Tribal. Non-Native Hip Hop's subaltern voice speaks to a glocal representation. A Tribal/Inter-Tribal/Multi-Tribal Native Hip Hop voice(s) speaks across a subaltern reference, negotiating Native/Indigenous/Indian identity. The collective Native artistic conscious strategy flips-the-script of racist references and dismissed historical traumas. Homi Bhabha's Third Space theory remains relevant in direct application by the second generation of Native Hip Hop artists. The Third Space is no longer limited to the margins or mediate spaces between colonizer-colonized. This critical rhetorical lens is expanded as contemporary Native Hip Hop artists view this colonial binary from a distance.

Providing a sovereign voice(s) and expressed directive of Hip Hop formalized on the grounds of Native/Indigenous/Indian self-determination, Native Hip Hop artists gaze at the circular dialogue of the Third Space. Native Hip Hop artists recognize the colonizer (read: ownership, power, authority) and the colonized (read: submissive voice, reactionary identity formation, controlled limited/localized visibility). Bhabha's theories of *Hybridity* (read: cultures as being malleable and shaped by the events and interactions of external socio-political and identity economic conditions) and *Mimicry* (read: the colonized subject constructs and reflects identity through the authenticity of the colonizer) are obfuscated by contemporary Native Hip Hop artists. Consciously willing to not participate in the colonizer-colonized discourse allows the second generation of Native Hip Hop artists to script their vernaculars and signifiers of Hip Hop. Native Hip Hop artists avoid the pitfalls of racist cultural reification and disenfranchisement by actively focusing upon their expressive arts founded upon sovereign self-determination.

The global-local uninformed knowledge of "(American) Indian Hip Hop" may potentially subject Native Hip Hop as an *other* – without proper posture or cultural relevance. To that affect, any one of the three theoretical positions of cultural expression, a Third Space, Hybridity, or Mimicry devalues the sovereign self-determined expressions central to Native artists.

Through Vizenor's trickster hermeneutics, Native Hip Hop artists took ownership, authority, and control of identity construction in the space, place, and agency of Hip Hop. The second generation of Native Hip Hop artists re-present the core Elements of Hip Hop and flip-the-script on what the larger non-Native Hip Hop community, infrastructure and media came to assimilate as "Indian rap," or "(American) Indian Hip Hop." The trickster – to employ Vizenor's theory – acted on the glocal non-Native Hip Hop culture at large. Native Hip Hop did not contribute to the dialogue circumnavigating within the Third Space. There was no tribal Hybridity. There was no Indian Mimicry. There was only to become a firm dialectic, tribal rhetoric, Native/Indigenous/Indian Hip Hop epistemology, and cultural contact maintained by tribal sovereignty and artistic self-determination.

The political strategies of the 1950s, 60s, and 70s, designed to reduce, eradicate, and terminate the Indian Policies, Indian governmental agencies, and nation-to-nation relationship between Indian Nations and the U.S. government, are re-presented by the younger Indian Hip Hop artists. Albeit urban or reservation, the second generation of Native hip Hop artists illustrates these termination policies as sites of active agency for cultural knowledge, customs, expressions, and sovereignty. Termination and assimilation policies become new vehicles for expression and language to be voiced by Native Hip Hop artists. This artistic agency was not for an isolated Native identity, but in response to the assumptions of power, privilege, identity economics, and socio-political visibility of the large non-Native glocal realities.

This chapter involved deconstructions of various Indian references each poised to determine, define, and use the Indian icon/image for its own purpose, point, and established place of privilege. It was important to endure this reading of American pop cultural references and inclusion of the Indian icon/image to see how Native Hip Hop artists at that time, 2009, displayed their tribally specific knowledge(s) of identity along a fluid continuum, Tribal/Inter-Tribal/Multi-Tribal, while capturing the necessary artistic techniques of Hip Hop. Post-2009, and ongoing into the subsequent 21st century years, the second generation of Native Hip Hop artists have established a Hip Hop canon securely recognized as being Native/ Indigenous/Indian, a Hip Hop Indigeneity identity.

As I argued previously, contemporary Native Hip Hop artists produced their creative works with exclusive tribal politics to illustrate a sovereign self-determined artistic voice(s). The second generation of Native Hip Hop artists established a genre of Hip Hop not to be a sub-genre within Hip Hop's authentic ideology, power, identity economic, or socio-political standards. The younger Native Hip Hop artists followed the firm lead of W.O.R., et al. and voiced a misuse of the Indian icon/image. The second generation of Native Hip Hop artists yelled against Hip Hop's early years of seminal cultural expression devoid of accurate Native/Indigenous/Indian representation. Continuing to use racist, limited, and token signifiers of Native/Indigenous/Indian, it was the founding Native Hip Hop artists (O.N. – Original Natives) who displayed their works in contest against the EuroAmerican pop cultural biased, racist, mis-informed, and derogatory socio-political agendas set toward Native Peoples. Extending this tribal agency, the second generation of Native Hip Hop artists actively codified what was only a minor articulation of Native reference at the start of Hip Hop. The importance and contemporary relevance of Indian artistic expression through the re-presentation of the Elements/Points of Hip Hop is recognized through a collective conscious in the Native Hip Hop canon. It is this articulated point within Hip Hop glocal culture where Native Hip Hop firmly yell, "I'm Native, I'm creative, I'm proud, and I'm re-presenting."

Chapter 3. The Location of Tribal Identity

"Indian people define themselves, their experience and significance every day in hundreds of variations."[96]

"I'm Proud of the Skin I'm In!"[97]

In this chapter I expand upon Du Bois' conception of double consciousness to illustrate that the three fluid forms of contemporary Native identity, Tribal, Inter-Tribal, and Multi-Tribal, constitute a triple consciousness. A summary of the migration of modern powwow culture into the urban center with the Relocation program will help explain the natural evolution of these identities. A deconstructive reading of the work by Stephen Cornell, Joan Nagel, et al, will further substantiate how these identities have become important in the present post-modern era. Finally, an analysis of two audio examples by WOR will assist in defining these Native identity formations.

The limitations of Double Consciousness

For many Native/non-Native scholars the complexity of Native identity is limited to a binary; reservation (rural) and urban (city). Du Bois' 1903 theory of "double consciousness," articulated "two souls, two thoughts, two unreconciled strivings ... in one dark body, whose dogged strength alone keeps it from being torn asunder" (Du Bois 3) and suggested early on that a complexity and multiplicity of identities could be defined within a single entity (person) or action. The anthropologist Roger Abrahams extends Du Bois' argument by suggesting that,

> "Performers...know that they may be playing to two audiences simultaneously – the black community and the white hipsters or weekend trippers. ...Black performers constantly recognize that the very performance that is conventional within the black community will be seen as strange, as pleasurably exotic to the hipster. Thus they operate out of a kind of double consciousness, knowing that they are called upon to present an image which will be interpreted as exotic to the outside world and not to the blacks in the audience." (Abrahams 155)

Thomas F. DeFrantz reinforces the same premise when he suggests that the history of "Black social dances contain dual transcripts of "public" and "private" meaning. These transcripts mirror constructions of outwardly entertaining and secretly derisive rhetoric articulated by black cultural theorists including W.E.B. Du Bois at the turn of the century." (DeFrantz 2 - 3).

Alfonso Ortiz in "The Earth Shall Weep" notes a "double vision" (Wilson12) in reference to how Native people have come to view history in a pre-contact/post-contact ideology. Henry Louis Gates, Jr. and Richard Wright echo these same ideas in their work by integrating the double consciousness/double-bind theories, and it is Wright who consistently referred to the "double vision" of African American people[98]. Regardless of how it is presented, the double consciousness/double bind theory can be viewed as a reflexive manner from the outside (other) toward the (self).

The influence of the Modern Powwow tradition

Jack Forbes, as quoted by Joan Nagel, illustrates the complexity of identity stemming from the hypodescent (the "one –drop rule"). He views the "one drop rule" as a strategic tool designed to not only limit "blacks" but also to categorize "Indians." (Nagel 71)[99] He further reveals that the "emphasis on the hypodesccent (the "one-drop rule") in categorizing Indians has the result that "blacks' are always 'blacks' even when mixed with white or American Indian. 'Indians', however, exist as a cultural category (or as a caste). They must remain unchanged to be considered 'Indian'. (qtd. in Nagel 71)

The principle dictates that Native people are required to be marginalized physically, consciously, and legally in segregation. Native people repeatedly face legal measures, such as the Termination Policies, and absorbed racialized stereotypes, defined by American popular media, that perpetuate misrepresentations and enforce a position of control over Native people. The Native sociologist Z.G. Standing Bear who, after concluding a discussion of urban Native people for non-Native school children in 1988, offered the statement that "there aren't any real Indians left." (qtd. in Nagel 71). To overcome this prescribed (un)consciousness of Native people one must view Native identity as a cultural continuum.

As stated previously, movement for Native people is not uncommon. From the first forced diaspora of Native people within the United States, c. 1830s with the Indian Removal Act (IRA) to the creation of the Indian New Deal policies of 1934, post-WW II economic conditions, P.L-280, the Indian Relocation Services Programs and P.L-959 (Indian Vocational Training and Employment Assistance Program), Native people have been moved from established reserved locations into urban centers throughout the U.S. (Neils 5 – 10) Upon first arrival to the urban centers Native people were exposed to other forms of creative expressions from cultures both Native and non-Native. Urban centers presented the location for a dynamic exchange of Native cultures for the growing Native population (Fixico 123 - 189, Nagel 114, Cornell 87 - 105) thereby leading to a resurgence and re-presentation of Native traditions and cultures (Nagel 158 - 184). Influenced by stereotyped Plains Native cultures, a re-vival of the powwow tradition began that led to the ultimate creation of the "inter-tribal"[100] powwow. (Buff 147 – 170, Nagel 201 – 205, Fixico 56 – 57, personal interview Means 2 Aug 2003) These social gatherings served the urban Native population as a point of articulation to re-present their "tribal"[101] identities both real and imagined (Anderson 37 - 46).

Further enhanced by the growing Red Power Movement of the 1970s, the inter-tribal powwow developed as a location where Native people could construct, de-construct and re-construct their own personal, and family, Native culture(s) within an empowered environment established to breed community awareness. (Means interview 2 Aug 2003, Nagel 158 - 184)

Native people now had an arena where their cultural artifacts were in sovereign control. This re-presentation of identity for urban Natives begs the critical and not so simple question; "what is a contemporary Native?" Through an active appropriation of Native and non-Native artistic expression, the image of the contemporary Native is presented as one engaged in both older, imagined (traditional) signifiers and constructs these with newer (contemporary) cultural and identity signifiers. (Nagel 43 - 79) Through the free form, dynamic exchange and creation of dance styles and regalia, songs and drum styles in the modern powwow tradition, new (contemporary) Native identities began to become present (McAllester 1982, Howard 1983, de Shane 1991, DesJarlait 1997, Ellis 1990/1999, Buff 2001, Krouse 2001, Beck 2002, TallBear 2003, Lawlor 2006).

It is here, within this newly transformed powwow arena, for contemporary Native people that the singular (Tribal) location of culture gave way to the development of and inter-tribal powwow (Inter-Tribal) that allowed multiple articulations of Native identity to become present and active (Multi-Tribal).

Tribal Identity Formation

Presently, there are a myriad of categorizations of Native identity; Sub-tribal (Cornell, Nagel), Tribal (Buff, Cornell, Fixico Lobo, Gonzales, Nagel, et al), Supra-tribal (Cornell, Nagel), Pan-Indian (Buff, Cornell, Fixico, Nagel, et al), Urban Indian (Fixico, Cornell, Gonzales, Lobo, Nagel), Regionalist (Gonzales), Reservationist (Gonzales), Traditionalist (Cornell, Gonzales, Nagel), Neo-Indian (Fixico), Retribalist (Cornell), Retraditionalist (Nagel), Multitribal Urban Indian (Gonzales), Enrollees (Gonzales), Automatic Enrollees (Gonzales), Adoptees (Gonzales) and postindian (Vizenor).[102] From this list it becomes clear that the majority of these terms were created with the emergence of the Red Power Movement in the 1970s.[103] bell hooks notes the formation of a postmodern Blackness that takes into account completely the issues of race, gender, identity and culture[104]. Replacing the term Black(ness) in hooks' theory with Native(ness), we can begin to see how a contemporary reading and application of Native identity is formed that requires a cultural definition that function on multiple levels. This exchange offers liberty to the first steps in the process of constructing a postmodern Native identity. The identity formation absorbs references to an "Other" (Native/non-Native) but is not limited by this reference. Rather, the resultant identity functions as an active critique of the self, by itself and ultimately for itself.

The philosopher Kwame Anthony Appiah offers a point of departure from the limited restrictions of the double consciousness/double bind theory. Appiah states that, "identities are complex and multiple and grow out of a history of changing responses to economic, political, and cultural forces, almost always in opposition to other identities....they flourish despite what I (call) 'misrecognition' of their origins; despite, that is, their roots in myths and lies." (Appiah 178)

Appiah includes cultural history constructed by those for whom the history exists. The complexity of change does not remain static. Rather, the movement of Native people into a connection with the non-Native community required dynamic change that created multiple identities. As Lawrence Grossberg noted, "[r]ap (read: Hip Hop culture) projects a critical voice, explaining, demanding, urging." (181) It is within and from this critical voice that Native identity is re-constructed in a fluid continuum that maintains cultural association and recognition as it is articulated individually.

The fluidity of identity allows Native people to integrate, communicate and cross-connect their tribal identity. Native people are offered tools for cross-cultural communication that are syncretic as well as adaptive, reflecting the dynamic state of Native identity. There is no singular point of arrival for Native identity, but rather a moment that encourages multiple methods of identity construction. These locations of identity engage within a dynamically complex rhizome (Deleuze and Guattari 3 - 25) that are constructed, de-constructed and continually re-constructed. Stephen Cornell's seminal work on Native identity makes clear the multiplicity of voices and identities available for contemporary Native people.

All through his research on Native identity, Stephen Cornell presents the transformation of the tribe through a process of tribalization to articulate a foundation for contemporary urban Indian identity.[105] Cornell explains that through,

"interaction with Euro-Americans and their institutions, Native American identities were focused increasingly at the maximal, tribal level. That was the tribal level of identity,...that received reinforcement...in large part to the nature and shape of that [Indian-White] interaction...the identity [tribal] itself was already

a significant element in Indian lives." (Cornell 102)[106]

Cornell continues this line of discourse by illustrating that tribal (read: singular) identity for Native people became dislocated from the limitation of this singular perspective. Multiple Native identities became possible in a new political climate with the realization of the IRA and the Indian New Deal (Cornell 87 – 101). The architecture of assimilation embedded within these policies became the pathway for multiple views of Native identity. Cornell notes that Native people during this period engaged and culturally developed "...broad boundaries of tribal identity..." (Cornell 102).

"The cultural and conceptual content of tribal identity was once largely the same for all members of the (read: singular) tribe but is no longer so. Change in the focus of identity has been convergent; the point of convergence has been the tribe. But change in the content of identity has been divergent. Many persons may identify themselves as Navajo, or Oglala, or Cherokee, but what that means to each one may be very different." (Cornell 102 – 103)

Cornell posits that the transformation of identity realized through the active and expressive construction/deconstruction of Native people. Although politics may have initiated this transformation, the end result reveals multiple perspectives of identity, a Multi-Tribal identity, along a fluid continuum.

Further, Cornell states that the "...meanings [culture and identity] are essentially continuous with the past, changed by time and circumstance and the influence of both Euro-Americans and other Indians..." (Cornell 103) This construction/deconstruction and now presented re-construction of Native identity remain culturally based in "aboriginal modes of thought and action and structures of social relations." (Cornell 103) From this we can conclude that Native artists continue to transform their artistic work in a continuously fluid manner balancing the dual realities of contemporary and traditional. Art re-presents the cultural currency of Native identity.

Cornell's critique, however, assumes that for Native people there is no intersection of identities. The extension of Native identity, as defined by Cornell, continues along a path that presumably is continuous, yet it flows linearly in one direction. It moves from a tribal (historic) identity to an urban supra-tribal or pan-Indian (political) identity. This theory does not consider the intersection or middle ground between other Native identities. Though Cornell, along with Nagel, acknowledges the emergence of American Indian identity with the cultural renewal in the post-Red Power era (c. 1970s), there is still an undercurrent present in his scholarship that limits the conflicting dialectic within identity formation.[107]

The construction of Tribal, Inter-Tribal, Multi-Tribal identity

With a critical reading of Stephen Cornell we are able to extend this area of discourse through a tribal [singular] focus into a tribalized [multiple] focus (Cornell 89 – 104). Native identity logically encompasses a continuum that flows through three identity areas: Tribal, Inter-Tribal, Multi-Tribal (Lechusza 2002). The "twentieth-century double-think" (Fischer 198) is no longer adequate because "audiences have become multiple" (Fischer 199). The "'bifocality' moreover must increasingly be a shorthand for 'two or more' cultures in juxtaposition..."Cultures and ethnicities as sets are more like families of resemblances than simple typological trees." Michael Fischer strives toward the same multifocality of identity in his assessment of ethnicity as,

> "not something that is simply passed on from generation to generation, taught and learned; it is something **dynamic**...",[108] "...flower[ed] only through struggle", "...discovered and reinvented in the new works...", "...a voice or style that does not violate one's several components of identity...", "a (re-)invention and discovery of a vision, both ethical and future-oriented.", where "...the meaning is abstracted from the past...is workable for the future." (Fischer 195 – 197)

To build on the work established by Cornell, et al, three identity formations become apparent: Tribal, Inter-Tribal and Multi-tribal (Lechusza 14). With the addition of the political work formulated by Stephen Cornell in 1999, we will be able to see how these identity areas are expanded to re-present a fluid dialogical continuum of contemporary Native identity.

A Tribal identity refers to a specific location of Native identity constructed through family history, heritage/identity and often defined as one's singular tribal enrollment. An example of this would be a family who identified wholly as being Diné. Cornell defines this perspective as an "anchored" tribal identity that maintains "specific historical experience(s) of the group [tribe]..." (Cornell 103). Cornell also identifies the need for tribal enrollment, "tribal membership" and the political capitol that comes with this identification (Cornell 103).

An Inter-tribal identity refers to the merging of two or more Native identities/cultures and histories within a singular person. This articulation became more present after the second forced Diasporic migration of Natives into urban centers with the Indian Reorganization Act (IRA) and the Indian New Deal. Here, inter-tribal mixing became more evident. Inter-tribal identity is like DuBois' historic concept of double consciousness; including by extension Frank Wright's and Henry Louis Gates' conception of "double vision." For Cornell, the two dimensions of Native identity are defined by their political organization and self-articulated identity (Cornell 103). This enables Cornell to move from a historic, tribal-based political organization of Native identity toward a self-identified concept of political Native identity. An example would be a person who identifies him(her)self firmly as two, or more, different tribal identities, i.e., Luiseño and Maidu.

A Multi-tribal identity refers to the further juxtaposition of Native identities within a person articulated by Native cultural appropriation. An example of this could be a person who is Mescalero (Apache) who participates as a powwow grass dancer, a dance style neither traditional nor indigenous to the Mescalero. (Lechusza14 - 15) The person in this example articulates his Multi-Tribal identity through the expansion of his original Native heritage [Tribal] into the powwow arena [Inter-Tribal] as a grass dancer [Multi-Tribal]. Stephen Cornell refers to this expansion as the point of "tribalization". Cornell defines the political transformation of the singular (Tribal) into the Inter-Tribal as it engages Indian-White political relations and finally into the Multi-Tribal that establishes a working political structure for Native people that is "capable of defending those rights (read: laws) and pursuing Indian interest within the framework of U.S. political and legal institutions." (Cornell 103 – 104) This viewpoint illustrates the movement, over time, from pre-Contact to the present, demonstrating how Native people have moved from singular to multiple realities in Figure 3.1 (Cornell 103).

<u>Political Organization Self-Concept or Identity</u>

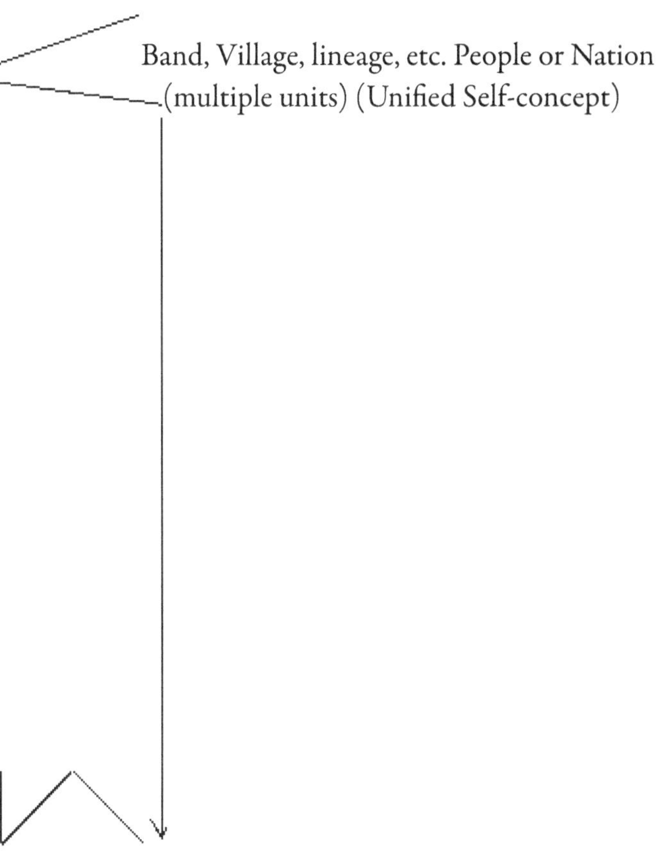

Band, Village, lineage, etc. People or Nation
(multiple units) (Unified Self-concept)

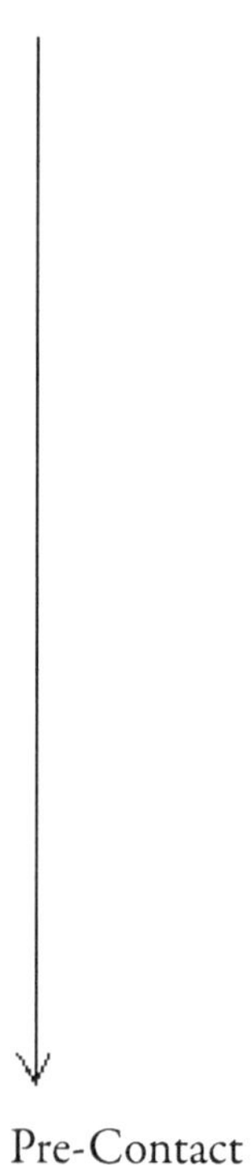

Pre-Contact

Conflict

Reservation

IRA

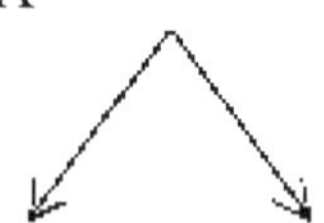

Today Tribe Tribe
(single unit) (multiple self-concept)

Figure 3.1: "Tribalization" by Stephen Cornell in <u>The Return of the Native</u> (103)

The Deconstruction of Native identity

Cornell establishes in this Tribalization diagram a hierarchy in Native identity.[109] Initially, Cornell refers to "multiple units" of political organization during the Pre-Contact era as unimportant to Native people. This is identified on the diagram by the lesser-than symbol that designates the pre-eminence of "People or Nation" over self-concept or identity. Following the "multiple units" line of logic into "Today", Cornell recognizes a movement toward a "single unit", the "Tribe" that according to this diagram, has greater importance than a "Tribe" with "multiple self-concepts". This is reflected using a greater-than symbol acknowledging the prominence of the "single unit Tribe."

Cornell's modus operandi illustrates the evolution of the tribe from the sub-tribal (band, village, kin, clan) to tribal (reservation-based, historic, politically official) and to the supra-tribal (national, pan-Indian)[110]. The framework of this scholarship rests on the political organization and activism of the Red Power Movement in the 1970s. This ideology consistently reifies a pan-Indian perspective as being quasi-ultimatum, for all Native people that, by definition, limits Native people to a singular perspective; a pan-reality[111]. Angela Gonzales asserts that, " [i]n most urban Indian communities, a form of pan-Indian culture and identity has developed that cuts across tribal lines. As both an identity and a culture, pan-Indianism draws heavily from popular images and traditions of Plains Indians. Such ethnic markers are normative, ahistorical, and often based on stereotypes." (Gonzales in Lobo 177)

Gonzales analyzes the political nature of identity construction by asserting that legal formations, such as Blood Quantum, are "crafted by the trajectories of history, science, and politics-replacing and devaluating relational ties... and other patterns of social interaction." (Gonzales 181 – 182). Additionally, Gonzales confirms what scholars elsewhere have noted; that these definitions of Native identity are recognized as debilitating, marginalizing, are without concern for Native views of self/tribal identification with the knowledge that "neither state nor federal agencies agree on a single definition." (Gonzales 1820)[112]

This sentiment is defended by Donald Fixico, who in his seminal work on termination and relocation, aptly entitled, Termination and Relocation, Federal Indian Policy, 1945 – 1960, surmised that the U.S. Federal government had to recognize that "no single (termination or relocation) policy can be devised that will successfully serve all Indians, who represent many different tribes, languages, and cultures" both on micro (tribal) and macro (national) levels. (Fixico 197)

Vine Deloria, Jr., offers a prophetic statement about the movement and direction of contemporary Native identity when he stated that, "[e]veryone (read: Native people) doesn't have to do everything that the old Indians did in order to have a modern Indian identity…tribal cultures-like all cultures-have changed, and will continue to do so over time." (qtd. In Lobo 178) In Deloria's reading of the "modern Indian identity" we find that attention is drawn toward a Multi-Tribal climate for Native people. This reasoning builds upon the consistency of Native people to engage Native/non-Native communities in an inter-cultural manner that affords the construction of an Inter-Tribal and/or Multi-Tribal identity. The application and maintenance of these inter-cultural connections will be on an individual basis. As there is no one singular Native identity, there cannot be one definitive process through which Native people construct identity. Susan Lobo defines this important point through her statement that, "…there is no such thing as pan-Indian today…"[113].

Similarly, Joan Nagel confirms that Native identity is "[m]ultitiered or multilayered". (Nagel 21) "Which of these identities" Nagel continues, "a native individual chooses to present in a social interaction depends partly on where and with whom the interaction occurs." (Nagel 21) Together these statements offered by Deloria, Lobo and Nagel define that there is a contemporary Native identity in place that exists beyond the static limitation of pan-Indian-ness. Cornell defines this point as realized in the political sphere through a linear trajectory [See Figure 3.2].

Examining Native identity through a Tribal/Inter-Tribal/Multi-Tribal lens reveals an identity formation that is fluid, negotiated and incorporated as a person/tribe deems necessary for a given context and/or situation. Figure 3.3 demonstrates how the application of these Native identity formations appear in practice and in contemporary reality.

Sub-tribal

Tribal

Supra-tribal
    (pan-Indian)
    Figure 3.2: Stephen Cornell Identity Categorizations

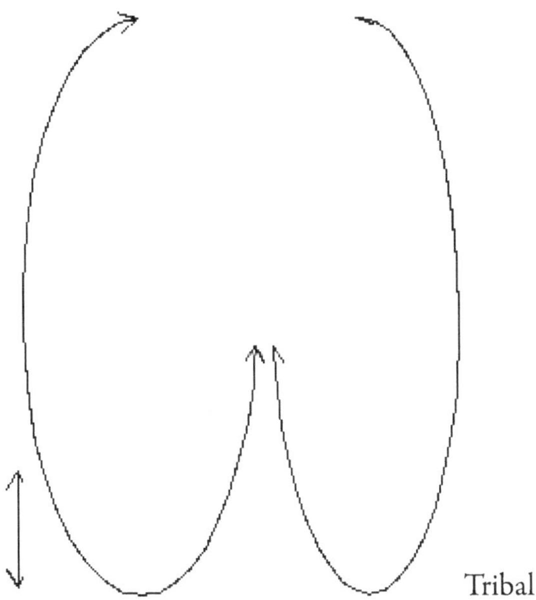

Inter-Tribal

Multi-Tribal

Figure 3.3: Tribal/Inter-Tribal/Multi-Tribal Identity Formations

Donald Fixico in his book The Urban Indian Experience in America notes the necessity of balance in the ongoing negotiation and reflection of self and communal Native identity (Fixico 183 – 189). Additionally, Fixico reminds us that, historically, Native people have prioritized the group, or community, over the individual. During the Relocation/Termination period the urbanized Indian made the shift from group to individual (Fixico 172 – 188). The identity formations of Tribal, Inter-Tribal, and Multi-Tribal offer contemporary Native people a balanced method of identity realization in a process that allows a dynamic intersection of identity and culture. This is graphically represented in Figure 3.4.

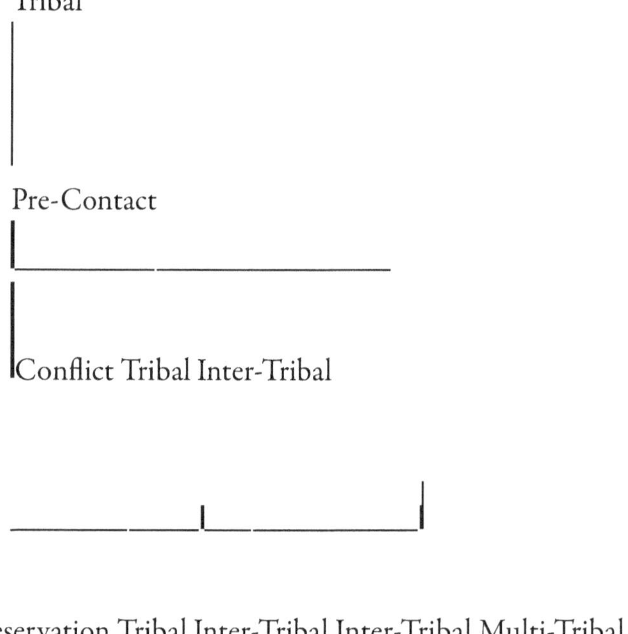

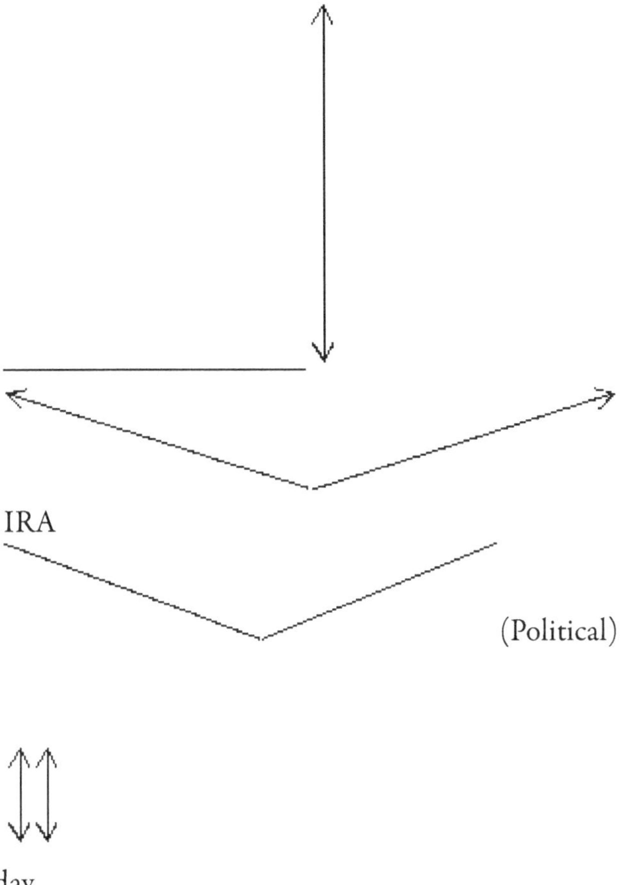

Figure 3.4: Tribal/Inter-Tribal/Multi-Tribal Identity Formations

Joan Nagel embraces the political "supra-tribal" identity formation defined by Stephen Cornell in defining an "urban Indian renewed identity" that arose out of the Relocation and Termination Policies (c. 1950s). This culminated in the political activism of the Red Power movement in the 1970s.[114] The identifier, supra-tribal identity, as used by Nagel creates a pan-Indian signifier that essentializes Native people.

Although Nagel works toward a post-modern, or rather post-indian, perspective of identity, the use of "supra-tribal" or "pan-Indianness" works against the mobility and fluidity of Native culture and identity. The term post-indian, as defined by Gerald Vizenor, is a literary device that re-contextualizes the "indian" as a simulation constructed by Euro-Americans. (Vizenor 4 – 5) This Euro-American action imposes a limitation upon the reality of Native people. "Indian", reinserts in pure "trickster" fashion the dynamic identity and cultural relevance of Native people. This "trickster hermenutical" transposition dislocates Native identity from the limited categorization of a colonialist structure[115]. Native identity then is a fluid continuum realized in the ongoing negotiation between Tribal, Inter-Tribal and Multi-Tribal formations. These identity formations do not construct the same model with a different name but strive to engage a sense of Native identity that is flexible while respecting self-determination.

Toward a New Native Identity

The Native identity formations presented above build on the work of Nagel, Vizenor, Cornell, et al. A fluid theoretical strategy for Native identity is outlined that embraces the historic, ideological, political, social, real/imagined continuum of Native identity. The application of these formations assists in the structuring of identity for any Native person regardless of their current location of culture.

The historic canon of scholarship that dealt with the critical arena of Native identity has a bifocal perspective fixed between urban and reservation identities. The different territories of physical, mental, environmental, spatial and political[116] bring to light multiple views of Native identity that become tested within each of these territories. Homi Bhabha's theoretical conception of Third Space[117] at first glance would appear to be a literary tool capable of articulating the dynamism of contemporary Native identity.

Bhabha states that the "Third Space displaces the histories that constitute it, and sets up new structures of authority, new political initiatives which are inadequately understood through received wisdom" (Bhabha qtd. in Pulitano 177 – 178). It is the enunciation of this split that, for Bhabha, "destroys the logics of synchronicity and evolution which traditionally authorize the subject of cultural knowledge." (Bhabha 36) However, Bhabha continues to operate along a structrualist binary position that subsequently restates the subject-other. For Native identity this binary reads as the "subject" being a Tribal identity and the "other" as being an Inter-Tribal identity. The Multi-Tribal identity, as outlined previously, does not find a position within this theory. Bhabha's Third Space is a critical tool that allows for a close identity reading, a dismantling of previous colonial concepts of identity, and assist in defining new areas for representation and the negotiation of meaning.[118] The Third Space, however, continues to define itself through a constructed "national text translated into modern Western forms of information technology, language, dress." (Bhabha 38) The dual territories of the Third Space are maintained by a colonialist paradigm that does not completely afford a Native translation of identity. The "diversity" and "hybridity" (Bhabha 38) to which Bhabha prescribes his theory are limited by their attraction to and definition from Western culture. As outlined above, Native people engage the composite location in which their identity is formed to construct a fluid dynamic of identity. The embodiment of Western culture within Native identity does not limit identity construction for Native people. Through a Native translation of Western culture identity then is extended and further dynamically expressed.

Frederic Jameson contributes toward the expressed dynamic, dislocation and re-articulation of Native identity. In his article 'Secondary elaborations',[119] Jameson is cited by Bhabha as being able to envision "the representation of global 'difference'"[120] through a focus on multiple existence of tension created spatially and historically. (Bhabha 218)

"Different moments in historical or existential time are here simply filed in different places; the attempt to combine them even locally does not slide up and down a temporal scale...but jumps back and forth across a game board that we conceptualize in terms of distance." (Jameson qtd. in Bhabha 218)

This "non-synchronous" (Bhabha 218) position speaks to the Native identity formations defined previously. Tribal, Inter-Tribal and Multi-Tribal Native identity formations, by the integration of Jameson's reading, can co-exist within and without permanent temporal or physical locations. They each can function as interdependent identities that "jump back and forth" as the application requires. Where Bhabha constructs identity along the lines of subject-other, nation-state, Gerald Vizenor reminds us that Nationalism is a simulation. (Vizenor 60) Native identity survives beyond the forced simulations of colonial dominance through the active transposition and the coherence of "shadows". (Vizenor 60) "Shadows" for Vizenor can "tease and loosen the bonds of representation in stories. The meaning of words is determined by the nature of language games." (Vizenor 72) Like Jameson previously, Vizenor's "shadows" move without permanence to accountability to time and space. They can "jump back and forth" engaging the moment, or rather identity at the present moment. The second point that Vizenor offers here, the "nature of language games", begs the application of these theories for Native identity.

Joan Nagel coined the term and idea of the "new Indian" (Nagel 36), as a Native person who resides within the urban center. The "new Indian" identity appears to be constructed through census data and research beginning in the 1960s and continues to be present well into the 1990s.[121] Nagel qualifies this perspective on the reservation Indian identity not by exploring the development of this specific identity, but by perceiving this Native identity through a binary lens tied to the termination policies.[122] The urban Indian experience defines the "new Indian" and the reservation Indian is terminated. Elvira Paulitino notes that for Native scholars this binary area is a "safe territory" from which to construct Native identity (Paulitano 129).

This reading of the "safe territory" articulates a polar division between urban/reservation proximities that reifies internal differences within the Native communities. With respect to contemporary Native identity, these differences remain susceptible to external stereotypes that may already be in place within the non-Native consciousness. Bhabah's Third Space is localized where the two points to divide are the urban and reservation. This leaves the Native person to reside within the Third constructed Space of the nation-state that is itself a colonialist apparatus of the Termination Policies.

Jacques Derrida's critique of logo-centrism offers a theoretical device in that leverages the difference, or "differance" between these two locations, urban/reservation, and their assumed Native identities[123]. For Derrida, the critique of logocentrism is the breaking down of binary oppositions by exploring their "mutual crossings and involvements." (Pulitano 171) Applying the device of difference to the binary of urban and reservation, the inherent difference, internal and external, does not create a separation, but are points of Inter-Tribal connection and dialogue. Nagel's concept of the "new Indian" identity avoids the reality that Native people express and re-present through their contemporary identities. By Vizenor's definition, Nagel's "new Indian" is a simulation of Indian identity that exists within the preoccupation of manifest manners. (Vizenor 59 – 60) "Manifest manners are the simulations of dominance; the notions and misnomers that are read as the authentic and sustained as representations of Native American Indians." (Vizenor 5 – 6) Nagel strives to constructs an Indian identity that articulates the current Native cultural complexities that originated through the socio-political climate of the 1970s. (Nagel 2001) The exact methodology (research techniques, social science vernacular, Native American socio-political studies) Nagel uses to structure the "new Indian" is itself the example of Vizenor's simulation. The forced creation of a Native reality through the tools and discourse of the dominant paradigm is how Vizenor realizes his term and use of simulation. (Vizenor 4) The simulated Native identity is void of substance, but full of rhetorical fantasy. Nagel positions the "new Indian" identity as one that will embrace inter-tribal difference and situate itself within the urban landscape. Vizenor counterbalances this placement by the creation of the postindian warrior. (Vizenor 4 – 6) "The postindian warriors are new indications of a narrative recreation, the simulations that overcome the manifest manners of dominance." (Vizenor 6) It is the postindian perspective that maintains a "surveillance" within the dynamic realities of Native identity (literature, culture, history, art and sciences).[124] The postindian is the literary antidote to hegemony. It is a Native post-structuralist application originating from contemporary Native "trickster" narratives that, among other things, transposes historical stasis.

Fredric Jameson positions both the rural and urban Native identity in consistent negotiation that defies a fixed point of space and place.[125] The fluidity across history and location for Jameson finds a playful partner in the "infinite layers" of Minh-ha T. Trinh. These "infinite layers" are the specific location from which static essentialist constructions of identity are departing. The layers acknowledge that there is not one single location of culture, or identity, but a multiplicity of identities that act in concert. (Trinh 90) Trinh's work establishes a balance for identity between these layers through which Jameson's theory can intersect, "jump[s] back and forth", in an improvisational manner. The concrete structure of identity begins to be disassembled through these collected theories to which Vizenor adds,

"The theories of structuralism, the myths of the universal and unexpected harmonies, and objective dissociations of natural tribal reason are dubious tropes to power in the literature of dominance. The simulations of manifest manners, casual evidence, objectivism, and transitive action have no referent, no sense of *postindian* play in language and experience, no shadows in silence, and no coherence of natural reason. The tribal referent is in the shadows of heard stories; shadows are their own referent,

and shadows are the silence and simulations of survivance."
(Vizenor 98)

By this accord, the location of Native identity is not limited in scope
but survives through the active amplification of existence and repetition of
process. The identity formations of Tribal, Inter-Tribal, Multi-Tribal are the
layers through which Native people "jump back and forth" improvisationally
through their own "self-identity" consciousness. (Vizenor 102) This process
outlines a self-referential fluid Native identity that resists static placement
but seeks contemporary indeterminate application.

The application of Identity formations: Nativist and Mixed-blood Identity

The identity formations of Tribal, Inter-Tribal, and Multi-Tribal act as a means for Native people to express and perform their identity(s) within a continuum that is continually influenced by contemporary environmental dynamics and global contexts. This section will describe how the three Native identity formations of Tribal, Inter-Tribal and Multi-Tribal are applied to both a Nativist and mixed-blood identity. Applying the three Native identity formations to both a Nativist and mixed-blood identity, we will see how these viewpoints are neither isolated nor singular.

A Nativist ideology is firmly and exclusively grounded in a Native perspective. Mixed-blood is a concept that is used to understand the mixing of various Native cultures, heritages and realities. Elvira Pulitano in her book, Toward a Native American Critical Theory,[126] insightfully examines this socially and politically charged concept as defined by both Native authors (Greg Sarris, Louis Owens, Gerald Vizenor, Paula Gunn Allen, Craig Womack, Robert Warrior, Elizabeth Cook-Lynn, Leslie Mormon Silko, N. Scott Momaday, Vine Deloria Jr.) and by non-Native authors (James Clifford, Minh-ha T. Tran, Arnold Krupat, Elaine Jahner, Rey Chow, Jean Baudrillard, Homi K. Bhabha, Kwame Anthony Appiah, Bill Ascroft, Griffiths Gareth, Helen Tiffin, Dipesh Chakrabarty, Gayatri Chakravorty Spivak)[127].

The term mixed-blood is used to articulate a racial position of a Native person both within and outside a Native heritage. (Cook-Lynn, Womack, Allen, Warrior qtd. in Pulitano 59 – 100) The term is predicated on a notion of authenticity based on an essentialized concept of blood quantum, tribal affiliation relating to a reservation system. (Cornell 104, Vizenor qtd. in Pulitano 175 – 176) The evolution of the modern mixed-blood identity has its origins in the Relocation and Termination Policies of the 1930 – 50s as described previously. As described in Chapter 1, the political intent of terminating the "Indian" was challenged by the persistent attitude and inter-cultural bonding of Native identity that took place during this era. The mixed-blood identity during the 1970s, Red Power movement, becomes the prominent means through which Native identity is maintained. This mixed-blood identity involves a binding together of multiple Native and non-Native cultures and histories. Ultimately, the mixed-blood identity strives to be the balanced position between a multiplicity of Native and non-Native identities.

The counterpoint to a political essentailized position of identity construction is a Nativist, or "tribalcentric" identity. (Pulitano 60) This view of race and culture maintains a legally protected definition of Native identity as authentic but does so through a singular tribal ideology. (Pulitano 59 – 62). A "tribalcentric" approach establishes and solidifies boundaries within the Native communities that are designed to house, foster, and protect a singular tribal perspective to confirm an ideological American Indian cultural cannon. As the critics Sarris, Owens, Deloria, Vizenor have noted (qtd. in Pulitano 60 - 100), this manner of cultural operation does more harm than good for the complex dynamic culture that contemporary Native people maintain.

These restrictions on the work of Native people deflate the cultural nuance, tribal subtleties and contributing global voice of Native people. The "purist" attitude of a Nativist ideology is prescribed by the dominant political laws that govern Native people within the U.S. The struggle for sovereign (read: singular) identity recognition of Nativist ideology must also maintain the political fractures that it is confronting. For Nativist identity to be realized political difference and struggle for a singular tribal identity is required.

The core values of each camp, Nativist and mixed-blood, are actually the same. Though it is obvious that their approaches are different, highly charged and ultimately politically centered (Cook-Lynn 152 – 158) each camp strives to present an authentic Native voice that can speak to and from the Native community.

A **Tribal Nativist** would be a person who identifies himself or herself by and within a singular Native culture. This is predicated on a limited sense of location (exclusively reservation) and contact (only tribal community) for this identity to exist purely. An example would be a person who is exclusively Dine (historically, culturally, spiritually, intellectually, artistically) and does not travel outside of the Dine culture.

An **Inter-Tribal Nativist** would be a person who connects, in any expressive manner, with another culture, Native or non-Native while retaining his/her singular tribal identity. The basis of this identity results from any cross-cultural contact, in any means possible, that maintains the individual tribal identity of the Native person. An example would be a Diné person who retains their singular tribal identity (historically, culturally, spiritually, intellectually, artistically) and who encounters another Native/non-Native culture. A prime example of this is when tribes share a common treaty or have some tribally centered disagreement with each other (i.e., Navajo-Hopi Land Dispute).

A **Multi-Tribal Nativist** intersects, again in any expressive manner possible or present, with other cultures, Native and/or non-Native, and who additionally engages or appropriates other Native/non-Native cultures. This third identity recognizes other Natives/non-Natives; their cultural artifacts are integrated and/or re-appropriated for the individual's own purposes, whilst retaining a singular tribal focus. Taking the same Diné person in question, s/he could be viewed as an author who composes literature, in English, about his/her tribe and culture from the perspective of a singular tribe who integrates "outside" literary devices and techniques to substantiate a singular tribal ideology. In other words, a Native author writes and appropriates the language of the colonizer (English) to re-present a singular tribal ideology and focus. The identity formations of Tribal, Inter-Tribal and Multi-Tribal can also apply to a mixed-blood ideology.

A **Tribal mixed-blood** person elects, in each situation or context (politically, socially, intellectually, spiritually, culturally, artistically) to focus specifically upon one of his/her tribal ethnicities. It is important to recognize that tribes maintain different ethnic constructions. The majority of these are done so politically, as discussed earlier in this chapter. This identity formation considers an underlying political agenda that is prescribed to a given tribe. Mixed-blood Native people negotiate this balance continually. This offers the ability of a Native person to focus specifically on one of their interwoven tribal identities for a particular situation as s/he maintains a passive association with their other tribal identity/identities.

Active and passive identity recognition for Native people allow their identity/identities to move from foreground to background retaining cultural relevance and personal importance.[128]. An example would be someone who is Choctaw/Cherokee and defines him/herself as a Cherokee while discussing an issue relevant to Cherokee history.

An **Inter-Tribal mixed-blood** person is one who acknowledges different tribal ethnicities that function in collaboration with each other in a given situation or context (politically, socially, educationally, spiritually, culturally, artistically). Using the Choctaw/Cherokee person as an example, he/she consistently balances each tribal ethnicity through an active integration of culture. The Inter-Tribal, for mixed-blood Native people, defines an area in which they are the most comfortable with their Native history/histories and ethnicity/ethnicities. It is here that the mixed-blood Native person can cross borders of their identity retaining a Native focus. To borrow a term from Krupat, mixed-blood people are the most adept "border intellectuals" since they must, as stated previously, consistently negotiate their identity through active definition and re-definition.

A **Multi-Tribal mixed-blood** person acknowledges his/her tribal ethnicities in functional collaboration with each other and engages an entirely different Native/non-Native culture that is then re-appropriated to enhance a Native identity. The Choctaw/Cherokee example balances each tribal ethnicity (Choctaw and Cherokee) actively integrating these two cultures within, for example, the San Ildefonso pottery style that results in a San Illdefonso pottery representation of Choctaw/Cherokee ethnicities.

This is the most common identity formation. Here, Native identity moves from foreground-background in a constant negotiation. This identity formation connects in Native cultural locations that can be understood by Mary Louise Pratt's notion of "contact zones"[129]. Within this identity formation Native people can intersect, clash and fluidly exchange their identities as they retain the cultural relevance of the tribe without the loss of the individual.

From these examples of Nativist and mixed-blood identity, we see that identity formations embrace the prescriptions of their culture. These identity formations allow agency for Native people regardless of their ideology, tribal affiliation or Native ethnicity while recognizing that there is a fluid continuum present within contemporary Native identity that necessitates this movement. Applying these identity formations to different Native cultural artifacts illustrates how these critical devices establish artistic agency for contemporary Native people. The double vision of Alfonso Ortiz, Native identity formations (read: "vision"), can be read as follows: **Tribal Vision** (pre-contact), **Inter-Tribal Vision** (post-contact). The extension of this concept for contemporary Native people yields a **Multi-Tribal Vision** (expressive contact) that exists in a fluid continuum of identity expressed freely within the arts and specifically within Hip Hop. WOR captures the creative energy that is centered within Hip Hop in order to collectively express their Multi-Tribal identity.

The Multi-Tribal identity of WithOut Rezervation (WOR)

WOR Native expand their work into a Multi-Tribal reality through signifyin' on the theories outlined above. Signifyin' is the celebrated theory of Henry Louis Gates Jr. that is defined as,

> "it functions to redress an imbalance of power, to clear a space, rhetorically. To achieve occupancy in the desired space, the Monkey rewrites the received order by exploiting the Lion's hubris and his inability to read the figurative other other than as the literal. Writers Signify on each other's text by rewriting the received textual tradition. This sort of Signifyin(g) revision serves, if successful, to create a space for the revisiting text. It also alters fundamentally the way we read the tradition, by defining the relation of the text at had to the tradition." (Gates 94)

Samuel Floyd describes Signifyin' as,

> "a way of saying on thing and meaning another; it is a reinterpretation, a metaphor for the revision of previous texts and figures; it is tropological thought, repetition with difference, the obscuring of meaning – all to achieve or reverse power, to improve situations, and to achieve pleasing results for the signifier." (qtd in Perry 61)

Signifyin' includes the theories and realities introduced into the formation of contemporary Native identity. The process of signifyin' alludes to movement and activity. The ability to re-read a text for political gain is an identity strategy that allows Native artists to re-present identity in a fluid fashion.[130]

The "already said" philosophy of Raymond Roussel considers the process of a "found language" that, through repetition and representation, "discovers an unexpected space [from which] to cover it with things never said before." (Shapiro 93)[131] Roussel's "unexpected space" and "it" can be signified through a Native Hip Hop lens. The location of Native identity within the "unexpected space" is Hip Hop and the "it" becomes Native identity. The multiplicity of interferences that arise from the involvement of the three identity formations, Tribal/Inter-Tribal/Multi-Tribal, continue to expand as Native Hip Hop artists gain an active political voice through Hip Hop. WOR actively embraces the "already said" philosophy of Hip Hop though they do not rely upon stereotypes of Hip Hop or Native culture. Rather, WOR applies a re-presentation, a reworking of the characteristics and dominant social-political themes of Hip Hop, by their own accord. WOR affirms their Multi-Tribal identity through their active reading and deconstruction of Native culture through the expressive vehicle of Hip Hop. The following section will focus on the audio examples "Tribal Shouts" and "To The Sell Outs" by WOR. These examples will illustrate how WOR came to be identified as a Multi-Tribal Hip Hop group.

The dynamic intersections of Ceremony, Powwow and Hip Hop

As urban Native people (a.k.a, "city redz", "city skinz", "urban skinz") in the later part of the 20th century searched their personal and collective memory for points of cultural definition the powwow arena became an increasingly important signifier[132]. New dance styles and songs containing contemporary narratives emerged as both Native and non-Native genres were learned and appropriated. As discussed earlier, Joan Nagel describes this cultural and community revival as support for the construction of a "new" Native identity and ethnicity. (Nagel 187 - 212) Within the urban center the location of culture was no longer isolated but influenced by its hybridity, it encouraged a dynamic re-presentation. When asked about the concept of Native identity, Russell Means stated,

> "I use the word "identities" deliberately — as there is no such thing as one, all-inclusive "Indian" identity. Just as it would be difficult, if not impossible, to lump Portuguese culture with Polish, and cover it with the broad brush of "European"; or Egyptian with Zimbabwean and pretend that "African" describes both equally — so, too with the countless different Native American cultures, nations, histories... and identities." (Means 2007)

The visual artist Ernie Paniciolli states that he prefers the term "Pre-American" to denote that Native People where present in the United States before any "other" contact. (Paniciolli email correspondence 13 Dec 2008)[133] The distinction of individual cultural identification by Means and the pre-contact realization by Paniciolli displays a strong sense of history embedded in multiplicity for Native people. These two points wedded together, along with the multifocal concepts of identity, Tribal/Inter-Tribal/Multi-Tribal, offer Native people the self-determining expressive agency required to expand beyond a limited, essentialized and marginalized identity.

WOR challenges a singular, stereotypical and racist perspective of Native music. The involvement of Hip Hop techniques (scratchin', sampling, call-response, rupture/flow, cut/mix and sermonizing)[134] WOR remains mindful of the history (social and political) and the complex African diaspora that brought Hip Hop to the United States. WOR engages both the urban African-American and Native (American) actions that fostered the development of popular music. WOR acknowledges the intersection of these two communities that re-present Native identity through the active agency of Hip Hop.

In a phone interview, Chris LaMarr simplified the construction and location of Native identity in music as the following, "...there's ceremonial music, powwow music and Hip Hop..." (phone interview 29 Dec 2008). These forms entertain the following Native identities within the construction of Native Hip Hop: ceremonial music (Tribal), powwow music (Inter-Tribal) and Hip Hop (Multi-Tribal). Hip Hop culture for urban Natives becomes a contemporary form of cultural ceremony, an agent of expression capitalizing on the impact of change. Jean Fischer defends this point when she states,

> "[N]ative systems of knowledge synthesize the paradoxes and heterogeneity of life experience. Alien to the European concept of progress, such systems produce art that is transgressive rather than progressive, and [are] resistant to easy commodification" (Fisher 338).

Paula Gunn Allen elaborates on the concept of ceremony and its relationship to the larger Hip Hop global community when she states that, "[t]he purpose of a ceremony is integration: the individual is integrated, fused, with his fellows, the community of people is fused with that of the other kingdoms, and this larger communal group with the worlds beyond this one." (Allen 119).

This quote supports the statement by LaMarr in defining how Native music functions on the three levels: as ceremony, powwow, and Hip Hop. The predetermined protocol of a ceremony is expressed in a Tribal identity where the signs and system function at the singular representation level. The transposing of this ceremonial process through the contemporary inter-tribal powwow re-presents an Inter-Tribal identity. Positioning the process of a ceremony through the transposed signifiers of powwow culture yields a Multi-Tribal identity. By integrating the music of these genres, each genre retains its own sonic identity. LaMarr/WOR does not construct a hierarchy but rather concludes that these musical genres unify sound and culture as discussed by Paula Gunn Allen. It is through this act of repetition and their intersection that these sonic identities begin to have form and develop agency.

Allen comes to a similar conclusion in analyzing form and structure in Native literature and ceremonies. Allen states, "the most significant and noticeable structural device (is repetition), which serves to entrance and to unify – both the participants and the ceremony." Allen continues to state that,

> "[i]t is reasonable, from an Indian point of view, that all literary forms should be interrelated, given the basic idea of the unity and relatedness of all the phenomena of life. Separation of parts into this or that is not agreeable to Native American systems, and the attempts to separate what are essentially unitary phenomena distorts them." (Allen 119 - 120)

The technical, literal, and physical integration of culture confirmed through the repetition that Allen reveals speaks directly to the creative process of LaMarr/WOR. In the following musical examples we will see how these intersections are realized by WOR in order to construct a Multi-Tribal identity.

Multi-Tribal Musical identity: "Tribal Shouts"

The closing track on the recording AYRFW? is "Tribal Shouts". WOR takes an active perspective within this track to demonstrate how they view and re-present a post-modern musical ceremony. Through the fluid involvement of the Native identity formations, Tribal/Inter-Tribal/Multi-Tribal, WOR expresses a "shout out" that resonates within and across tribal identities.

At its core, this work is a toasting and tribute song very much in line with the African/African-American form noted by Gates, et al.[135] This form of paying homage is also present in the powwow arena during the "Giveaway".[136]

Generally speaking, this is the moment, most often pre-determined in modern powwow situations, that the powwow timeline is paused. This momentary pause allows a family, most normally Native, to recognize other important members of the Native community. The members themselves being recognized may be of Native or non-Native ethnicity. Honor songs, special dances and gifts are offered from one family to the recipient. Though a Giveaway can occur at any time during a powwow, they are most often reserved for the final days or event. Capitalizing upon the placement of the Giveaway within the Powwow schedule and the important cultural meaning that it retains, WOR uses this form to "shout out" to those who have inspired and supported their work. WOR situates this track at the end of the recording that is consistent with the form of a powwow. Those being recognized include family, friends and organizations, which is consistent with the operational protocol of the Giveaway.[137] In this manner, WOR is giving away what they have created, their music. They are offering their Hip Hop work as an acknowledgement of the support that they have acquired from their surrounding community.

Through this selection WOR articulates their complex Multi-Tribal identity. To begin, each of the gentlemen are offered a moment to "shout out" to their own tribal community. This references their individual Tribal identity.

It is important to remember that the gentlemen who comprise the group WOR all come from one or more different tribal heritages. This added layer demonstrates how WOR flows through the identity formations of Tribal into Inter-Tribal. This fluid and active re-presentation of a cross-cultural connection between the identity formations, Tribal/Inter-Tribal/Multi-Tribal, is one mode of operation that WOR maintains within all their works.

WOR infuses an inter-tribal powwow sonically reality that is transposed through Hip Hop. As in other examples on AYRFW?, WOR incorporates a digital drum loop that is representative of the style and genre of Hip Hop present in the Bay Area c. 1990s. Mobb Music, as stated in Chapter 1, maintains a heavy bass and drum foundation. The accentuated emphasis of this sonic foundation is on the second and fourth beat establishing a back-beat that is a seminal characteristic in popular music. The signifyin'[138] use of this sonic foundation for Native people directly represents the "heartbeat" of the powwow drum. As defined throughout this chapter, there is no singular Native identity and, therefore, no singular Native heartbeat. The transcription of the Hip Hop backbeat into a signifyin' re-presentation of powwow culture defines an Inter-Tribal and/or Multi-Tribal sonic identity. Inter-Tribal, in this case, is referenced through the dialogue of two or more identities. Musically speaking this is Hip Hop and Native music. A Multi-Tribal identity is constructed through the extended incorporation of the different Tribal heritages of the gentlemen within WOR that are expressed via Hip Hop which is then transposed through a reference to powwow music.

As noted earlier, the inter-tribal powwow itself is constructed dynamically through Tribal, Inter-Tribal and Multi-Tribal identities. In a similar fashion, Hip Hop can be realized as an Inter-Tribal and/or Multi-Tribal music. The active incorporation of two different cultures represented within Hip Hop would yield a Hip Hop Inter-Tribal identity. For example, a Latino individual who involves Hip Hop within their work is expressing their identity, at minimum, as an Inter-Tribal identity. However, if this Latino individual acknowledges two or more Latin identities, alongside Hip Hop, they are then expressing a Multi-Tribal identity. Because of its complex cultural inception, Hip Hop cannot be viewed as a singular Tribal identity. Therefore, any culture in which Hip Hop becomes involved is, by this definition, operating at either an Inter-Tribal or Multi-Tribal level. Appling this Inter-Tribal/Multi-Tribal definition to Native identity it becomes clear that Native Hip Hop will either be realized as Inter-Tribal or Multi-Tribal. The gentlemen within WOR maintain either a Tribal, Inter-Tribal or Multi-Tribal identity depending upon a given context. WOR, as already stated, is either an Inter-Tribal or Multi-Tribal group. Hip Hop is the elected vehicle of expression for WOR. The composite identities involved yield a Multi-Tribal identity for WOR. Simply stated, WOR is a Multi-Tribal Hip Hop group.

Multi-Tribal Musical identity: "To The Sell-Outs"

James Clifford states that, "[i]dentity is conjunctural, not essential" and that it "must always be mixed, relational and inventive". (Clifford 10 – 11) Applying this statement by Clifford to contemporary Native people, we see that the intersections of identity are complex and are not limited to a singular view. When Native identity is expressed vis-à-vis Hip Hop culture, the dynamic mechanics of Native identity are then actively re-presented. Taking a close reading of the selection WOR's "To The Sell Outs" we are able to see the mixed, relational and inventive connections Clifford identifies

The selection "To The Sell-Outs" involves samples, a stable repeated verse-chorus form, and a musical textured designed in reference to and R&B style. . As stated earlier, LaMarr expresses his interest in "...old school Hip Hop, R&B, the Blues..." (phone interview 14 Dec 2008). This work reveals many layers of identity. To begin with, the sampled voices that are first heard, and that return throughout this selection, come from, as LaMarr noted, the Oprah Winfrey show. (LaMarr phone interview 14 Dec 2008) In 1992 The Oprah Winfrey show produced the episode "Too Little Too Late: Native Americans Speak Out" during Oprah's self-proclaimed investigation of the roots of racism.[139]

The sampled voices here, all male, are taken from non-Native men who are granted authority, by Oprah Winfrey, to speak about the issues of alcoholism in the Native American community. The sampled male voices fix this trope within a male pan-Indian reference; "...adult males on many Indian reservations..." as well as "...and their leading cause of death is alcoholism..."[140]. Taking a closer look at these sampled phrases we see both Inter-Tribal and Multi-Tribal identities present. The Inter-Tribal identity is defined using pan-Indian references. The Multi-Tribal identity is incorporated through the non-Native male reference to the issue of alcoholism with Native men. When the rapper, here LaMarr, enters, a Tribal identity is brought into focus. However, this work does not remain in a singular position, but rather quickly shifts into a Multi-Tribal identity formation that is the resident location for this selection.

The verse-chorus form of this work references LaMarr's before stated interest in R&B, the Blues and old school Hip Hop.[141] This recycled musical and poetic structure allows LaMarr to detail his complex perspective toward alcoholism. This reference begins as a Tribal identity formation that quickly slides through an Inter-Tribal identity, resolving within a Multi-Tribal identity. LaMarr self-identifies as a Pit River/Paiute Native. The visual positioning of these tribal cultures together begs an inherent Inter-Tribal identity formation. This does not pose to limit LaMarr as his understanding and inclusion of these two Tribal identities work, in tandem, to assist an Inter-Tribal identity formation. The further addition of Hip Hop to this construction yields, in reality, a Multi-Tribal identity.

The poetry of this selection acknowledges a pan-Indian understanding of a strict anti-alcohol stance, yet this is not stated directly by LaMarr. The closest point is in the statement, "...this is for those who sold their true ways...," meaning those Native people who have traded their traditional values for the path of alcoholism.

The repetition of words "you", "your" and "you're" throughout this selection articulates a Multi-Tribal identity. When asked about this usage LaMarr states, "...I wanted to say something to those old folks who know how hard it is to be involved with alcohol and still be able to speak to the kids (Native youth) about the issues of alcoholism...the kids don't want anyone comin' around preaching to them...so I had to find a way to speak to them so they could hear what I was sayin'..." (phone interview 29 Dec 2008)

This statement brings into focus the application of the three identity formations, Tribal/Inter-Tribal/Multi-Tribal, and how they can function beyond a generational divide.

Native people of all generations are able to gather a perspective (cultural and individual) with regard to the thesis of this selection, "To The Sell Outs". The meaning of the title begs the question, Who is the "sell-out?" It is presumed by LaMarr, that listening audience will know, through context, what this title is referencing; a person who opts to sell his/her culture for exchange of a better life and treatment. But LaMarr cannot predict is who will be the audience (listening and/or reading) of this work and what specifically is their generational perspective. This is not understood as a limiting position, but one that seeks to further enhance Native identity through dialogue with those who encounter the selection. By dislocating this selection, in time, location and space, the meaning gathers more re-presentational status for the applicable Native/non-Native community.

The text of this work functions through all three Native identity formations. Repeated listening, a change of time, enhances a new contextual understanding of this work and how it articulates Native identity.

The musical landscape of this section can be seen in an equally complex Multi-Tribal fashion. The delicate piano laced with light reverb in the upper register produces an ominous character reminiscent of old school Hip Hop. The light organ melody that comes in and out in this track echoes the R&B and funk styles.

The main feature of this selection is the drum machine, a virtual drum kit, often used in old school Hip Hop. The high, clear snare, the quick crescendo of the high-hat sample, the shaker pattern, and the low, partially masked kick drum, add further detail and body to this selection. The timbre and tonality are in a minor key that rhythmically oscillates between a tonic-dominant giving a sonic character to the verbal and literal theme of the work. The two piano chord pattern that enters at the start of the selection is repeated adding to the ominous character of the work while creating a timeless quality to the overall composition. The distorted string patch that comes in during the second part of the verse conjures images of a lightly distorted guitar sound that is not overbearing but rather stylistically fitting.

The musical body of this example locates itself within the framework and design of R&B and old school Hip Hop. By adding multiple sonic layers to the already thick identity mix, we can see the active involvement of each of the three Native identity formations at work. By incorporating the theoretical identity formations outlined above, it becomes evident that R&B as well as Hip Hop are both Multi-Tribal genres of music. Each genre developed through African diasporic music and found expressive locations in the urban post-industrial centers of the United States in the later part of the 20th century.

Given the diasporic motion, active cultural involvement, and the global postmodern resolution that both genres afford, R&B and Hip Hop can be understood as Multi-Tribal music. R&B and Hip Hop could not have come into existence without the cross-cultural connection, discourse and intersection of multiple cultures that create their tribal identity. WOR appropriates the sonic signifiers of these genres to further expand their rhizome of identity. Each of these formations coalesce in what George Lipsitz refers to as "musical syncretisms" that work together to express the process and dynamics of culture in the larger global community (Lipsitz 126).

Transposing all of the before stated musical attributes through a Native identity, we are able to see that this selection functions as a Multi-Tribal identity. The fluid movement between Tribal, Inter-Tribal and Multi-Tribal is readily apparent in the music of WOR. The ebb and flow through their works depend upon a different variables including; what genre is being reference?, what is the compositional strategy?, which poetic lyric or Native rapper is performing?, et al. This demonstrates that WOR works within, and between, the fluid strata of Native identity.

Robert Farris Thompson surmises just how intertwined identity and the creative process are as they are redefined, recycled, and re-presented. Although the quote here specifically addresses African-American culture, the same process and conceptualization is evident in the creative work of Native artists, "Art, life, land, philosophy, religion and politics are interconnected with the divine spark that Thompson calls 'the flash of the spirit': an improvisational individuality informed by a transcendent spiritual presence that energizes all of African-American culture and creates a powerful resistance to total Western encapsulation." (Thompson qt. in Da Vasques 163)

Conclusion

This chapter begins with a discussion of DuBois' double-consciousness and how, for contemporary Native people, this viewpoint is not entirely sufficient. Applying a deconstructive analysis through Stephen Cornell, Joanne Nagel, Gerald Vizenor, et al who work in identity construction and identification for Native people, it became evident that contemporary Native identity is a complex, multifaceted issue. Currently, Native identity functions beyond the historically prescribed definition of a pan-Indian identity. Through these critical readings, it became evident that there is a need for an integrated approach to understand contemporary Native identity.

The three identity formations of Tribal/Inter-Tribal/Multi-Tribal can be recognized, defined, and applied to both a Nativist and mixed-blood ideology. The focus of these identity formations is not to create another categorization for Native people, but rather to allow for any/all dynamic possibilities. These identity formations function as a means for Native people to express and re-present their identity within a continuum that is continually under the negotiation and influence of contemporary environmental dynamics and global contexts. Two audio examples, "Tribal Shouts" and "To The Sell-Outs" from WOR demonstrate the direct integration and application of these identity formations.

WOR illustrates how Hip Hop functions as agent for Native identity moving freely and fluidly within areas of identity formation. From this analysis we can see that Native identity does not maintain a singular locus, but rather is inter-dependent upon many layers of constructed meaning. Identity for Native people is a composite of all the actions, objects and events that can occur in a continuously negotiated, fluid dynamic.

The signifyin' identity for Native people is beholden to the ongoing, never quite unified, multiple structures of identity construction. The signifyin' Native, in pure Vizenoresque trickster fashion, eludes the previous signifiers of the Native persona (Indian, pan-Indian, supra-tribal, et al) and finds a location of identity within a fluid ambivalence that continuously is constructed and deconstructed through musical negotiations.

BONUS TRACK

This chapter set in motion a Native critical epistemological trajectory that has found comfortable company with the artistic expressions of the second Native Hip Hop generation.

The original writing of this chapter only took into account the initial recording by W.O.R., *Are You Ready For W.O.R.? (AYRFW)*. At the time, there were only a limited number of printed recordings of the second recording by W.O.R. *WWII*. Since that time, an analysis of *WWII* has taken place. It is beyond the scope of this present work to delve further into *WWII*, but this extended analysis is ongoing and seeks to be a future project.

The critical Native theories of Hip Hop identity formation and dynamic expressions outlined in this chapter opened a dialogue to the importance of Native expressive identity and the timely recognition of Native/Indigenous/ Indian Hip Hop. What could not have been anticipated was that these outlined theoretical points apply equally to the foundations of Native Hip Hop and the second generation of Native Hip Hop. The disciplined analysis and critical Native epistemology stated, outlined, and argued helped to center the forthcoming creative works and sovereign self-determined expressions of the younger Hip Hop generation. These analytical and critical theories were applied in action-meaning-content within the growing Native Hip Hop canon and contribute to foundations of a sonic agency for identity and sovereign/self-determined re-presentations.

In earlier chapters (re)presentation was used to define a dialectic of Native expressive culture at the formation of a Native Hip Hop canon. Given the evidence of time and display of the collected works by the second generation of Native Hip Hop artists the term "representation" can, now, embrace an ambivalent space that is not hinged upon earlier scripted narratives of what Hip Hop is and how Hip Hop should remain. Extending Homi Bhabha's (2017) theoretical use of ambivalence the fluid interactions within the sphere of Hip Hop are between the historic identity of Hip Hop culture and the developing articulated voice of Native Hip Hop. Though Bhabha illustrates this action-repulsion from a colonizer-colonized perspective, the re-presentation of ambivalence is characterized through a Native expressive trajectory as one that disrupts historic cultural definitions of Hip Hop. This re-presentation demands – by way of repetition and echoing a Native voice through production value and volume – that Native Hip Hop be involved within the levels of comfort that the glocal cultural communities were entertaining toward Hip Hop.

Denying Native inclusion at the early stages of the Hip Hop artistic industrial complex forced Native artists to generate references to the relevance of tribal identity and socio-political sovereignty. This artistic act of self-determination re-presented the gaps within Hip Hop culture. Bhabha (1998/2017) these gaps as being disturbances within cultural definitions that lead to hybridity. Power, dominance, definitions, and knowledge, therefore, are open to being re-presented from alternative views and positions of culture. A EuroAmerican/Western ideology would frame this action as point of colonial dominance to remain in control of and establish a colonial rhetoric.

At the developing stages of Hip Hop a colonial discourse was not the preview. Hip Hop was born out of the necessity for urban youth to artistically resist and counter oppressive actions and definitions that were in practice. As Hip Hop culture grew, the ownership, definition and expectations of the directions of Hip Hop culture were central to those at ground level of this revolutionary cultural paradigm shift. It was the composed language, the tribal identity and the artistic expressions by the younger Native Hip Hop generation that noted – rhetorically as well as specifically – the gaps in the dialectic of Hip Hop. This dissection of the gaps within Hip Hop's forming industry complex is where the Native voice(s) began to speak. The sounding Native expressive voice(s) did not speak as a subaltern. (Gramasci 1971, Spivak 1985, Piermarco Piu. n.d.) This critical Native voice(s) was heard as a constructed culturally centered sovereign voice(s). The exposition of Hip Hop representation(s) were not singular, but were in fact being narrated by a Tribal/Inter-Tribal/Multi-Tribal identity continuum. This action is the re-presentation of Hip Hop by the second generation of Native Hip Hop artists.

The hyphen in the critical use of re-presentation serves as a signifying cypher, bridging the gaps between the forming scripted Hip Hop narrative and the developing Native Hip Hop voice(s), leading to a canon. The hyphen is not a separating apparatus. The hyphen connects social agency for Native and non-Native expressions to coexist in an ambivalent space fueled by dynamic indeterminate interactions. The second generation of Native Hip Hop artists did not succumb to a hegemony of cultural identifiers, socio-political economic values or assumed glocal racist knowledge of Native/Indigenous/Indian Peoples. Native Hip Hop artists, at this second generation turning point, actively applied a re-presentation of the Six Elements/Four Points of Hip Hop. While the attention of the growing Hip Hop artistic industrial complex was focused upon itself, Native Hip Hop artists were consciously collecting their tribal experiences that were expressively to become the Native Hip Hop canon.

To construct a sovereign proper posture of Native identity, through the active agency of Hip Hop, the younger Native Hip Hop artists embrace each of the Three Tribal Identities outlined here: Tribal/Inter-Tribal/Multi-Tribal. What the second generation of Native Hip Hop artists have been able to sculpt is a Native canon utilizing and re-presenting each of the Six Elements of Hip Hop (Dj-ing, Mc-ing, Rap, Breakdancing, Graffiti, Fashion) and the Four Points of Hip Hop (Sermonizing, Rupture/Flow, Cut/Mix, Layering). As discussed, these active Hip Hop Elements/Points have been culturally re-presented by the second generation of Native Hip Hop artists. This act of codification established an expressive artistic vernacular of Native identity.

Current (2023) Native Hip Hop artists have taken possession of Hip Hop's visibility, glocal influence, and cultural acceptance to organize and further structure the Native Hip Hop canon. The growing number of Native musicians, groups, and collectives from the reservations and urban locations satisfy this canonic development. Following the lead of such prominent Native Hip Hop artists as, Supaman, Frank Walen, Drezus, DJ Redcloud, Nataanii Means, The Halluci Nation, Xiuhtezcatl Martinez, Michelle Lee Runns (aka MZShellz), Tall Paul, Linday "Eekwol" Knight, Shibastik, et al., are the living evidence of a founded, firm, and ever-growing Native Hip Hop canon. What the second generation of Native Hip Hop artists have been able to provide to the larger non-Native Hip Hop glocal community is the importance of re-presenting Hip Hop in a position of proper posture, identity agency, cultural sovereignty, and the economy of socio-political self-determination.

The Native Hip Hop canon did not accept the scripted racist identity or cultural colonial bias of being an "Indian rapper." Native Hip Hop inverted this stereotyped identity as it would cement the immense artistic contributions of this younger Native Hip Hop generation. Even as most of the Native centered news and media were learning how to contend with and understand the corpus of work being produced by the younger generation of Native Hip Hop artists, Native Hip Hop was re-presenting the Six Elements/Four Points of Hip Hop culture as flexible Tribal/Inter-Tribal/Multi-Tribal locations of sovereign culture. Hip Hop was being manufactured and voiced by Native/Indigenous/Indian sovereign self-determination.

Taking a bold step forward, it can be said that Hip Hop has been appropriated by Native artists. The Elements/Points of Hip Hop were being transposed, re-scripted, and expressed by Native acculturation. This is a reverse operation and counterpoint from how other cultures have come to engage Hip Hop. Native artists applied Smitherman's flip-the-script theory on Hip Hop' Six Elements/Four Points. Appropriation and acculturation both employ an act of containing, manipulating, and reframing an object. Native Hip Hop artists influenced Hip Hop's core cultural values vis-a-vis sovereign cultures, customs, knowledge, traditions, and expressions. The growing Native Hip Hop canon would not allow itself to be a possessed object. The collective conscious canon of Native Hip Hop serves as evidence that Hip Hop did not appropriate or acculturate Native identity(ies)/culture(s). It is the Tribal/Inter-Tribal/Multi-Tribal fluid identity dynamics that inverted this dialectic. In doing so, Native Hip Hop sheds light on a positive Native/Indigenous/Indian cultural posture that is in contest to misunderstanding and historic racist doctrines of Indian Peoples.

The historic lineage of Hip Hop comes through an African-American diasporic expressive lexicon. This defined and repeated lineage gained a pop cultural standing and reference to authenticity for future Hip Hop definitions and cultural exchanges. Infusing the core Elements/Points of Hip Hop with Native/Indigenous/Indian Tribal/Inter-Tribal/Multi-Tribal identity signifiers removed Hip Hop from pop culture's limited focus and skewed refence to authenticity over Hip Hop. This action is the reverse of what a non-Native media industry would assume to take place from an assumed marginalized American Indian reference. Discounting Native involvement, operation, manipulation, and tribal scripting of the Six Elements/Four Points of Hip Hop was not an oversight by the Hip Hop cultural artistic industry complex. Perspective and attention to the evolving Native Hip Hop vernacular was not even considered. Hip Hop was liberated by the second generation of Native Hip Hop artists from socio-political protected privilege and became a Native/Indigenous/Indian identity signifier sermonizing, cutting/mixing, rupturing/flowing, and layering along the back-and-forth Tribal/Inter-Tribal/Multi-Tribal points of cultural contact.

The hyper focused aspects, pretense and cultural expectations of what Hip Hop was and should remain fortified a limited pedigree of Hip Hop culture. The younger generation of Native Hip Hop artists recognized the liberal resistance agency at the thriving core of Hip Hop. Native Hip Hop artists influenced that pulsating dynamic core with Tribal/Inter-Tribal/Multi-Tribal identity signifiers structured along the socio-political economic lines of sovereignty and self-determination. It is this embodiment of the Hip Hop politic, identity, and cultural interactions that welcomed the second generation of Native Hip Hop artists. This action was not developed by mistake from Native artists. Instead, the younger Native Hip Hop artists recognized the importance of this sonic, cultural, and political vernacular. The infusion of tribal ethics, as a proper position of culture, customs, traditions, knowledge, and expressions is what became the voice(s) of the Native Hip Hop canon. No error or happenstance was made. Native artists were specific in their focused attention to how Hip Hop would serve their Tribal/Inter-Tribal/Multi-Tribal cultures, customs, traditions, knowledge, and expressed contemporary identities.

The second-generation of Native Hip Hop artists inverts, flips-the-script, and reverses the critical lens normally pointed at Indian icon/images. This refocused gaze, where Native identity is looking at non-Native artistic expressions, brings into focus the abject relationship between the establishing Native Hip Hop canon and the larger non-Native Hip Hop community. Barbara Creed (1993) notes abject relationship as being:

[t]he place...where meaning collapses, the place where I am not...The abject threatens life, it must be radically excluded from the place of the living

subject, propelled away from the body and deposited on the other side of an imaginary border which separate the self from that which threatens the self.

Samantha Petony (1996) secures this use of abject re-presentation from a Native Hip Hop gaze as the, "[forced exclusion of] the abject which…draws our attention to the place where meaning collapses."

The assumptions of power in the abject self, the "body," is the non-Native Hip Hop cultural industry complex. The Native Hip Hop canon becomes the proverbial "threat" to the body, as the second generation of Native Hip Hop artists did not allow their expressed artistic identities to be codified along racist, colonial rhetoric or discourse. Any biased agenda or marginalized perspectives of Native/Indigenous/Indian identity counter the abject body and advance their own tribal artistic agenda on the grounds of expressed socio-political sovereignty and self-determination. The EuroAmerican pop cultural icon/image of the defeated Indian was "radically excluded" (Creed 65) as the imaginary borders of artistic expression were erased through the sounding Native Hip Hop voice(s). The "place of meaning" is "collapsed" (Petony para. 2). At the time, space, and place of Hip Hop's glocal magnification, Native Hip Hop voice(s) co-opted the Elements/Points of Hip Hop and set forth to elaborate these along the lines of a complex tribal identity continuum, socio-political sovereignty, and the cultural economics of self-determination.

Reference:

Abdennebi Ben Beya. <u>Mimicry, Ambivalence, and Hybridity</u>. *scholarblogs*, 1998/2017. scholarblogs.emory.edu

Creed, Barbara. *Horror And The Monstrous Feminine: An Imaginary Abjection*. London Routledge, p. 65, 1993, otago.ac.nz/deepsouth/vol2no3/pentony

Gramasci 1971, Spivak 1985 – Piermarco Piu. (n.d.). <u>Subalternity</u>. *Global Social Theory*, globalsocialtheory.org

indianz.com/news/2022, *Native America Calling*: <u>Honoring the top Native Hip Hop artists</u> 9 September 2022

Indian Country Today News. <u>8 Great Native Hip-Hop Artists</u>. 13 September 2018, ictnews.org

Nasrullah Mambrol. <u>Ambivalence in Post-colonialism</u>. *Literary Theory and Criticism*, 27 September 2017, literariness.org

Pentony, Samantha. School of Humanities, Oxford Brooks University, *Deep South* v.2 n.3, Spring 1996.

Chapter 4. The Signifyin' Frybread

"For those of us who bridge the gaps within our culture in possession of Indian knowledge, as well as trained artists, I coin the label of "Contemporary Traditionalist"

– James Luna[142]

This chapter investigates how WOR signifies[143] on Hip Hop culture through lyrics, Hip Hop technical devices (Sermonizing, Cut/Mix, Flow/Rupture, Layering) and sampling. The chapter will deconstruct song lyrics and identify how issues of stereotyping, gender and sexual politics, oral tradition and the construction of personal/tribal histories are re-presented. Audio examples are selected from the recording "Are You Ready For W.O.R.?"[144]

A Lyrical Native Identity

The organization of poetry in Hip Hop follows the long-honored tradition of the blues. Many scholars have discussed this relationship emphasizing the importance of this poetic and musical source in Hip Hop (Smitherman 1977/1999, Alim 2004/2006/2009, Campbell 2005, Perry 2005, Baugh 2007, Cobb 2007, Androutsopoulos 2009, Pennycook 2009, Ibrahim 2009). Hip Hop poets prioritize the pulse of the text and the relationship of the words to the beat. Literary analysis is important to understand how WOR negotiates the intricate complexities of contemporary Native identity in their lyrics. The re-presentation of important literary techniques, such as double-entendre, metaphor, rhyming, et al., creates a variety of lexicons in Native Hip Hop. With an understanding of the cultural politics in the lyrics, this chapter will address a range of musical techniques including, sampling and the beat.

The art of syncopation (words) and knowledge of the pulse (beat) allow the poet in Hip Hop to create his/her own style (Cobb 84 – 89). From the elemental "simple syncopation – matching beats to syllables" (Cobb 84) of the late 1970/80s, to the evolved "computer style" (Cobb 92) of the 1990s, Hip Hop artists continue to create and expand their use of literary devices. The artists have developed a post-modern lexicon defined in a global/local political climate.

Chris LaMarr recalls the infamous quote from Chuck D from Public Enemy, who in 1988 stated that rap is the "Black CNN" (Kitwana 201). This statement speaks to the importance of Hip Hop as the voice of complex cultures being constructed, de-constructed and re-constructed, in real time, for African-American communities within the urban industrial complex. Chuck D challenges the local/national news networks that in 1988, mis-represented Black urban youth in a rapidly developing Hip Hop culture (Kitwana 201, 206 – 15). Chuck D inverts the (mis)representation into a (re)presentation in Hip Hop culture. Kitwana develops this idea when he states that, "[a]s the national forum for Black youth concerns and often as the impetus for discussion…, rap music has done more than any one entity to help our generation forge a distinct identity" (Kitwana 201). WOR transposes the genre of Hip Hop to re-present the complexity of contemporary Native identity.

WOR captures the social dynamic of Indian Country on their 1994 recording AYRFW?. [145] The lyrics address socio-political issues and help to construct a post-structuralist Native identity. As a contemporary Native Hip Hop group, WOR does not define the Native cultural climate of the late 20th century in the linear trajectory of EuroAmerica. In their lyrics (poetry) WOR negotiates a dialectic between the urban and reservation systems articulating a contemporary Native identity. WOR offers the listener and, more importantly, the Native community an opportunity to listen beyond the Third Space.[146] As defined in Chapter 3, Homi Bhabha's Third Space enunciates a colonial doctrine that stabilizes a subject-other relationship. Through the agency of Hip Hop, WOR creates an intermediate area allowing a flexible re-presentation of Native identity that simultaneously is constructed, de-constructed and re-constructed. In doing so, WOR offers a companion to Chuck D's "Black CNN" in Native Hip Hop.

A Literary Survey of WOR

Mohawk scholar Gerald Alfred states, "It has been said that being born Indian is being born into politics. I believe this to be true; because being born a Mohawk of Kahunawake, I do not remember a time free from the impact of political conflict" (Alfred 1). A deconstructive analysis of the lyrics by WOR illustrates their political awareness of Indian Country. According to William Cobb, MC styles advanced "dramatically" through the 1980s, with the use of literary devices such as rhyming, metaphor, onomatopoeia, personification, simile, analogy, double entendre, and comparison. (Cobb 91 - 105).[147] The selection "Red, White, and Blue"[148] demonstrates that WOR uses these literary devices to re-present Native identity.[149]

Rhyming

A wonderful extended rhyming scheme in the final verse deserves to be quoted in its entirely:

> White man in blue beating on you what's the clue
> black on black, blue on red, blue on brown
> keeping us down
> got a gat a license to cap
> a power trip how about that beat Rodney King,
> didn't do a thing
> caught it on tape a judicial rape
> a white cop free but if it were me
> where I'd be the penitentiary
> but that's the system set up to miss'em
> if you're white in blue you'll never lose
> so some advice you'd better think twice
> you rolling the dice if you call the vice
> so end of story kinda gory
> it's the red, white, and blue
> straight from WOR to you! (40 – 55)

The rhyming pattern, and internal rhyme, in the first line flows through the entire section of the song: "White man in blue beating on you what's the clue" This internal rhyme is also evident in other segments of this verse "caught it on tape a judicial rape...so end of story kinda gory".

A double rhyme is used in the line: "but that's the system set up to miss'em". Another literary device used with rhyming is Enjambment. Enjambment breaks the line in a midpoint but still connects the rhyme across the lines. This is apparent in the lines: "black on black, blue on red, blue on brown/keeping us down" and "a white cop free but if it were me/ where I'd be the penitentiary".

This selection speaks to the political injustice toward people of color. Specifically, the selection deals with the Los Angeles Riot of 1992, as spurred by the Rodney King beating. WOR further signifies on the political displacement of Native people by the U.S. Federal Government.[150] WOR questions the neglect for people of color that is understood and presented as American. When racist social norms are unchallenged, stereotypes prevail. WOR recognizes the liminal negative attitudes toward people of color in popular media. To subvert the racism of the mainstream press, WOR addresses socio-political issues from a Native perspective.

Onomatopoeia

The onomatopeia offers an interesting insight into the meaning of slang for WOR.[151] In the lines:

I got the lines ready to rhyme

cuz[152] now it's the time, for me to get mine

hold me back and I'll attack

and you don't want that *cuz* whcn I rap

it's about the truth so how about you

do you want the facts, a heart attack

how about a payback

anyway I'll have my say *cuz* I'm here to stay

and when I'm through you can say you knew about the true

red, white and blue (4 – 13)

but I ain't trippin' *cuz* they're slippin' (24)

Man in white, thinks he's right

but that I'll fight, *cuz* I'm MC Hiddese

cuz I know better soon they'll be deader

better change their ways *cuz* we're here to stay

better dead *cuz* this sh** is real (27 – 31)

The word "cuz" is used as an abbreviation for the word "because". The switch between English and slang within this phrase works quite well. No meaning is lost. The sound and use of the letter "z" cuts the word short without losing its meaning. Switching is an understood technique that allows the replacement, or substitution, of terminology without the loss of intent or meaning. This shortening of the word coupled with the sound of the word offers a cultural perspective on these, and similar words that use the letter "z". For example, the use of "z" in the name "Rezervation"[153] is defined by Chris LaMarr when he states that: "that's how you say it, "rezzzzz"...there's an emphasis on the "z"....it's been shortened a bit, made to fit for Native people and for Hip Hop that is just what it is, 'the rez'" (phone interview 20 Dec 2008).

Obviously, the use of the letter "z" is an onomatopoeia specific to Native slang and common in the Native community. Geneva Smitherman defines the Black Experience in language as a form of "Recreolization" of language that works consciously to "recapture and reconfigure" forms of Black speech that will yield an "African-in-America linguistic identity" (Smitherman 38). The spontaneity, concreteness, call and response, rhythmic patterning and signifying (signifyin') that we see in the poems of WOR are representative of the "Recreolization" discussed by Smitherman.

Personification

In the lines:

> we shed no tears instead putt'em in fear
> but that's today the American way
> where might makes right
> so America prepare to fight (36 – 39)

WOR personifies the object "America." Taking into account the Termination Policies, as discussed in Chapter 1, the process of assimilation into American culture is represented through the lines "where might makes right" (line 38). The process of assimilation constructs a power struggle between Native/non-Native people where "the American way" (read: assimilation) becomes the dominant political force, ("where might makes right"; the American assimilated way is the correct way to live). In line 39, "America" is personified as an entity that embodies these ideological views. WOR stands as a challenger to "America" in this ideological struggle. "America" is asked to take arms against those who challenge their dominant position, ("America prepare to fight"; if the American lifestyle is challenged then a violent struggle must arise). WOR is clear not to define any one particular struggle with "America." Rather, they allow all the possibilities to find support in this legal struggle.

The following poetic forms (Analogy, Simile, Metaphor and Double-Entendre) are related. According to the Handbook of Rhetorical Devices (2008),[154] a Simile is, "a comparison [using like or as] between two different things that resemble each other in at least one way." An Analogy then:

> compares two things, which are alike in several respects, for the purpose of explaining or clarifying some unfamiliar or difficult idea or object by showing how the idea or object is similar to some familiar one. While simile and analogy often overlap, the simile is generally done briefly for effect and emphasis, while analogy serves the more practical end of explaining a thought process or a

line of reasoning or the abstract in terms of the concrete, and may therefore be more extended (Harris 2008).

A Metaphor, "compares two different things by speaking of one in terms of the other. Unlike a simile or analogy, metaphor asserts that one thing is another thing, not just that one is like another." The Double-Entendre is, "a word or phrase having a double meaning, especially when the second meaning is risqué."

In Geneva Smitherman's "Black Semantic" (Smitherman 35 – 72) Smitherman identifies three types of word formation that arise from the socio-historical context of West African language, "words of direct African origin; words that are loan-translations; [and] inflated vocabulary" (Smitherman 43). These "common English words that are direct African survivals" and reflect a "posturing [that] provides the speaker with inflated word choices for ordinary situations" (Smitherman 45 – 46). The "semantic interpretation" allows an interpretation for Smitherman that is originally a "black or white" reading (Smitherman 59). However, the selection of words, their application and persistent use "grounded in ...common linguistic and cultural history" (Smiterhman 43) creates a "highly context-bound lexicon" (Smitherman 59). Changing the reference from black-white to Native-non-Native allows a complex reading of this text.

Analogy

The entire poem itself, "Red, White, and Blue" is a larger analogy between Native and non-Native cultures. Stanzas 2 and 3 of the poem each represents a different culture, respectively Native and EuroAmerican. For example, stanza two (lines 14 – 26) refer to Native cultures:

Blood shed red, a bullet to the head
better off dead that's what they said
but that was their plan to get our land
won't you understand
annihilation of my nation
my people died, they tried to hide
all the lies but realize
that the red in the flag is a blood rag
a body bag it makes me sad
what we had to compared to what we have
but I ain't trippin' cuz they're slippin'
and we're coming back strong
back to where we belong (14 – 26)

The analogy here between the color red is the Native slang for being Natives "being red". Smitherman notes this technique as a form of signifyin' through "Black Semantic language and verbal concepts" (Smitherman 43) that can be categorized in three linguistic formations: words of direct African origin; words that are loan-translations; inflated vocabulary (Smitherman 43). The color red participates in two of these three linguistic formations: "loan-translation" and "inflated vocabulary". The loan-translation is recognized with the term "red", that refers to a color, as well as to the skin color of Native people, "red skin." Through an "inflated vocabulary," "red" is more meaningful because it refers to a culture of people. This inflated vocabulary is evident in the historical references within this stanza:

annihilation of my nation
my people died, they tried to hide
all the lies but realize

that the red in the flag is a blood rag

a body bag it makes me sad

what we had compared to what we have (18 - 23)

This refers to the political and literal termination of Native people through war.

The third stanza refers to the color white:

Man in white, thinks he's right

but that I'll fight, cuz I'm MCHiddese

cuz I know better soon they"l be deader

better change their ways cuz we're here to stay

better dead cuz this sh** is real

I saw LA so whatcha gotta say

better stop dissin' take time to listen

if you refuse were all gonna lose

been this way for 500 years

we'll shed no tears instead putt'em in fear

but that's today the American way

where might makes right

so American prepare to fight (27 – 39)

Applying Smitherman's three Black Semantic language and verbal concepts once again we see that the color "white" refers to EuroAmerican culture. The line, "Man in white, think he's right" (line 27) refers to white privilege. An acknowledgement of this political situation comes in line 35, "been this way for 500 years", that is alighted with line 37, "but that's today the American way". The analogy here is referring to the dominant political force of EuroAmerica. The color white is subject to a loan-translation that then is inflated through integration. The power-based authority gained through white privilege is challenged by the lines, "I saw LA so whatcha gotta say/better stop dissin' take time to listen" (line 32 – 33). The first part of the line is in reference to the LA riots of 1992. The implied conclusion is that those in a position of authority (read: white) may not be as powerful as once believed. The second portion of the line, "so whatcha gotta say [?]", begs the unanswered question regarding the position of power for the "Man in White" (line 27). How is the "Man in White" going to address and maintain his position of power? How does the "Man in White" retain a hegemonic structure that he (read: white male) has erected for himself? This reading of man as "The Man", or a person in power is an example of Semantic Inversion (aka "flippin' the script") (Smitherman 270 – 282). This literary tool inverts the power structure. Smitherman recounts the same reference of "the man" (read: white) in African-American culture:

> Historically, *the Man* was not *any* man but,...derogatorily, the white man. In the 1960s and 1970s, the term came to be applied not only to the white man but also to the policeman. Among Hip Hoppers, this script has been flipped again, as *the Man* has come to mean a person with great power, knowledge, skill, and so forth (Smitherman 280).[155]

This reading defines "White" as a "man" of power that, in the following section becomes the police.

The last two lines of this stanza recall the historic confrontations for Native people within America, "where might makes right/so America prepare to fight" (lines 38 – 39). This inflated reference to political dominance connects the second and their stanza of the poem.

The fourth and final stanza of this work completes the overall analogy of the red, white and blue through a reference to police violence:

> White man in blue beating on you what's the clue
> blue on black, blue on red, blue on brown
> keeping us down
> got a gat a license to cap
> a power trip how about that beat Rodney King,
> didn't do a thing
> caught it on tape, a judicial rape
> a white copy free but if it were me
> where I'd be the penitentiary
> but that's the system set up to miss'em
> if you're white in blue you'll never lose
> so some advice you'd better think twice
> you rolling the dice if you call the vice

so end of story kinda gory
it's the red, white, and blue
straight from WOR to you! (40 – 55)

The color "blue" in a loan-translation refers to the police force. This stanza illustrates the dominance of physical power over non-EuroAmerican culture groups, "blue on black, blue on red, blue on brown" (line 41) where the cultures respectively are African-American, Native American and Mexican American. WOR elects not to refer to any one method of "keeping us down" (line 42), but rather invites the listener to draw from their own experience with forms of social-political oppression. WOR casts police brutality as white (read: blue) privilege through the lines:

White man in blue beating on you (40)

got a gat a license to cap / a power trip how about that beat Rodney King, / didn't do a thing (43 – 45)

a white cop free but if it were me/where I'd be the penitentiary / but that's the system set up to miss'em / if you're white in blue you'll never lose (47 – 50).

This poetry here details the 1992 Los Angeles Watts Riots that began after the beating of Rodney King by three police officers that were later acquitted. The inflated vocabulary here is not evident as in the previous stanzas. However, the directness of the words captures a politically charged point in history.

Simile

The simile by WOR is self-evident in this selection. An example of the simile is in the line, "do you want a fact, (like) a heart attach" (line 9). The simile word connective word, "like" is not present, but is implied. The line could be read as implying a severe shock to the recipient of the information, "do you want a fact, (as though you would like) a heart attack". In line 14, another implied simile is found, "Blood shed red, a bullet to the head" (line 14). This could be read as, "Blood shed red, (like) a bullet to the head". Replacing the "like" in this line allows the line to be read as a simile. There is also a simile referring to the cultural power-base of America in the line, "but that's today, the American way" (37). This line then can be read as, "things should be viewed today in the world like they are in America." Again, the "like" is implied and, when replaced, the line reads as a simile. The simile illustrates an American prominence, first world bias, and hegemony upon global perspectives. This reading points to a simultaneous local/global fuzzy border that Pennycook and Mitchell identify as a "complexity of location" (28) within Hip Hop that Jannis Androutsopoulos coins "glocal" (56).[156]

Metaphor

"Red, White, and Blue" provides an interesting metaphor. These colors represent Native and non-Native positions in a political power struggle. As before, the colors are deconstructed as, "Red" being Native, "White" for Euro-American, "Blue" as the police force. These three cultural references (Native, Euro-American, police force) also represent the colors in the American flag. I refer to this as a first step since the continued deconstruction of these "colors" yields a metaphor and a double-entendre.

Here is an interesting display of metaphor:

I got the gat ready to blast

I got the lines ready to rhyme (3 – 4)

Blood shed red, a bullet to the head

better off dead that's what they said (14 – 15)

keeping us down

got a gat a license to cap (42 – 43)

Line 3 refers to a gun ("gat") that is prepared to shoot ("blast") and, presumably, cause a murder. Line 4 invokes the poetry ("the lines ready to rhyme"). The "gat" becomes a metaphor for knowledge and the "blast" is the experience of stating the poetry that follows in line 4.

Lines 14 – 15 appear to refer to a legal murder by a gunshot to the head. However, applying the same reading from lines 3 – 4, the "bullet" becomes a metaphor representing knowledge ("a bullet to the head"; knowledge going into the mind). The second metaphor is the "gat" (gun) and the application of the knowledge, ("got a gat a license to cap"; I have ownership of knowledge and the ability to use it to write). These lines refer to the gathering and expression of knowledge. The subtext of EuroAmerican fear (referenced in line 36) is based upon the premise that if Native people gain knowledge, then they will gain political power through education. In these lines WOR transforms, through metaphor, an act of physical violence into a political act of poetry.

Another metaphor is visible in the lines:

that the red in the flag is a blood rag

a body bag it makes me sad (21 – 22)

These lines refer directly to three colors in the United States flag, red, white and blue. The "flag" as a "blood rag" is a metaphor for America's oppressive violence. This transposes the U.S. "flag" as an understood symbol of freedom it into a symbol of violence and death. The bloodshed through violence is simultaneously real and a metaphor.

Double Entendre

The example of the colors "Red, White, and Blue" demonstrates that each of these colors developed first through an analogy. The three colors through a loan-translation connect as an inflated vocabulary. WOR uses the American flag as a metaphor in a political critique of the U.S. government. For WOR, the American flag has a double meaning of solidarity with a first world nation, as well as the power-struggle between Native and non-Native people. Double-entendre subverts language as in Smitherman's Black Semantic thesis, here exchanging an African with a Native perspective. This signifyin' results in the multiple codes of meaning through a Native perspective.

Comparison

Finally, WOR illustrates the use of comparison in the lines:

I got the gat ready to blast/ I got the lines ready to rhyme (3 – 4)

This line empowers poetry (rhyme) as a weapon (gat), a means of self-defense. Words are aimed and riddle the listener's ears with the social injustices waged against Native people. WOR initiates an act of (re)education of Native issues in an arena that is non-violent but charged with knowledge.

Another comparison is in the lines:

been this way for 500 years (35)

WOR compares the current situation, c. 1994, and the past 500 years. This refers to the arrival of Christopher Columbus to the "new world," the beginning of the historical conflict between Native and EuroAmerican society.

WOR continues, "and when I'm through you could say you knew about the true/ red, white and blue." (lines 12 – 13); "so end of story kinda gory/ it's the red, white, and blue/ straight from WOR to you!" (lines 53 – 55)

Lines 12 – 13 compare "true" to an unspoken truth that underlies the "American way" (line 37). One will know the "true" (read: untold truth, "red") about the American political system ("white") and policing agencies ("blue").

Line 53 - 55 depict a history of violence and brutality, "so end of story kinda gory" (Line 53). The following line compares the American flag once again, "it's the red, white, and blue" (line 54) to the preceding line that refers to the historic violence. The last line establishes WOR as the author of the truth, "straight from WOR to you!" (line 55). The text compares visible truth (read: American) with an invisible truth (read: Native). The start of line 12 reassures the listener that "when I'm through you could say you knew about the true" (when this text is completed the listener will know an underrepresented truth about American history, history from a Native perspective).

Born at 18

In Born at 18,[157] WOR reaches beyond binary constructions (urban/reservation, Native/non-native, colonized/colonizer) to explore a dynamic Multi-Tribal identity.[158] WOR refutes the simplified insider/outsider binary and resists the temptation to replace this with yet another binary, urban/reservation. For purposes of this analysis, signifiers within this selection are labeled: [1] Militant/Political/Social, [2] Despair/Demise/Defeat and [3] Optimism/Hope/Empowerment.[159]

WOR's signifying text grounds Native identity in Native culture. WOR transposes Hip Hop lexicon into Native culture. The group employs urban slang most often in the breaks between the verses. The introduction incorporates the phrase, "definitely in the house" that positions the entry of WOR, "Ah yeah, WithOut Rezervation is definitely in the house" (Introduction line 1). The group features in Break #3 a lengthier exchange between two of the members of WOR:

> Kevin Nez, "Yeah, you checkin' out the sounds of WithOut Rezervation
>
> (sample, "we were born at 18")
>
> Kevin Nez, "comin' out to ya live and direct from the rez'vation...hey yo MC Hiddie man, waz up' G?,
>
> Chris LaMarr, "waz up' Mo?, MC Hidde WithOut Rezervation comin' up wit a strong Native American tip, lettin' every body know what's really goin' on in the Red Nation...so we kickin' this out to all our brothas and sistas...young and old...let the story be told...(Break #3)

With the words and phrases "checkin'", "waz up 'G", "wit", "Native American tip", "we kickin' this out", "brothas and sistas" WOR echoes the Hip Hop lexicon of the urban landscape. WOR re-contextualizes the Hip Hop lexicon through a Native perspective. This is most significantly illustrated in the middle of this exchange when LaMarr states, "wit a strong Native American tip" ("with a strong Native American influence"). Acknowledging the fluidity of Native identity as outlined in Chapter 3, this phrase speaks to all three Native identity formations as confirmed in the opening lines, "both in the land and in the inner cities" (Introduction line 1).

MC (re-)naming is viewed in Break #1:

> Chris LaMarr, "MC Hidde was born at 18
> Kevin Nez, "Red Shadow was born at 18"
> Corey Aranaydo, "Nazze was born at 18"
> LaMarr, Nez, Aranaydo, "Natives proud, Native strong...born at 18!...

The MC (re-)naming of members of WOR reveals another Multi-Tribal dimension that intersects traditional practice and Hip Hop culture. The MC/rapper name is a personal signifier in the toasting/boasting African tradition that informs Hip Hop. The MC names for the members of WOR also function as a re-tribal naming consistent with the vocabulary of Native identity.[160] This allows the names to simultaneously represent a Multi-Tribal identity and MC status in Hip Hop culture.

Other characteristics influenced by Hip Hop culture include: the use of digital distortion as a masking technique (similar to the masking styles and techniques of the Hamatsa, Tlingit, Yu'pik, et al of the Pacific Northwest),[161] the collective shout chorus at the end of a phrase (similar to the technique used within contemporary powwow songs), the inflated-vocabulary of Native language (as coded/re-coded signifiers, i.e., the "z" in "reservation" or "rez'), and the use of samples (placing importance on a single event that has larger meaning).[162] These semantic characteristics interpret/invert, de-cod/re-code or loan-translate the text reflecting a Multi-Tribal identity. With the application of these literary analytical tools, this text entertains multiple Native voices.

WOR's Multi-Tribal voices engage in a dialogue with the audience. Applying Jannis Androutsopoulos' "system of interrelated spheres," three spheres of influence are recognized: 1. Artistic expression 2. Media discourse 3. Fan/activist response (Androutsopoulos 44). Each sphere bases its influence on their interrelationship. As a result of this interrelationship, the spheres operate on a Multi-Tribal level. The interrelationship in these spheres of influence establishes a platform for audience response to the text.

The lyrics speak to the complexity of Native politics (gender, spatial, tribal, economic, local/global) and how these are re-presented and negotiated. Bakhtin's concept of the Polyphonic Novel allows us to view the text as "representing the multileveled, multivoiced, nonfinalized, dialogical nature of all character, idea, human experience, [and] life itself" (Jackson 271). Multiple voices participate in this deconstructive act. Each of these perspectives encompasses additional multiplicities such as, Native (mixblood), urban (Native and non-Native), political (American government system, tribal governments), gender (male and female). Through the lens of Hip Hop, WOR balances, presents and re-presents the juncture of literary technique and multiple identity perspectives.

The repeating poetic structure of the text demonstrates WOR's use of repetition on a micro level as well as a macro level.[163] The text employs 4 – 5 lines per verse, or stanzas, throughout the work. In the last line of each phrase there is a short sample that functions as a cadence that coincides with the cadence of the text. With a blues inspired sample WOR signifies on an urban Native identity that displays the influence of non-Native music such as rock, punk, blues, etc. (LaMarr phone interview Dec. 22, 2008). The brief blues influenced sample contrasts with a sample of a female powwow vocal. This juxtaposition draws attention to the female situation being addressed in the song. The title itself, "Born at 18," directly refers to a young woman, just entering adulthood, who gives birth to a child:

> We were born at 18, what that means
> a child screams, with a life of no hopes and no dreams (14 – 15)

The decision to use a powwow sample emphasizes the Inter-Tribal reality of the powwow arena for Native people. Further, as discussed in Chapter 3 and will be expanded later in this chapter, the powwow for many Native people is an Inter-Tribal and Multi-Tribal signifier of their Native identity. The female vocal sample represents the identity formations (Tribal,

Inter-Tribal, Multi-Tribal), to use another sample may have run the risk of deflating, marginalizing or even silencing the Native female voice.

WOR states that this selection is for and from the "young and old...let the story be told" (Break #3). The group inverts this reflection on a seemingly negative situation, having a child at 18 years of age into a positive re-presentation of Native culture. This inversion empowers the next generation deflecting a negative stereotype of Native people.[164]

Sermonizing, Cut/Mix, Flow/Rupture and Layering

Jon Michael Spencer has identified Sermonizing, Cut/Mix, Flow/Rupture and Layering as underlying theoretical concepts in Hip Hop (Spencer 15). In the following sections each of these concepts will be deconstructed demonstrating how WOR integrates these concepts within a Multi-Tribal identity.

Sermonizing

Jon Michael Spencer discusses the evolution of the sermon and sermonizing in relation to popular Black music. Incorporating Spencer's analysis of sermonizing we see that the Native Hip Hop MC (Master of Ceremony) continues, in a similar tradition. Spencer traces the history of sermonizing from Black worship, particularly the antebellum spiritual:

> melodious declamation delineated into quasi-metrical phrases with formulaic cadence was customarily enhanced by intervening tonal response from the congregation. Responsorial iteration of catchy words, phrases, and sentences resulted in the burgeoning of song to which new verses could be contemporaneously added (Spencer 225).

In the tradition of sermonizing, Spencer notes that "favorable creations were remembered and perpetuated through oral transmission" (Spencer 225). It is here, that Spencer speaks about the most important components of sermonizing that remain ever-present in the works and poetry of the Hip Hop MC. Spencer acknowledges that preaching, as witnessed through the Black Church is "truly a manifestation of power" (Spencer 226).[165] Spencer cites William C. Turner Jr., who describes theophany as the "manifestation of a deity, some object is present which opens to the transcendent while simultaneously being rooted in the world of the tangible, historical reality" and characterizes the power of preaching as, "there is no modality more indicative of the presence of deity, power, and intrusion from another order than that of the preached word entrenched in musicality" (Turner 27 - 28). Spencer identifies this concept as, "a word coming from another world" (Spencer 226-7) that Turner previously stated as, "the preacher becomes an oracle through which a divinely inspired message flows" (Turner 4 – 9). Spencer outlines the prime elements used in sermonizing; melody, rhythm, call and response, polyphony, structure/anti-structure, form (rational content) and improvisation (glossal content) (Spencer 227).

Sermonizing within the works of WOR is supported by a Native activist ideology relevant to both urban and reservation contexts. LaMarr notes that he was inspired by political discussions at the Intertribal Friendship House (Oakland, CA). It was here that LaMarr was introduced to the musical, poetic and political works of John Trudell, Nilak Butler, Russell Means and Susan Lobo (LaMarr Phone interview 18 Dec 2008). These poet/activist/scholars would become pivotal mentors for LaMarr as he forged ahead with his own work in Hip Hop. Joining with two other urban Native men, Mike Marin (aka Sice the Merciless) and Kevin Nez (aka Nez the Nemesis) Chris LaMarr (aka M.C. the Messenger) created the Hip Hop group WithOut Rezervation.

In reviewing the MC names of WOR (the Merciless, the Nemesis, the Messenger) with the name of the group (WithOut Rezervations), it becomes apparent that WOR is working on a metaphorical political level. The MC names, the Merciless and the Nemesis, are representative of the act of toasting and boasting in Hip Hop. They signify on political conflicts that continue to plague Native people within the United States. The metaphorical meaning of the names is subject to semantic inversion/interpretation. The merciless acts of violence perpetuated against Native people are inverted/interpreted to re-present an unforgiving ("mercy less") rhetorical attack on the American political system (read: the nemesis, the adversary).

The 1982 album The Message,[166] by Grandmaster Flash and Furious Five, includes Melle Mel's voice and poetry that has been identified by Hip Hop scholars as establishing the genre of Rap in Hip Hop culture (Rose 55, Nelson 1 – 22, Keyes 39 – 66, Perkins 1 - 48). Following this heritage, "The Message" by Public Enemy's Chuck D., is one of the signifiers in socially conscious Hip Hop (Ramsey 173 – 180, Kitwana 201). For WOR, and more specifically Chris LaMarr, Public Enemy's socially conscious message functions as a role model for the presentation of their work (phone interview 14 Dec 2008).

With the name the Messenger, LaMarr sermonizes on the influence and importance of the message for Native people. LaMarr and WOR deliver "the message" (read: conscious Native centered political meaning) to Native people through the expressive and active agent of Hip Hop. LaMarr follows a model established by Public Enemy, Wu Tang Clan and other socially conscious Hip Hop artists (phone interview 14 Dec 2008). The message expressed is not simple, static or singular, but rather is complex, fluid and multiple. As the Messenger, LaMarr sermonizes on culturally relevant Native themes. Re-presenting these themes through Hip Hop he creates a cross-cultural connection with the non-Native Hip Hop community who hear another "message."[167]

These DJ names function in the same Hip Hop DJ lineage, speaking with authority, conviction, confidence and power (Rose 55). The names employ an inflated vocabulary that involves multiple cultural signifiers (American, Africa-American, Native). The loan-translation of these names through a Native perspective presents a sermonizing voice within a Multi-Tribal identity.

The name of the group, WithOut Rezervation (WOR), identifies another form of sermonization. The group originally decided on the name Without Rezervation because it signifies on "reservation." WOR recuperates this Native signifier through transposition, first in spelling followed by meaning. The capitalized the "o" in "Without" creates the acronym "WOR" (LaMarr phone interview 18 Dec 2008). The substitution of the "s" for "z" within the word "reservation" actively transposes the literal and limited prescription of this term.[168] Tricia Rose remarks that throughout the history of Hip Hop rap groups have reinvented phrases, terminology, and words that "emerge from complex cultural exchanges and larger social and political conditions of disillusionment and alienation" (Rose 59). This is an example of Smitherman's semantic inversion or "flippin the script" of English lexicon (Smitherman 279 – 282). This transposition paves the way for the acronym WOR.

Chris LaMarr relates that the primary "message" of Without Rezervation is to speak beyond the real and imagined structures of the reservation system (LaMarr phone interview 18 Dec 2008). The signification of the name, WithOut Rezervation (WOR) is designed to articulate a contemporary Native identity beyond the imposed restrictions of the reservation.

Upon hearing the word WOR (read/hear: war) one may immediately conjure images of battle, aggression and violence. The group capitalizes on the real/imagined violence that has occurred historically between the U.S. government and Native people. Through the transposition of this term, "war," WOR inverts, or rather, "flips the script" on the real/imagined violence that has controlled Native people for multiple generations. Chris LaMarr notes that with the appropriation of the acronym and MC names, WOR sermonizes through a Native post-industrial ritual of re-naming. This ritual reflects the complexity of Native and non-Native Hip Hop communities (phone interview 28 Dec 2008).

In 1992, the 500th anniversary of Columbus' "discovery" of the "New World" served as the impetus for critical discourse. WOR began to compose work that spoke to the Grand Native Narratives as referred to by Vine Deloria Jr. (Chapman 152 – 169). The group engaged highly charged topics such as alcoholism ("To The Sellouts"), teen pregnancy ("Born at 18"), criminal injustice ("Guilty 'til Proven Innocent")[169], the US political/government system ("Red, White, and Blue", "Time For Some Action"), stereotypes and misrepresentation of Native history ("502 Years", "Was He a Fool? (Columbus)", "Mascot", "Are You Ready for WOR?"), and Native pride ("Skin I'm In").

Nearly half of this recording (four out of ten tracks) focuses on issues of stereotyping and misrepresentation. LaMarr refers to this important time for WOR as crucial to their attaining visibility through numerous features on radio programs and concert performances. This visibility offered WOR the opportunity to rap in the tradition of "conscious Native Hip Hop" that was inspired by the need for education and the political unifity of Native people in the late 20th Century (phone interview 28 Dec 2008). Quoting LaMarr:

> if we could do something to help the kids through hip hop and rap then we were all for it...we were encouraged by the older generation to do it our way as they saw the kids listening to what we were saying...and we were very aware to say it in a good way... (phone interview 28 Dec 2008).

The political climate of 1992, their visibility on a national stage and the signifyin' transposition of Hip Hop culture through a Native identity helped shape the sermonizing voice that became WOR.

Cut/Mix

The concept of Cut and the Mix, theorized by Jon Michael Spencer, addresses not only the deconstruction ("cut") but also the reconstructive ("mix") in Hip Hop (Spencer 20). Cut/mix deepens the understanding of cultural issues, artistic interpretations, and the re-presentation of Native identity. Tricia Rose illustrates the significance of cut and mix to the corporeal of "hip hop's lyrical, musical and visual works" as they "accumulate, reinforce and embellish" (Rose 39) the complex signifyin' aesthetic and cultural lexicon of Hip Hop. Cut/mix juxtaposes cultures (Hip Hop, Popular Music, Native music, et al) and identities (Native, non-Native, Tribal/Inter-Tribal/Multi-Tribal, reservation, rural, urban, et al), mixing these components as they are re-presented in music. When flow/rupture is applied to rhymes (Rose 39), the cut/mix re-constructs identity on micro and macro levels. With Cut/mix, Native Hip Hop artists can signify on a specific area (identity, culture, or politics).

WOR engages cut/mix through their collective mixblood identities that cut and mix different Native cultures. The members of WOR identify themselves as Pima, Navajo (Dine) and Pit River/Paiute.[170] WOR embraces their diverse tribal and cultural backgrounds and they do not seek to create a unified Native identity or pan-indian identity.[171] No singularity is reified. This multifaceted dialogue speaks to a diaspora of cultures that freely exchange and cross-connect within the Hip Hop arena.

WOR captures these cross-cultural connections as they cut between their different tribal identities (Pima, Dine, Pit River/Paiute). WOR then mixes these identities together transforming a singular (Tribal) into a plural (Multi-Tribal) representation. For example, a "shout out" to the Aztlan Nation articulates a singular Tribal reference as well as a collectively conscious relationship that contains multiple factors, "aztlan nation, and all our relations" (line 52).[172] The members of WOR define (cut) as an individual relationship to the Aztlan Nation in a dialogical process via the "shout out" (mix). Through repetition in performance, analytical reading, and poetic writing, WOR expresses a re-constructed, fluid identity in Hip Hop culture.

Elvira Pulitano reminds us of the statement by Trinh T. Minh-ha who states that, "fragments of/in life, [are the] fragments that never stop interacting while being complete in themselves." [173] WOR remains open to numerous Native and non-Native cultural viewpoints, expressions, and signifiers. WOR realizes Trinh's "fragments" in a Tribal, Inter-Tribal, Multi-Tribal perspective that is dislocated and reconfigured.

and all our relations (52)

what's really goin' on in the Red Nation…so we kickin' this out to
all our brothas and sistas…young and old (Break #3).

These lines cut through Multi-Tribal identities ("all our relations", "Red Nation"). The text also features a generational cut and mix, "young and old…let the story be told" (Break #3). The process here is the generational exchange of "[T]he story" that intersects generations and is complicated by a Tribal, Inter-Tribal or Multi-Tribal identity. Identity becomes an on-going activity that is performatively expressed and culturally relevant. Identity is never static as Minh-ha stated, identity "never stop[s] interacting while being complete in themselves."[174]

The original record cover art demonstrates another example of the "fragments of/in life."[175] AYRFW? features a background in concrete that defines the urban center. The members of WOR define two locations of home, one being the urban center and their individual reservation[176] (LaMarr phone interview 28 Dec 2008).

Embedded within this concrete slab is a fracture, a shard that contains five different Native silhouettes all without eyes. These figures are crossed diagonally with barbed wire that meets in the middle of the shard. WOR uses this image to signify that they are in a state of combat, battling the presumed hierarchy of the US government as well as referencing the imprisoned circumstances of Native people within the U.S. WOR challenges the strategic tactics that the U.S. has forced upon Native people, "both in the land and in the inner cities".[177] The lettering on the album cover features capital block letters in red to signify a war-like (read: WOR) attitude. The use of the color red signifies the cultural representation of birth, the blood of the ancestors and the rejuvenation of life that blood offers (LaMarr phone interview 20 Dec 2008).

The limited use of color represents another aspect of the cut/mix principle, this time in traditional Native and popular culture. The Gourd Dance specifically uses the colors blue and red.[178] This Southern Plains dance style comes from the home areas of WOR members, namely the Southern part of the United States. The Gourd Dance is traditionally a "warriors dance." One can be initiated into this "society" as a veteran of war and or after serving time in a branch of the armed forces.[179] WOR follows this militaristic thread placing an image of a map describing the land from Alaska through Central America on the cheek of the lower silhouette that is mainly in red and blue. These two colors are seen on the Gourd Dance Blankets that Lassiter notes as, "...half red, half blue – draped over the shoulders and hanging to the knees or draped across the chest" (Lassiter 110). James Howard adds more detail to the discussion noting that veterans wear red and blue woolen broadcloth shoulder blankets with "the red end of the blanket over the heart" (Howard 249). The veterans place medals and ribbons on the meeting point of the blue and red (Howard 250). Specifically limiting their color choice to blue and red, WOR signifies on the symbolic re-presentation of these colors, as well as the Gourd Dance itself, as recognized in the contemporary powwow arena.[180]

The six stars atop the map represent the Iroquois Nation after the addition of the Tuscarora in 1722 and the six different worlds from Navajo cosmology (phone interview 28 Dec 2008). The lightning bolts that are glazed along the opposite cheek of the larger silhouette are in red and blue, again drawing on the before mentioned representation of these colors. Their shape, the lightning bolt, represents the force and power of nature in southwestern Native art.[181] The lightning bolts are parallel to each other that signifying a balance between two worlds (Native/non-Native, traditional/contemporary) (Berlo 36 – 63). The silhouettes without eyes recall the provocative works of the California mixblood Native artist Fritz Scholder. Scholder's works caught the attention of radical Native and non-Native communities alike.[182] Images with darkened faces and absent expressions create an eerie sensation that speaks to the invisibility of the Native person. The philosophy of the Anishnabe author Gerald Vizenor also defines the "indian" as an invented image in literature and history, controlled by constructed structures of Euro-American society (Vizenor 6 – 8).[183] Finally, the eagle feather is presented as an Inter-Tribal signifier. The large single feather is placed in a prominent position that speaks directly to a collective Native identity, "both in the land and in the inner cities".[184]

WOR mixes and re-presents a dynamic identity continuum[185] that embraces Native history, politics, urban and reservation cultures. Native signifiers that are distrurbing (i.e., barbed wire, concrete block, "indian" silhouettes) are cut and situated (read: mixed) alongside affirming Native signifiers (i.e., an eagle feather, Gourd Dance colors, lightning bolts, multiple meaning of the color red) that are transposed through a Multi-Tribal logic. The mixing is performed outside restrictions of time, place, and Native/non-Native identity. The transposing process performed through a Multi-Tribal identity re-presents a complex re-contextualization of Native identity.

Flow/Rupture

H. Samy Alim defines "flow" as a "narrative sequencing" that is "defined generally as the relationship between the beats and rhymes in time" (Alim 95). Flow's foundation is rhythmic but, as Alim notes, "flow" is not a limited concept but assist in creating an artist relationship in congruence with Hip Hop culture (Alim 93 - 101).[186] The flow is what allows an artist/poet to glide through simile, metaphor, double-entendre, rhyming, et al., while constantly re-shaping and re-mixing the representation of the subject in question. The flow allows the interplay of different signifiers to operate on both an artistic and technical level. Therefore, flow assists a Hip Hop artist/poet in defining and re-presenting his/her work.

Tricia Rose discusses circulation as one of the main functions of flow (Rose 39). Through repetition the Hip Hop artist flows between different strata in which they find their works: cultural, post-industrial/urban, artistic, historic, artistry (musical, literate, et al.), etc. (Rose 39 – 61). Native Hip Hop artists embrace the dynamic of flow with their own cultural signifiers across identity (Tribal/Inter-Tribal/Multi-Tribal), culture, urban/reservation (consciousness, location), political history, and artistry (musical, literate, et al).

WOR demonstrates their use of flow as they navigate and weave through the complexities of identity. This is evident in the diverse perspectives in Born at 18: Militant/Political/Social, Despair/Demise/Defeat, Optimism/Hope/Empowerment. WOR challenges perceived contradictions and limited points-of-view. The flow is re-presented in a fluid form of Native identity that, as phrased by Chris LaMarr, "speaks to the kids on the rez and in the city" (phone interview 18 Dec 2008).

The counterpoint to Flow is Rupture. Rupture becomes a very useful device in that the poet leaves his/her their constructed and sometimes confined literary space to draw attention to a word, phrase, or sound. William Cobb refers to rupture as the "anti-flow" that is defined as the precise and seemingly out-of-place location of phrasing and text (Cobb 89). The anti-flow normally introduces a different idea for the poet. Elongated phrasing and unstable climactic cadences are two examples of anti-flow. The principle of "anti-flow," however, neglects the interaction between flow and rupture. Cobb creates a hierarchy that favors flow. The balance between flow and "rupture in the line" (Rose 39) confirms that rupture does not work against flow, but to functions as an active extension of the line. It is rupture that captures the improvisational moments within flow allowing the artistic work (Rap, DJ-ing, Breakdancing, Graffiti, Aesthetics, Journalism/Writing) to interact within a cultural context. Rupture represents the unrehearsed, unexpected, inconsistent, and indeterminate moments that arise in an artistic practice. The DJ, MC, graffiti artist, breakdancer, fashion designer and author embrace these creative improvisational moments as defining the depth of their craft.[187]

WOR embraces the principle of flow/rupture across a multitude of levels: tribal, urban, gender, and political. WOR ruptures from the stereotype of the silent, stoic male warrior and illustrates the persistent complexity of the contemporary Native poetic voice. WOR, or more precisely Chris LaMarr, does not rest comfortably on a predetermined understanding of Native culture or history. LaMarr balances contemporary Native and non-Native perspectives in his raps. The selection Skin I'm In[188], LaMarr writes:

I'm a dog, a rez dog (1)

I'm proud of the skin I'm in (13)

Red brother (14)

coming up strong in the Native race (31)

These lines exemplify LaMarr's political flow that travels between numerous Native identities. With the word "dog," LaMarr ruptures the meaning of a domesticated animal into one that is "down" (read: up and supportive with the current context) (Smitherman 280). This exhibits Native pride. The "Red brother" and "Native race" do not refer specifically to any particular tribe or Native culture. LaMarr flows between Native identities rupturing any limitations. The representation of a "Native race" acts as a political rebuttal to the EuroAmerican dominant culture within the U.S. This racial signifier localizes WOR's ideology in a Nativist perspective.[189] LaMarr embraces the ruptures that extend from cultural and political (mis)representation.[190] By flowing across the lines of presumed cultural demarcation and rupturing political positions infused with cultural insensitivity, WOR/Chris LaMarr re-presents the complexities of a post-modern Native vernacular.

Layering

"Layering," as defined by Tricia Rose, is the reaffirmation of the collective strata, discussed above, that resound in Hip Hop culture (Rose 40 – 60). Joseph G. Schloss redefines the concept of "digging" for rare records that assist a DJ in creating an audio identity through samples (Schloss 60 – 80). Layering is where antithetical properties coalesce. "Rappers layer meaning by using the same word to signify a variety of actions and objects; they call out the DJ to 'lay down a beat,' which is expected to be interrupted, ruptured" (Rose 39).

The selection Born at 18, illustrates the concept of layering through the multiple meaning of the term "born". A literal translation is the act of childbearing, where a metaphorical translation may signify the arrival of an action. WOR is aware of both these meanings and layers poetic text that refers to youthful childbirth with the sampled voices from female powwow singers[191] and the low, booming, distorted voice of John Trudell who repeats (layers) his prophetic statement, "We were born at 18". WOR builds this song on the fact that Trudell is the "Voice of Alcatraz Island" (Johnson 106).

While working for KPRA as a broadcast/radio host during the Occupation of Alcatraz Island from 1969 – 1971 (Johnson 107 – 113), John Trudell began the legendary "Radio Free Alcatraz" radio program that broadcast world issues and discussed conditions in "Indian Country."[192] For Trudell, the Occupation of Alcatraz Island is the rebirthing place for Native sovereignty, solidarity, and unification (personal interview 4 Dec 2008). WOR follows Trudell's lead, layering both the political and social meanings of Born at 18.

Chris LaMarr notes that his personal contact in the Bay Area with those involved with the Occupation of Alcatraz Island as integral to the establishment of WOR and inspired the use of positive Native signifiers. LaMarr confirms that WOR's use of samples, Native slang, drumbeat patterns, powwow samples, colors, images, et al collectively create a layered meaning and re-present contemporary Native identity in Hip Hop (phone interview 28 Dec 2008 – 2 Jan 2009).

This approach to an entire body of work that stretches through history, unifying dynamic and multiple signifiers is a textbook example of layering. WOR provides a model for the growing genre of Native Hip Hop of how to construct and work within the four critical areas of Hip Hop (Sermonization, Cut/Mix, Flow/Rupture, Layering). This gives Native communities the dialogical framework that represent the omni-present complexities implicit within Native identity.

A summary of the analysis of Born at 18 demonstrates how the techniques of Sermonization, Flow/Rupture, Cut/Mix and Layering interact. The sample of the female powwow voice cuts and mixes between verses of the song. This is symbolic of the collaboration between traditional and contemporary powwow music (LaMarr personal phone interview Dec. 20 2008). The spoken word comments by WOR, and distorted voice of John Trudell ("We were born at 18"), rupture the poetic flow established by LaMarr and the other MCs in this example. However, this rupture does not interrupt the consistent and persistent "heartbeat" of the bass line that flow signifies the heartbeat of the Native community "both in the land and in the inner cities."[193]

Sermonization is expressed by the poetic text of the MCs, the distorted voice of John Trudell, the female powwow singers' sample, and the persistent heartbeat of the music. All these layers demonstrate how WOR is signifies on contemporary Native culture through their cultural appropriation of Hip Hop. Both Schloss and Rose reaffirm these techniques as the Native "blueprint for social resistance and affirmation" (Rose 39), where the "creat[ive] aspiration, moral beliefs, political values and cultural realities" (Schloss 60) "create sustaining narratives, accumulate them, layer, embellish, and transform them" (Rose 39).

Samples and the Beat

The technique, art, and ideology of sampling work in collaboration with the construction of identity for Native Hip Hop artists.[194] The sample is a sound object removed from its original context and repeated by the use of electronic assistance, most often a sampler. Tricia Rose reminds us that, "samples were used to 'flesh out' or accent a musical piece" (Rose 73). The practice of sampling itself dates to the early 1980s (Rose 79).

Sampling, according to Joseph G. Schloss is, "the electronic borrowing and manipulation of recorded sound" (Schloss 29). The techniques of borrowing and manipulation in Hip Hop are not new. DJ Marley Marl refers to the development of the sample as a happy "accident" that launched a musical generation (Rose 79). It is important to recall that samples were mostly used in the late 1980s to recreate or rather, "mask the sample and its origin; to bury its identity" (Rose 73). The reality is that the original identity of a sample is disguised and re-presented for a different purpose.

In practice, the sample is a fluid signifiyin' agent in a cross-cultural glocal[195] arena. The sample is not stable and derives cultural energy from each point of contact. Each contact point for a sample creates another signifyin' layer. The cultural representation of the sample gains a new identity that is multiplied by repetition and context. The choice of what to sample may include signifiers that are appropriated from another culture. The sample re-presents a Multi-Tribal rhizome complicated by its location in sonic culture.

Chris LaMarr refers to the samples originating from powwow culture (phone interview 29 Dec 2008). The use of powwow signifiers for WOR allows them to cross-connect with the complexity of identities that are involved in powwow culture.[196] LaMarr states that to connect with the large (glocal) Native population, both on the reservation and the urban context, it is important to incorporate signifiers that converse within these cultural arenas (phone interview 29 Dec 2008). Once a sample is used it is no longer a static signifier.

A sample highlights a signifier from a culture. A structuralist understanding of a sample requires a signifier-signified binary. This minimizes the complexity and does not allow multiple re-presentations. The repetition and re-contextualization of a sample exists within Androutsopoulos' three spheres of influence.[197] Therefore, the sample re-presents the complexity of identity in sound.

The sample encounters a multitude of identities along its dialogical journey. For Native people the meaning of a sample can speak to their own real/imagined understanding of "Indianness", and re-present the modern complexity of urban and reservation Native people. Signifyin' does not abandon nor neglect any of the history, identities, or other signifiers (real/imagined) in Native communities. Hip Hop establishes a dialogue that continues to sermonize flow/rupture, cut/mix and layer as it signifies identity.

AYRFW? has fourteen tracks that include eleven tracks with samples. Like Born at 18, a heavy ground bass beat signifies on the idea of the heartbeat in two ways: first, the heartbeat of the people (i.e., the drum) and second, the heartbeat of the newborn child.[198] Chris LaMarr states this clearly when he surmises that "for Native people that drum is the heartbeat of the people...and it's the same in Hip Hop where the drumbeat is the beat of the people who are hearin' it" (phone interview 22 Dec 2008). West Coast Hip Hop of the mid 1980s/early 1990s (i.e., Mobb Music, G-Funk, Gangsta Rap), focused on the "high-lighted bass-and-synth" (Cobb 93) that becomes the groove for rappers/poets to glide, ebb and flow. The Hip Hop "beat" during this time period is transposed into Native Hip Hop with the drum as the "heartbeat" for both the powwow and Hip Hop culture.

WOR repeats a short two bar phrase that represents the persistence of the heartbeat. The signifier of the heartbeat is not limited to any of any particular culture. It remains open to Native and non-Native connections.

The first sample we hear are the voices of female powwow singers.[199] These voices first enter at the introduction of the song and are repeated during the chorus. The sample fades slowly gliding out of perception like female powwow singers (LaMarr phone interview 20 Dec 2008). WOR strategically places the sample at the beginning and juncture points of the song to construct a positive view of Native women. The female voices are heard above the male voices as they repeat in a two-cycle phrase.[200] It is important here to note that female powwow singers can be heard singing high above male powwow singers regardless of the tessitura of the male voices (Browner 66 – 87). The sampled female voices crescendo slowly at the start of each cycle and are cut slightly at the end of the first cycle. The second repeated cycle begins with the same crescendo and is allowed to diminuendo slowly.

The repetition of the sample serves as a foundation for the entire work. When the sample fades leaving only the male voices, who rap or speak rather than sing, their absence is not, at first, noticeable. The female presence evades erasure. The first cycle slightly clips the female voices that becoming part of the landscape of the two-cycle phrase. This is augmented by electronic manipulation that in turn becomes a marker for the sample itself.

WOR, as an all-male rap group, does not attempt to make a statement for Native women. They recognize the importance of the woman's position in the dynamic of Native culture. The repetition of the sample dismantles the stereotype of the silent, complacent, and docile Native female. WOR realizes the importance of the female voice, perspective, and identity as a core component of powwow and Native Hip Hop culture. The song bonds Hip Hop technique (sample/sampling) and Native culture (powwow).

The Scratch

One minute and twenty-six second into Born at 18 we hear a word "scratched" out of the rhyme, "but you know that we won't go out like that cuz we're too damn strong it's time to take our sh** back"[201] (19). Hip Hop authors and performers define the technique of the "scratch" as the act of moving a record back and forth in a groove of a record producing a scratching sound (Keyes 2002, Rose 1994, Perkins 1996, X-Ecutioners 1997/98). WOR does not take advantage of the artistic possibilities of scratching but rather uses it sparingly. The scratch technique that WOR does involve amounts to little more than editing.

WOR assumes that people from different generations will hear their work. WOR made a conscious decision to scratch out profanity in their selections so that the elder audience would not reject or dismiss the meaning of their songs. This prompted a level of self-editing prior to recording. Consistent with their working ethic, WOR strives to retain Native cultural sensitivity and Hip Hop credibility. According to Chris LaMarr, WOR desired to have their works recognized by, "young Indian kids...who were into Hip Hop..." but also needed to balance these same works "...paying respect to the elders..." (phone interview 14 Dec 2008). Operating with these restrictions explains why scratching is limited in its use.

Conclusion

WOR challenges stereotype re-presenting a contemporary, Native political viewpoint that addresses gender identity. With the four critical Hip Hop devices (Sermonization, Flow/Rupture, Cut/Mix and Layering), WOR engages and deconstructs (mis)representations as it reconstructs Multi-Tribal identities. Through Native ideology, WOR transposes Hip Hop techniques and tools reflecting a multiple tribal reality.

BONUS TRACK

This chapter focused upon the use of text in selected works by W.O.R. This useful process can further be expanded, given the time since the original writing of this work. What stands as an unquestionable act is that the collective vernacular of Hip Hop has been acculturated by the second generation of Native Hip Hop artists. It is this tribal rescripting, use, and sociolinguistic transposition that helps solidify the Native Hip Hop canon.

The BONUS TRACK of chapter 3 noted the acculturation contact between non-Native and Native Hip Hop artists. Hip Hop culture has, in effect, reified a stereotype of the Indian image/icon by discounting the importance of Native Hip Hop artists. Hip Hop's artistic-media industry complex has not granted full access nor attention to the growing Native Hip Hop canon. This denied approach to contemporary Native Hip Hop reverts to a referential politic of scripting Native/Indigenous/Indian identity as a marginalized other. In effect, Native Hip Hop is forced to survive outside of borders constructed by ownership, authenticity, and a pop cultural glocal discourse of Hip Hop identity.

From a critical literary perspective, Native Hip Hop speaks directly to the importance of identity, cultural political issues, gender politics, health and welfare programs, and the right of legal sovereignty and self-determination. These core principles are in company with the seed of the inner-city resistant youth movements that helped outline Hip Hop. Yet, sociolinguistic scholars and others working within the Hip Hop artistic-media industry complex have yet to embrace how these contributed values of Hip Hop are shaped from a Native/Indigenous/Indian lens.

Native Hip Hop linguistics and vernacular content is not the stereotyped "whoops," "screams," or "hollers." Native Hip Hop is not super-saturated with tribal linguistics. This activity would be foreign to non-Native audiences and displace Native Hip Hop into a stereotyped reference of the Indian. Native Hip Hop artists are well aware of the omnipresent racially structured Indian icon/image in EuroAmerican pop culture.

Native Hip Hop embraces the language of the colonizer, English. Native Hip Hop artists utilize Hip Hop sociolinguistic structures, semantics, and signifiers to ensure that the realities of contemporary tribal contexts are clearly understood. In this decolonizing process, Native Hip Hop artists re-present and contemporarily activate their tribal voices. Gayatri Spivak notes that the complexities and realities of those whom the Western ideological canon situate as marginalized are misunderstood and inadequately represented by Western pedagogy and cultural theories. (Singh2023) For Spivak, there is a crisis in knowledge.

Spivak continues:

The crisis in knowledge indicates the presence of...privilege...[toward colonial] intellectuals...[who] make political claims on behalf of the oppressed or [referenced] marginalized people. This [action-meaning-content] leads to the silencing of their voices and omission of their lived experiences...it also implies that the lives and struggles of these [people]...will only continue to be misunderstood and misrepresented with respect to the [privileged] western [canon]. (qtd in Singh 2023)

I extend this concept to note how and why Native Hip Hop artists protect their use and incorporation of tribal language, words, signifiers, and vernacular. As noted in chapter 2, the theory "Distortion-for-Protection" is still at play with this protected linguistic strategy. This theory is stretched further as Native Hip Hop artists actively take charge of colonizer discourse, rhetoric, signifiers, vernaculars and, in the case of Hip Hop, words/expressions/poetry. Native Hip Hop artists recognize and pronounce that Hip Hop language has no imminent domain. The present glocal Hip Hop canon, founded upon culturally expressed action-meaning-content, Native Hip Hop artists announced a contested dialectic to Hip Hop authenticity and ownership by any one culture, community, or identity.

Native/Indigenous/Indian connections of culture(s) is expressed through an artistic practice of Hip Hop sociolinguistic formations. In the evolution of the Native Hip Hop canon, Native/Indigenous/Indian artists coalesced the artistic dynamics of culture, framed a socio-political economy of resistance, and re-presented the relationship between Native/Indigenous/Indian and non-Native communities. This action-meaning-content indicates a sovereign Native value of self-determination as well as an intellectual trajectory narrated by Native Hip Hop artists. The realities of contemporary Native/Indigenous/Indian Peoples are witnessed using colonial discourse and rhetoric, English. Native expressive agency occupies Hip Hop sociolinguistic troupes and references present throughout Hip Hop's glocal identity and subgenres.

It is from this point of sociolinguistic contact that I propose an added level of Native discourse using sociolinguistic structures. I argue that tribal-sociolinguistic critical theory expands the discourse of Native/Indigenous/Indian identity beyond a linguistic core. Language, for Native Hip Hop artists, is not singular, limited, nor illusive. The use of Hip Hop signifiers allows Native artists to speak across a colonial rhetoric. Native Hip Hop artists narrate pop cultural glocal semantics from their sovereign/self-determination locations of tribal culture(s). The identity of language, in the voices of Native Hip Hop artists, becomes Tribal/Inter-tribal/Multi-tribal. Language is expanded to be a principle of proper tribal cultural posture aligned with contemporary relevance. Tribal "[v]ocabularies...have...[the ability] to define experiences, history, and struggle[s]". (Singh 2023)

Native Hip Hop artists pose a strategy for tribal linguistic survival. Hip Hop sociolinguistic pedagogy is transposed by Native/Indigenous/Indian Hip Hop artists as an academic vehicle for language survival pedagogy and practice. Native/Indigenous/Indian Hip Hop artists infuse tribal specificities in Hip Hop semantics as agency for cultural sovereign/self-determination politics. Hip Hop language becomes a survival apparatus structuring the dynamic growth of the Native Hip Hop canon. It's important to critically understand that the use of English/African American Vernacular English, and other sociolinguistic pedagogical approaches, are culturally re-presented into a composite location of Native/Indigenous/Indian identity. This process is a firm reference to the accuracies, realities, socio-political economic issues, welfare, and identity complexities for Native/Indigenous/Indian Peoples. In the words/rhymes/poetry of Native Hip Hop artists language is a referral of traditional-contemporary identity. Language is more than words for Native Hip Hop artists.

Chuck D coined Hip Hop as being the "Black CNN." Perry Imani notes the African American Vernacular English (AAVE). In chapter 2, Imani further defines AAVE with the following standards:

(1) the primary language is African American Vernacular English (AAVE); (2) it has a political location in society distinctly ascribed to black people; (3) music and cultural forms [are] derived from black American oral culture and; (4) it is derived from black American musical traditions. (Perry 10)

Geneva Smitherman (1977) reads Hip Hop vernacular from the characteristics of the three Black Semantic foundations:

(1) words derive or have a direct African origin; (2) words entertain a loan-transformation; (3) words result in an inflated vocabulary.

In chapter 2, I posed a Native reading of these points of vernacular contact and semantic characteristics. That early Native influenced theory of a cultural exchange in language and semantics read as the following:

(1) the primary language is Inter-Tribal using black American vernacular within Native signifiers; (2) it has a political location in society distinctly associated with Native people, music and cultural forms that include black American popular culture; (3) it is derived from Native oral culture and; (4) it is derived from Native musical traditions that inclusively involve black American musical traditions.

Perry Imani (2005) expands the contextual elements of text (read: cultural encounters) when it's stated that:

[w]e read...texts, not simply alone, but in context, in relationship with other texts. We also read them intertextually,...we are concerned with how texts "speak" to each other. What is the cultural conversation being had between and within different...texts?"

H. Samy Alim (2007) unpacks the importance of socio-linguistic representation in Hip Hop. Taking a critical approach to how Hip Hop language is continued to be used by disenfranchised youth. Alim notes the "cultural tension" in language that needs "critical language pedagogies." Alim continues his critical Hip Hop language pedagogies (CHHLPs) argument pointing to the cultural "obligation to present [a] current sociolinguistic reality." It is this sociolinguistic pedagogical approach that needs to see a critical reality of how language is utilized for a clear "vision...[of] reflexive pedagogies and a call to mobilize the full body language, social, and cultural theory to produce consciousness-raising pedagogies." (Alim 2007)

Qualifying these points, Lynsey K. Wolter (2018) makes the distinction of African American English (AAE) along the lines of conscious, gangsta and contemporary rap/Hip Hop. Wolter (2018) restates Smitherman's analysis of Hip Hop language in three closely related points already identified by Smitherman, (1) AAE/ Hip Hop language stands equal to any other; (2) has systematic patterns; (3) functions as powerful expressions of identity.

In addition, Wolter (2018) reads H. Samy Alim's critical theory of AAE/ Hip Hop language as being a "national language [that] is separate from AAE." (Wolter 2018) Awad Ibrahim "argues that AAE[/Hip Hop language has] features...[that] are [defined] characteristics of membership."

This research by Wolter (2018) realized and concluded that AAE/Hip Hop language reviewed as "conscious rap utilized AAE[/Hip Hop vernaculars is used] less, [whereas] gangsta rap utilizes [AAE/Hip Hop vernaculars] more, and contemporary [2018] rap...[demonstrates a] fluctuation [based] on changes in the landscape of the [Hip Hop] genre."

A collective consciousness of Native Hip Hop artists follow the epigraph from James Luna as being "contemporary traditionalist," linguistically speaking. Hip Hop language, semantics, and signifiers are transposed along contemporary lines of a Tribal/Inter-tribal/Multi-tribal identity continuum. Binding Native/Indigenous/Indian identity construction together are the values, traditions, customs, cultures, knowledge, expressions, and sovereignty. These positions of cultural identity exemplify Luna's term, contemporary traditionalist. Applying an exclusive critical Native reading of language and its central value to the construction of contemporary Native/ Indigenous/Indian identity, values, traditions, customs, cultures, knowledge, expressions, and sovereignty, the First Nations Native Language Immersion Initiative (n.d.) states that language is:

a vital asset for Native people and communities...[i]t defines who we are, where we come from, and the value systems that in many ways cannot be translated into English.

This recognition of the importance position language maintains for Native/Indigenous/Indian Peoples presents the necessity for the second generation of Native Hip Hop artists to convey contemporary Native identity extended from a traditional/cultural point of self-determination. Benny Shendo Jr. – First Nations Board Chair – structures the necessity of cultural language preservation as the following:

Language is a core part of who we are as Indian people. Each of us has our respective languages that connect us to our place of birth, teach us how to pray, and show us who we are as Indian people. ***Language is sacred***. (emphasis in the original. firstnations.org, n.d.)

The question remains, why don't more Native Hip Hop artists use traditional languages to express their tribal sovereignty and cultural identity? Wouldn't this further secure the contemporary traditionalist philosophical doctrine?

The immersion of Hip Hop vernacular with tribal language has the potential to lean toward the exclusion of a functioning corpus of Native Hip Hop. An unspoken yet vividly relevant colonial discourse – re-presenting colonial linguistics - is central to how Native Hip Hop artists express contemporary identity, sovereignty, and self-determination. If sovereign, self-determined tribal identity is to be maintained and build upon a contemporary traditionalist agency, then, it is necessary to irradicate potential stereotypes of Indian Hip Hop such as, bigotry (read: illegitimate language), misunderstanding (read: nonsense words), racist ideologies (read: whoops and hollers), and historic socio-political stereotypes (read: Tonto speak – fractured incoherent thoughts and use of English).

Native Hip Hop artists specifically pronounce their use of Hip Hop's Elements/Points to contest colonial narratives and expressions set to minimize Native/Indigenous/Indian identity. The activation of Hip Hop semantics, signifiers, and vernaculars by a contemporary traditionalist sovereign self-determined identity frames a pedagogical "practice of freedom." (Freire 1968) The tribal-political economics of language repeat "generative themes" (Freire 1968) constructed through Luna's contemporary traditional theory. Paulo Freire (1968) points to how these "generative themes" are activated as methodologies that awaken the "critical consciousness through [the] investigation of 'generative themes.'" Native Hip Hop artists script themes of sovereignty and self-determination within their words/rhymes/poetry and use of Hip Hop signifiers. Using tribal specific terms, words, signifiers, and expressions within the language of the colonizer forces colonial discourse to recognize Native/Indigenous/Indian values, traditions, customs, cultures, knowledge, expressions, and sovereignty as narratives of self-determination for contemporary traditional identity.

Being linguistically pointed, Native Hip Hop artists focus applied attention to the use of their own tribal language, signifiers, and expressions in their words/rhymes/poetry as the binding cypher in Luna's contemporary traditionalist theory. The markers of tribal locations of culture(s) is Freire's "practice of freedom" (1968) in pedagogical approach, artistic reference, anti-colonial discourse, and Tribal/Inter-tribal/Multi-tribal identity continuum. The narrativity of the Native Hip Hop canon is a Multi-tribal complex voice(s). These voices are fueled by tribal specificities and articulated along contemporary traditional lines of sovereignty and self-determination as a pedagogical practice of freedom.

The fluid Tribal/Inter-tribal/Multi-tribal identity construction and colonial language transposition articulates a sovereign Native Hip Hop vernacular. This voiced agency is a tribal dialectic that produces an Indian Hip Hop Lexicon (IHHL). Native Hip Hop artists frame colonial language (American English), semantics, signifiers, and vernacular of contemporary Hip Hop (African American English, African American Vernacular English, Critical Hip Hop Language Pedagogies). The specificity of sovereign self-determination for Native Hip Hop artists is what repositions the conversation away from a reified sociolinguistic structure toward one that is narrated by Native Hip Hop artists. Native Hip Hop artists engage the Elements/Points of Hip Hop culture and re-present the critical lineage of language through a tribal lexicon inclusive of cultures, customs, traditions, knowledge, and expressions.

Sociolinguists argue for specific use and glocal cultural use of Hip Hop language. This sociolinguistic reading provides a structure to delve deeper into the meanings, expressions, use, and application of language in Hip Hop vernacular. The critical analysis and application that I present, for Native Hip Hop, expands the sociolinguistic discourse. Language, as a critical Native theory, is established first by aligning the Elements/Points of Hip Hop. Native Hip Hop artists then bind Hip Hop culture-vernacular together along tribal lines of an Multi-tribal identity continuum. This methodology opens the area of discourse for a Native/Indigenous/Indian cypher of a sovereign self-determination Indian Hip Hop lexicon (IHHL).

The Indian Hip Hop Lexicon (IHHL) is not limited to language. The lexicon is traversed by Native Hip Hop artists to embody cultural themes and Tribal/Inter-tribal/Multi-tribal socio-political ethics.

At the early years of Hip Hop there was not enough of an Indian voice(s) to be soundly expressed. Given the aging evolution of Hip Hop, and the progression of Native inclusion within this glocal genre, it is now of value and relevance to coin an IHHL. This critical Native expressive theory is a supporting pillar of the Native Hip Hop canon. Just as Chuck D stated that Hip Hop was the "Black CNN," so too does the collected conscious work of the second generation of Native Hip Hop artists outline the structure of a dynamic lexicon. Further, following the recognition of the "African American Vernacular" (AAV) – see chapter 1 – a tribally expressed lexicon stands on the foundational ground of Freire's (1968) theoretical voice of the oppressed.

The IHHL embodies Native critical theories, a Tribal/Inter-tribal/ Multi-tribal identity continuum, the collected socio-political economy of sovereig self-determination, cultures, customs, traditions, knowledge, and expressions of Native Peoples. As agency, IHHL moves the social discourse of Hip Hop toward the necessity to involve Native artists. The IHHL is not a hermetic theory. This Native epistemology should not be limited to the transparent borders between Native/non-Native cultural expressions. The ambivalent energy of IHHL points to the value of Native ontological discourse to be integrated beyond the invisible borders constructed by the Hip Hop artistic industry complex.

Using the IHHL in practice, by non-Native Hip Hop communities offers the opportunity for those additional communities to magnify the lens on their use of the Hip Hop semantics, signifiers, and vernacular. This artistic identity agent is malleable for Native/Indigenous/Indian Peoples and gives leverage to the future critical voices of Native Hip Hop artists. The IHHL is not static, frozen in time, nor limited in a theoretical agenda. The IHHL is not set to overstep any one perspective of Hip Hop. IHHL opens the eyes of those interested in Hip Hop. This critical Native theory is its own referential pedagogical vernacular that allows IHHL to operate on its own terms. Equally, this is a co-operative critical theory that engages the glocal cultural discourse of Hip Hop. Serving both the non-Native and Native Hip Hop communities, the IHHL maneuvers dynamic contemporary traditionalist realities of Native Hip Hop into view without losing the heartbeat of Tribal/Inter-tribal/Multi-tribal identity formulations.

References:

Alim, H. Samy. <u>Critical Hip-Hop Language Pedagogies: Combat, Consciousness, and the Cultural Politics of Communication</u>. *Journal of Language, Identity, and Education*, Vlm 6:2, pps 161-176, 5 December 2007.

firstnations.org, <u>First Nations Native Language Immersion Initiative</u>, n.d.

Freire, Paulo. *Pedagogy of the Oppressed.* <u>Dialogics</u>, Chapter 3, historyisaweapon.com

Freire, Paulo. *Pedagogy of the Oppressed,* 1968/1970/1983.

Imani, Perry. *Cultural Studies, Critical Race Theory and Some Reflections on Methods*, 50 Vill. L. Rev. 915 (2005), digitalcommons.law.villanova.edu

Singh, Pallavi. "Understanding Gayatri Chakravorty Spivak: Key Theories and Ideas." *Literary Theory*, 25 July 2023, literatureandcriticism.com

Smith, E.T. <u>bell hooks – Ideas for Social Justice</u>. *The Commons:Social Change Library*, n.d. commonlibrary.org

Smitherman, Geneva. <u>Talkin' and Testifyin, The Language of Black America.</u> Boston: Houghton Mifflin Company, 1977 (43).

Wolter, Lynsey K. *What it Do: An Analysis of African American English in Hip-Hop.* University of Wisconsin, May 2018, Minds@UW.edu.

Chapter 5. Conclusion and post-thoughts

"Hip-Hop was the power of the streets and the voice of thevoiceless manifested before this artform became Hip-Pop"[202]

– Ernie Paniciolli

During the researching process a question arose, "How many articles can be found on Native Hip Hop?" After careful examination, "Native American Hip Hop" produced 832 articles where "American Indian Hip Hop" produced 681 for a total of 1, 513 articles. Of these over 1,000 articles only one dealt with any facet Native Hip Hop: " Break Dancing and Breaking out: Anglos, Utes, and Navajos in a Border Reservation High School".[203] It goes without question that Native people of the Americas are present and thriving as diverse cultures and nations of people. Hip Hop is quickly approaching its fourth decade of existence and is well beyond its fertile youth. However, given this critical lack of scholarly attention dealing with Native Hip Hop it appears that there is an urgent need within the current 21st century for such scholarship to become present. Touré and H. Samy Alim both acknowledge that there is a Hip Hop Nation,[204]

"a country no map maker will ever respect. A place with its own language, culture and history. It is as much a nation as Italy or Zambia, a place my countrymen call the Hip-Hop Nation...We are a nation with no precise date of origin, no physical land, no single chief...The Hip-Hop Nation is a place as real as America on a pre-Columbus atlas...The Nation exist in any place where hip-hop music is being played or hip-hop attitude is being exuded." (qtd in Shapiro 96)

The reality of this location, the Hip Hop Nation (HHN), as an articulator of identity holds a strong, firm ground. The inclusion of Native identity within this 1999 quote is quite telling. Within Hip Hop, the repetition of Native identity persists as a modifier of strength and struggle for this culture and "Nation". Recalling the historic inclusion of Native identity at the formation of Hip Hop as a genre, the HHN has come to signify upon a Native identity to localize and realize culture. As outlined from throughout this compiled work, there is a persistent Native identity within Hip Hop culture. Hip Hop is a Multi-Tribal artistic form.

H. Samy Alim actively strides toward Hiphopography (Alim 11) that he has been conceptualizing throughout his educational/scholarly career. This work takes "integrates the varied approaches of ethnography, biography, and social, cultural, and oral history to arrive at an emic view of Hip Hop Culture." (Alim 11) Alim continues to note that "Hiphopography began as the study of Hip Hop cultural practice, a Hip Hop Culture Studies, if you will - not as a sub paradigm within cultural studies, but as a movement lying somewhere between cultural studies and cultural anthropology." (Alim 11) Clearly defined, "Hiphopography humanizes Hip Hop." (Alim 12) This placement of Hip Hop within the fertile grounds between cultural studies allows for and requires an interdisciplinary studies approach to the discipline. Likewise, Native (American) research, scholarship and education require a similar level of engagement along multidisciplinary lines. The final and contextually necessary discipline to engage is musicology and ethnomusicology.

These three research disciplines, Hip Hop (Hiphopography), Native Studies and Musicology/Ethnomusicology as a combined research field focus the discipline of Native Hip Hop into a profitable scholarly area. Yet, this insurmountable task of documenting and researching Native Hip Hop is not without its many challenges. To start, there is a lack of unification within Native Hip Hop itself. It has only been within the last nine years that Native Hip Hop has been applying a "serious" reflexive look at itself to gain a stable foot within the Native community. The First Nations Hip Hop groups in Canada have become a valuable model for Native Hip Hop artists in the U.S. These groups provide a positive model of expressing a "Hip Hop-conscious beings existing in a home, street, hood, city, state, country, continent, hemisphere"[205] and now reservation, reserve, and rancho. It is time for Native Hip Hop as a movement to obtain unification as a community. The historic Hip Hop divide noted in the binary between the East-West should not extend into Native Hip Hop. Nor should this be translated into a North (Canada)-South (U.S.) conflict. For the Native voice to be heard within Hip Hop it is important that the Native imprint to be more than just a passing sample on the digital drum(machine). By taking charge of the dynamic, fluid, flexible and global recognition that Hip Hop maintains, this genre serves as an ongoing expressive Native cultural agent. The nexus for Multi-Tribal identity and Native artistic sovereignty is within Hip Hop culture.

Bakari Kitwana outlines a working methodology for the Native Hip Hop to transpose. (Kitwana 2002, 2005) Kitwana's methodology identifies the historical, political and cultural elders for the African American community illustrating how their work has influenced the "Hip Hop Generation". (Kitwana 2002) WOR produced a similar result collaborating with Native political activists of the 1970s. Samples of these elder voices were incorporated within raps enabling WOR to stretch beyond a generational divide and complete the prophetic postmodern powwow circle in an inclusive break-round dance with history.

With Hip Hop now arriving in its Middle Ages the multiplicity of sub genres begins to expand. The time now beckons that Native Hip Hop artists rupture from a prescribed context of Hip Hop those forces limitations and negative simulations upon the youth. In his article, "A New Enemy",[206] Ernie Paniccioli speaks about power, place and culture identifying Native artists who marginalize their culture through the limited, romantic, and uninformed view of non-Native people.

Building upon this energy and "warning" from Paniccioli it becomes quite evident and fitting that Native Hip Hop artist introduce different ways in which Hip Hop culture can be viewed with respect to Native cultural authenticity. Paniccioli's statement directly and pointedly addresses the need for a more culturally conscious Native Hip Hop. The form Paniccioli recognizes involves the Tribal, Inter-Tribal, Multi-Tribal urban/reservation voices of Native people that function beyond linear limitations, political hegemony, and stereotypical segregation. This form of culturally conscious Native Hip Hop follows the pace established by the late Vine Deloria Jr. when he stated, "We Talk, You Listen" (Deloria 2000). If Native people listen to the postmodern (digital)drum they will hear the voice(s) of the men and women which repeat and reverberate across, and in, time.

Like the powwow arena that is the communal circle where Native people gather to express and relate as Tribal, Inter-Tribal, Multi-Tribal people, Hip

Hop culture is the repetitive circle that continues to recycle itself through Six Elements (Rap, DJ-ing, Break Dancing, Graffiti, Aesthetics, Journalism). (LaMarr phone interview 2008)

This dissertation only begins to touch upon the issues of importance for Native people that can be analyzed through a critical investigation of Hip Hop. The focus of this dissertation is specifically upon the Hip Hop group WOR. Future work will expand the model and methodology implemented here and being the Herculean, but necessary task, of applying this research to the larger Native Hip Hop community. Once it was known in Indian Country that someone was completing a dissertation that dealt with Native Hip Hop numerous emails and correspondence from droves of Native Hip Hop artists, promoters and producers arrived seeking to get their name and work out into the eyes/ears of the Native and non-Native public.

This illustrates the point that there has been little in the means of critical or scholarly work completed in the field of Native Hip Hop. True, there are Native bloggers and Native Hip Hop websites which daily discuss Native Hip Hop. However, the fact remains that there is a plethora of work to be completed within this cultural genre.

Future research necessary within Native Hip Hop is the importance and influence of Native women within Native Hip Hop, the critical involvement of the internet as a means of Multi-Tribal identity for Native Hip Hop, a critical reading of Native Hip Hop videos, the integration of Hip Hop on Native sports, an analysis of positive/negative Native inspiration upon glocal Hip Hop, the use of traditional language(s) in Native Hip Hop, etc. The joy of this research area is that it is plentiful, dynamic, and welcome to interdisciplinary studies.

Within the present post-modern era there lies a very exciting definition of ethnicity presented by Schermerhorn who states,

> "A Collectivity within a larger society having real or putative common ancestry (that is, memories of a shared historical past whether of origins or of historical experiences such as colonization, immigration, invasion or slavery); a shared consciousness of a separate, named, group identity; and a cultural focus on one or more symbolic elements defined as the epitome

of their peoplehood. These features will always be in dynamic combination, relative to the particular time and place in which they are experienced and operate consciously or unconsciously for the political advancement of the group." (Schermerhorn 12).

This definition of ethnicity establishes the realization of a Multi-Tribal Native Hip Hop Nation (NHHN) that supports the advancement of the creative Native. Critical advancement along this line will assist in confirming a conscious Native Hip Hop. Ernie Paniciolli should be proud to know that the next generations of Native Hip Hop artists are able to invest themselves to cultivate an identity within Hip Hop that stems from the origins of Hip Hop that began with Native music.

The political supra-tribal identity is now expanding into a Vizenoresque postindian model. Embracing the energy of this movement Native Hip Hop can ascertain a larger fluid form of identity construction/deconstruction that extends toward a meta-tribal context. H. Samy Alim's Hiphopography can be translated through a Multi-Tribal ideology into a genre that balances multiple Native identities within Hip Hop culture. Native Hipology is realized as a genre within Hip Hop defined by Native artist that embraces the Six Elements of glocal Hip Hop culture. These Elements are transposed through devices, tools, and techniques within the fluid continuum of Native identity that re-present Native Hip Hop in a postnative fashion. Native Hipology is the signifyin' frybread in the glocal sonic arena that feeds beyond the limits of commodities and stereotypes, sermonizing the raps of young mixed-bloods who shall not find early retirement in a crypt.

It is with this empowered attitude, direction and understanding that Native Hip Hop forges ahead re-appropriating Hip Hop culture within and by their own Multi-Tribal identities. The new drum is the multiple drums of the turntable and powwow arena simultaneously sermonizing, cutting/mixing, flowing/rupturing, layering lyrics and beats for the singers, dancers, elders, and youth. Native Hipology is the Multi-Tribal fabric for Native culture(s) that are amplified through continuous variations. This genre realizes Ernie Paniccioli's dream of an art form that, "...reflect[s] the life, lifestyle and experience of the person [people] rapping the story". [207]

BONUS TRACK

At the time of this writing Hip Hop has advanced into its middle years. No longer is Hip Hop a sacred space for youth rebellion, conscious action, or cultural expressions outside EuroAmerican norms. Hip Hop has become an EuroAmerican/global norm.

Many of the questions posed in the original Conclusion have been addressed. There has been a growing Native Hip Hop canon. Women in Hip Hop have become visible. Cultural strategies of sovereign self-determination for Native Peoples have and are taking place within the Hip Hop sphere. Even these minor developments by Native Hip Hop artists beg the question, has Native Hip Hop become successful? Is Native Hip Hop moving into communication within the larger Hip Hop glocal sphere? Has Native Hip Hop arrived at a place of acceptance?

Earlier in the Conclusion I recognized H. Samy Alim's pedagogical work that sought to establish a Hiphopography (Alim 11). Alim was on-point with the importance for the collective Hip Hop glocal community to embrace all the available vernaculars of Hip Hop. Quoting Alim again, his Hiphopography, "integrates the varied approaches of ethnography, biography, and social, cultural, and oral history to arrive at an *emic* view of Hip Hop Culture." (Alim 11) At the stages of Hip Hop's growing pains into pop culture norms, this pedagogical approach would include the practitioners in all the Elements/Points of Hip Hop. What comes to light in relationship to Alim's Hiphopography is that it remains an academic discursive approach.

lim denotes that "Hiphopography began as the study of Hip Hop cultural practice, a Hip Hop Culture Studies, if you will - not as a sub paradigm within cultural studies, but as a movement lying somewhere between cultural studies and cultural anthropology." (Alim 11) Alim – and his fellow Hip Hop scholars - define Hiphopography as the pedagogical practice that "humanizes Hip Hop." (Alim 12) The developed Native Hip Hop canon accounts for the production of Alim et al.'s Hiphopography. The younger, second generation of Native Hip Hop artists completed this pedagogical theory through the establishment of an expressive Multi-tribal Hip Hop vernacular.

In contrast to the O.G. (Original Gangsta – read: historic origins of Hip Hop) that has been afforded the foundational voice for Hip Hop identity, ideology, sociolinguistics, vernaculars, and signifiers, Native Hip Hop evolved outside these culturally codified expressive norms. Having very little academic or non-Native attention Native Hip Hop articulated what Alim et al. sought to see manifest in the African American Vernacular (AAV) of Hip Hop. Native Hip Hop has consistently utilized cultures, customs, traditions, expressions, knowledge, and sovereign self-determined references in the production of the Hip Hop arts. In the broadest scope, each of the conscious and nonconscious levels of Native Hip Hop convey some attachment or signifier of tribal identity. The desire for academics to realize the human element of Hip Hop, Native Hip Hop localizes as its core sensibility on a human anti-colonial discourse of Multi-tribal identity.

The proposed development and complexities of Native identity theorized within this work have begun to find their value and relevance in pop cultural and the Hip Hop glocal world. Vizenor's *postindian* model has been realized. The theory of a *supra-tribal* identity has found its justification and livelihood. The expected ongoing use of the pan-Indian identity product has given away to a *postnative* dialectic. Each of these Multi-tribal identity complexities exist within the construction of the Native Hip Hop canon. There is a thriving female Native Hip Hop collective. Native artists from various tribal backgrounds are working across reservation borders to announce the unification of tribal solidarity, sovereign socio-political justice, and self-determined expressive identity. What is amazing to recount is how far Native Hip Hop has grown since the writing of this original work.

Native Hip Hop has come to the age where it takes active possession of Hip Hop vernacular, norms, semantics, sociolinguistic dialectics, Elements/ Points. In response, Native Hip Hop artists react to colonial discourse, yet continue to remain centered upon their own expressive self-determined and sovereign issues. Through the Native urban diaspora (read: relocation policies, termination policies) Native Hip Hop artists elect not to draw those historic traumas into question. In contrast, Native Hip Hop artists have used these collected termination policies as platforms of expression. Native Hip Hop artists captured the arts of the colonizer, reframed these expressions as their own for Multi-tribal identity formation and sovereign self-determined socio-political liberation.

Where the racist colonial history of the term, "Indian," was once culturally accepted in the larger discursive memory of EuroAmerica, a post-Indian ideology and dialectic (see Gerald Vizenor, et al.) moves the Indian image/icon from a horrific stereotyped marginalized racist colonial American history. The repetition of the traumatic Native/Indigenous/Indian colonial history in the West/New World secures a constructed fantastical EuroAmerican perspective absent of any contemporary Native/Indigenous/Indian identity. Native scholars, artists and activist have argued to remove biased terms, icon/images from colonial control. Native Hip Hop provides the example for how this tribal operation can be set forth.

Embracing Smitherman's flip-the-script theory and cultural practice, a Multi-tribal identity, dialectic and expressive discourse recognizes the fluid critical socio-linguistic tribal voice that speaks for, by, and on its own cultures, customs, traditions, expressions, and knowledge points of sovereignty. Colonialism holds no current value for Native identity. EuroAmerican colonial practices against Native/Indigenous/Indian Peoples deny contemporary sovereign self-determined expressions and tribal realities. Native Hip Hop defies colonial rhetoric, argues against assimilation policies, contests social, legal, welfare, and educational strategies to eradicate Native sovereignty and self-determination. This consistent repeated discourse for Native activist, scholars, and artists - Native Hip Hop artists - remains fundamental to a rhetoric traversed into an active voice speaking through and from an IHHL (Indian Hip Hop Lexicon).

It can no longer be denied that there is a Multi-Tribal glocal Native/Indigenous/Indian Hip Hop identity, a glocal Hip Hop Indigeneity.

The break beat, the MC, the rap/poetry/words, the clothing, the media attention, the business owner, and community support; the incessant unwavering core of the Hip Hop landscape. When you next cross the Hip Hop path and start to sway to that phat beat, double and triple check what caught your attention. Because that turntable just might be scratchin' a powwow drum beat and the MC just might be a kid from the (urban/rural) rez. That phat beat is the contemporary traditional heartbeat of The People.

Appendix: Born at 18 Lyrics

Introduction

Chris LaMarr, "Ah yeah, WithOut Rezervation is definitely in the house...and we're kickin' this out to all our brothers and sisters living on the reservation..both in the land and in the inner cities, 'cause we know what it's like to be born at eighteen..."

"Born at 18, not a dream, an evil scheme (1)
America's way to keep our people triple teamed (2)
but we've been through this damn thing before (3)
they try to knock us out but you know we always
come back for more***"
"It's not to say that I like it that way (1)[1]
cuz we fight and fight to make it through a single day
but you know that's life on the rez
original plan was a land that left us for dead***
makes you wanna ask why it hasta be like that
cuz I stand for my culture must I stand with a gat (1)
but you know they wouldn't have any other way
so I'll say it's hell to be born today [1]***"

Break #1

Chris LaMarr, "MC Hidde was born at 18"
Kevin Nez, "Red Shadow was born at 18"
Corey Aranaydo, "Nazze was born at 18"
LaMarr, Nez, Aranaydo, "Natives proud, Native strong...born at 18!..."
Chris LaMarr,
"We were born at 18, what that means [2]
a child screams, with a life of no hopes and no dreams
it's their plan to keep the good people down
without a sound, six feet underground***
but you know that we won't go out like that

cuz we're too damn strong it's time to take our sh(it)** back [2]
but like you heard from the first verse [3]
the battle's on, on 'til the break of dawn***
cuz their people won't let my people be
another form of a racist society
to think their culture's better than mine
but I'll drop a rhyme justa make you change your mind***
cuz they know what we got's just to strong
that's why they always try to do my people wrong
make us struggle and fight just to stay alive [3]
over they years so many of my people died (2)***
but you know that's life when your born at 18 (2)
cuz America always tries to end our dream [3]
but they can't cuz the strong will survive
stay alive I got posse on my side [3]***"

Break #2

Chris LaMarr, "Yeah, we've been strugglin' since the day we were born
Kevin Nez, *("What's up?")*
(sample, "*we were born at 18*")
Chris LaMarr, "That's what it means to be born at 18, but we've got the
Great Spirit on our side"
Kevin Nez, *("I'm with that ya'll")*
Chris LaMarr, "given us strength, culture and pride to stay alive"
Kevin Nez, *("Hell yeah!")*
LaMarr, Nez, Aranaydo, "WithOut Rezervation"
(sample,"*we were born at 18*")
LaMarr, Nez, Aranaydo, "WithOut Rezervation"
(sample, "*we were born at 18*")
LaMarr, Nez, Aranaydo, "WithOut Rezervation"
(sample, "*we were born at 18*")
LaMarr, Nez, Aranaydo, "kickin' it hard 'cause this is my Nation."
Kevin Nez,
"Last verse one time I'll kick a funky rhyme (3) [1]
for my people with the guts and strength justa stay alive

cuz they've tried and lied for 500 years
keep my people in fear but no where near***
knocking us out with their genocidal blows
but here we stand true and we'll take you on toe to toe
but you should know not to mess with the red bro
on the flow, one true Navajo***
but this rhyme is going back to my people
lucky that we're stronger than the white man's evil
our strength, lives, culture, pride
we were just too tough for them just to push aside***
but they tried with all their might anyway
and I'm here to stay and I'll make'm pay [1]
cuz there's one thing about being born at 18 [3]
you can't fade my people cuz we've seen everything***
so peace and shouts out to the red nations,
to those with and without reservations, (LaMarr, Nez, Aranaydo, unknown woman voice) aztlan nation, and all our relations,
the creator for this grand creation [3]***"

Break #3

Kevin Nez, "Yeah, you checkin' out the sounds of WithOut Rezervation (sample, "we were born at 18")

Kevin Nez, "comin' out to ya live and direct from the rez'vation...hey yo MC Hiddie man, waz up' G?,

Chris LaMarr, "waz up' Mo?, MC Hidde WithOut Rezervation comin' up wit a strong Native American tip, lettin' every body know what's really goin' on in the Red Nation...so we kickin' this out to all our brothas and sistas...young and old...let the story be told...WithOut Rezervation...

(unknown male voice) "Ah-ho!"

LaMarr, Nez, Aranaydo, "WithOut Rezervation...WithOut Rezervation...WithOut Rezervation (pause)

LaMarr, Nez, Aranaydo, "WithOut Rezervation...WithOut Rezervation...WithOut Rezervation kickin' it hard 'cause this is my Nation."

Appendix: Red, White, and Blue Lyrics

1 Red, white, and blue, let me tell you

    2 who's the fool and who is true

    3 I got the gat ready to blast

    4 I got the lines ready to rhyme

    5 cuz now it's the time, for me to get mine

    6 hold me back and I'll attack

    7 and you don't want that cuz when I rap

    8 it's about the truth so how about you

    9 do you want the facts, a heart attack

    10 how about a payback

    11 anyway I'll have my say cuz I'm here to stay

    12 and when I'm through you could say you knew about the true

    13 red, white and blue

    14 Blood shed red, a bullet to the head

    15 better off dead that's what they said

    16 but that was their plan to get our land

    17 won't you understand

    18 annihilation of my nation

    19 my people died, they tried to hide

    20 all the lies but realize

    21 that the red in the flag is a blood rag

    22 a body bag it makes me sad

    23 what we had compared to what we have

    24 but I ain't trippin' cuz they're slippin'

    25 and we're coming back strong

    26 back to where we belong

    27 Man in white, thinks he's right

    28 but that I'll fight, cuz I'm MC Hiddese

    29 cuz I know better soon they'll be deader

    30 better change their ways cuz we're here to stay

    31 better dead cuz this sh** is real

    32 I saw LA so whatcha gotta say

33 better stop dissin' take time to listen
34 if you refuse were all gonna listen
35 been this way for 500 years
36 we'll shed no tears instead putt'em in fear
37 but that's today the American way
38 where might makes right
39 so America prepare to fight
40 White man in blue beating on you what's the clue
41 blue on black, blue on red, blue on brown
42 keeping us down
43 got a gat a license to cap
44 a power trip how about that beat Rodney King,
45 didn't do a think
46 caught it on tape a judicial rape
47 a white cop free but if it were me
48 where I'd be the penitentiary
49 but that's the system set up to miss'em
50 if you're white in blue you'll never lose
51 so some advice you'd better think twice
52 you rolling the dice if you call the vice
53 so end of story kinda gory
54 it's the red, white, and blue
55 straight from WOR to you!

BIBLIOGRAPHY

Abrahams, Roger D. <u>Singing the Master: The Emergence of African-American</u>
   <u>Culture in the Plantation South.</u> New York, Penguin Books: 1992.
Alfred, Gerald R. <u>Heeding the Voices of our Ancestors. Kahnawake Mohawk</u>

   <u>Politics and the Rise of Nationalism.</u> Toronto: Oxford University
   Press, 1995.

Alim, H. Samy. <u>Rock the Mic Right: The Language of Hip Hop Culture.</u> New
   York/London: Routledge, 2006.
Alim, H. Samy, Ibrahim, Awad and Pennycook, Alastair, ed. <u>Global Lingusitic</u>

   <u>Flows: Hip Hop Cultures, Youth Identities, and the Politics of</u>
   <u>Language.</u> New York/London: Routledge, 2009.

Allen, Paula Gunn. <u>Off the Reservation, Reflections on Boundary-Busting,</u>
   <u>Boarder-Crossings, Loose Canons.</u> Boston: Beacon Press, 1998.
Allen, Paula Gunn. "The Sacred Hoop: A Contemporary Indian Perspective on

   American Indian Literature". <u>Literature of the American Indians:</u>
   <u>Views and Interpretations.</u> New York: Meridian Books, 1975: 111
   – 136.

Anderson, Benedict. <u>Immagined Communities, Reflections on the Origin and</u>
   <u>Spred of Nationalism.</u> London/New York: Verso, 1983.
Anderson, Walter Truett, ed. <u>The Truth About The Truth, De-confusion and</u>

Re- constructing the Postmodern World. New York: Penguin Putnam
Inc.: 1995.

Appiah, Anthony Kwame. In my father's house: Africa in the philosophy
of

culture. New York: Oxford University Press. 1992.

Appiah, Anthony Kwame and Gates, Henry Louis, Jr., ed. "Race into
Culture:

A Critical Geneology of Cultural Identity. " Identities. Chicago/
London:

University of Chicago Press, 1995: 32 – 63.

Arlyk, Kevin. "By All Means Necessary – Rapping and Resistence in

Urban Black America." Globalization and Survival in the Black
Diaspora – The New Urban Challenge. Charles Green, ed. New
York: State University of New York Press, 1997 269 – 287.

Baker, Houston A., Jr. Black Studies, Rap and the Academy. Chicago/
London:

University of Chicago Press, 1993.

Barton, Carig E., ed. Sites of Memory: Perspectives on Architecture and
Race,

New York: Princeton Architectural Press, 2001.

Baudrillard, Jean. Simulacra and Simulation (trans. Sheila Faria Glaser).
Ann

Arbor: University of Michigan Press, 1994.

Berlo, Janet Catherine and Ruth B. Phillips. Native North American Art.
New

York: Oxford University Press, 1998.

Bhabha, Homi K. The Location of Culture. London/New York:
Routledge,

1994.

Bigenho, Michelle. Sounding Indigenous: Authenticity in Bolivian
Music

Performance. New York: Palgrave, 2002.
Born, Georgina and Hesmondhalgh, David, ed. Western Music And Its Others,

Difference, Representation, and Appropriation in Music. Berkley/ Los Angeles/London: University of California Press: 2000.

Browner, Tara. Heartbeat of the People – Music and Dance of the Northern
Pow- wow. Urbana and Chicago: University of Illinois Press, 2002.
Bruyneel, Kevin. The Third Space of Sovereignty, The Postcolonial Politics of

U.S.-Indigenous Relations. Minneapolis/London: University of Minnesota Press, 2007.

Buff, Rachel. Immigration and the Political Economy of Home; West Indian

Brooklyn and American Indian Minneapolis, 1945 – 1992. Berkley/Los Angeles/London: University of California Press: 2001.

Campbell, Kermit E. Getting' Our Groove On, Rhetoric, Language, and

Literacy for the Hip Hop Generation. Detroit: Wayne State University Press, 2005.

Canby, William C. Jr. American Indian Law (Fourth Ed). Minnesota: Thomas
West Publishing Co., 2004.
Cepeda, Raquel. And It Don't Stop! The Best American Hip-Hop Journalism of
the Last 25 Years. New York: Faber and Faber, Inc., 2004.
Chapman, Abraham, ed. Literature of the American Indians: Views and Interpretations. New York: Meridian Books, 1975.

Chang, Jeff, ed. Total Chaos: the Art and Aesthetics of Hip-Hop.
Massachusetts: Basic Civitas Books, 2006.
Churchill, Ward. Acts of Rebillion: The Ward Churchill Reader.
New York/London: Routledge, 2003.
Churchill, Ward. Indians Are Us? Cultural Genocide in Native North America.
Maine: Common Courage Press, 1994.
Churchill, Ward. Fantasies of the Master Race, Literature, Cinema and the
Colonization of American Indians. Maine: Common Courage Press,

1992.

Churchill, Ward and Vander, Jim Wall. Agents of Repression – The FBI's
Secret War Against the Black Panther Party and the American Indian
Movement. Boston: South End Press, 1990.
Clifford, James. The Predicament of Culture; Twentiety-Century Ethnography,

Literature, and Art. Cambridge/Massachusetts and London:
Harvard University Press, 1988.

Clifford, James. Routes, Travel and Translation in the Late Twentieth Century.
Massachusetts/ London: Harvard University Press, 1997.
Cobb, William Jelani. To The Break of Dawn: A Freestyle on the Hip Hop
Aesthetic. New York/London: New York University Press, 2007.
Cook-Lynn, Elizabeth. Anti-Indianism in Modern America: A voice from
Tatekeya's Earth. Urbana/Chicago: University of Illinois Press, 2001.

Connell, John and Gibson, Chris. soundtracks; popular music, identity and
place. New York/London: Routledge, 2003.

Conyers, James L., Jr. <u>African American Jazz and Rap: Social and Philosophical Examinations of Black Expressive Behavior.</u> North Carolina/London: McFarland & Company, 2001.

Cornell, Stephen. <u>The Return of the Native: American Indian Political Resurgence.</u> New York/Oxford: Oxford University Press, 1990.

Costello, Mark and Wallace, David Foster. <u>Signifying Rappers: rap and race in the urban present.</u> New York: Ecco Press, 1990.

Da Vazquez, Sheryl Tucker. "African-American Art and Architecture."

Barton,Craig E. <u>Sites of Memory: Perspectives on Architecture and Race.</u> New York: Princeton Architectural Press: 2001.

Debo, Angie<u>. A History Of The Indians Of The United States</u>. Oaklahoma: University of Oklahoma Press, 1970.

Debo, Angie. <u>Geronimo: The Man, His Time, His Place.</u> Norman/London: University of Oklahoma, 1976/1986.

DeFrantz, Thomas F. "The Black Beat Made Visible: Hip Hop Dance and Body Power." <u>Of The Presence of the Body: Essays on Dance and Performance</u> Theory. Massachusetts: Wesleyan, 2004.

DeFrantz, Thomas F. <u>Dancing Revelations: Alvin Ailey's Embodiment of African American Culture.</u> New York/Oxford: Oxford University Press, 2006.

Deleuze, Gilles and Guattari, Felix. <u>A Thousand Plateaus; Capitalism and Schizophrenia.</u> Minneapolis/London: University of Minnesota Press, 1987.

Deloria, Philip J. <u>Indians in unexpected places.</u> Kansas: university of Kansas, 2004.

Deloria, Philip J. Playing Indian. Yale: Yale University Press, 1994.

Deloria, Vine, Jr. Custer Died For Your Sins – An Indian Manifesto. New
     York: The Macmillan Company, 1969.
     Deloria, Vine, Jr. We Talk, You Listen: New Tribes, New Turf. New
York: The
     Macmillan Company, 1970.
     Deloria, Vine Jr. God Is Red: A Native View of Religion. Colorado:
Fulcrum
     Publishing, 1994.
     Dyson, Michael Eric. *Performance, Protest, and Prophecy in the Culture
of
     Hip- Hop.* The Emergency Of Black And The Emergency Of Rap.
     Spencer, Jon Michael, ed. Black Sacred Music: A Journal of
     Theomusicology 5.1 (Spring 1991) Duke University Press: 12 – 24.
     Ellis, Clyde. A Dancing People, Powwow Culture on the Southern
Plains.
     Kansas: University of Kansas, 2003.
     Fine-Dare, Kathleen S. Grave Injustice: The American Indian
Repatriation

     Movement and NAGPRA. Lincoln and London: University of
     Nebraska Press, 2002.

Fire, John/Lame Deer and Richard Erdoes. "The Circle and the Square."

     Literature of the American Indians: Views and Interpretations.
     New York: Meridian Books, 1975. 77 – 86.

Fisher, Michael M. J. "Ethnicity and the Post-Modern Arts of Memory."
Writing

     Culture, The Poetics and Politics of Ethnography. Berkeley/Los
     Angeles/London: University of California Press,

1986: 194 – 233.

Fixico, Donald L. <u>Termination And Relocation: Federal Indian Policy, 1945 –</u>
<u>1960</u>. Albuquerque: University of New Mexico Press, 1986.

Fixico, Donald L. <u>The Urban Indian Experience in America</u>. Albuquerque:
University of New Mexico Press, 2000.

Fletcher, Alice C. "The Relation of Indian Story and Song." <u>Literature of</u>
<u>the</u>

American Indians: Views and Interpretations. New York:
Meridian Books, 1975: 235 - 239.

Forbes, Jack D. <u>Africans and Native Americans: Color, Race and Caste in</u>
<u>the Evolution of Red-Black Peoples.</u> New York: Blackwell, 1988.

Forbes, Jack D. <u>African and Native Americans; The Language of Race</u>

<u>and the Evolution of Red-Black Peoples.</u> Urbana/Chicago:
University of Illinois Press, 1993.

Gabbard, Krin, ed. <u>Jazz Among the Discourses</u>. Durham and London: Duke
University Press, 1995.

Gansworth, Eric, ed. <u>Sovereign Bones: New Native American Writing,</u>
<u>Vol. II.</u>
New York: Avalon Publishing Group, 2007.

Gates, Henry Louis. <u>The Signifying Monkey: A Theory of</u>
<u>African-American</u>
<u>Literary Criticism.</u> New York: Oxford University Press, 1989.

Garroutte, Eva Marie. <u>Real Indians, Identity and the Survival of Native</u>

<u>America.</u> Berkeley/Los Angeles/London: University of
California Press, 2003.

Geertz, Clifford. The Interpretations of Cultures. New York: Perseus Books
Group, 1973.
George, Nelson. The Death of Rhythm & Blues. New York: Penguin Books, 1988.
George, Nelson. Hip Hop America. New York: Penguin Books, 1998.
Giglio, Virginia. Southern Cheyenne Women's Songs. Norman and London:
University of Oklahoma Press, 1994.
Gilroy, Paul. The Black Atlantic, Modernity and Double Consciousness.
Cambridge: Harvard University Press, 1993/1994.
Gracyk, Theodore. Rhythm And Noise: An Aesthetic Of Rock.
Durham/London: Duke University Press, 1996.
Harvey, Graham and Thompson, Charles D. Jr., ed. Indigenous Diaporas and
Dislocations. England/Vermont: Ashgate Publishing Company, 2005.

Hebdige, Dick. Subculture; the Meaning of Style. London and New York:
Routledge, 1979, 1987.
Hertzberg, Hazel W. The Search For An American Indian Identity: Modern
Pan- Indian Movements. USA: Syracuse University Press, 1971.
Holm, Bill and Bill Reid. Form and Freedom: A Dialogue on Northwest Coast
Indian Art. Houston: Institute for the Arts, Rice University, 1975.
hooks, bell. Black Looks: race and representation. Boston: South End Press, 1992.
hooks, bell. "Gangsta Culture – Sexism, Misogyny: Who Will Take the Rap."

Outlaw Culture: Resisting Representations. New York/London: Routledge, 1994: 115 – 123.

Hoxie, Frederick E., Peter C. Mancall and James H. Merrell. American

Nations, Encounters in Indian Country, 1850 to the Present. New York/London: Routledge, 2001.

Igliori, Paola. Stickman – John Trudell – poems, lyrics, talks, a conversation. New York: Inanout Press, 1994.

Iverson, Peter. "We Are Still Here" American Indians in the Twentieth Century. Illinois: Harlan Davidson, Inc. 1998.

Jackson, Robert Louis. Dialogues with Dostoevsky; The Overwhelming Questions. Stanford: Stanford University Press, 1993.

Jones, Blackwolf and Jones, Gina. Listen To The Drum: Blackwolf Shares His Medicine. Minnesota: Hazelden, 1995.

Jones, LeRoi. Blues People, Negro Music in White America. New York: Harper

Colins, 1963, 1999.

Johnson, Troy R., ed. Alcatraz: Indian Land Forever. Los Angeles: American Indian Studies Center, 1994.

Johnson, Troy R., ed. You Are On Indian Land: Alcatraz Island, 1969 – 1971.

Los Angeles: American Indian Studies Center, 1994.

Johnson, Troy R. The occupation of Alcatraz Island: Indian self-

determination and the rise of Indian activism. Illinois: University of Illinois Press, 1996.

Johnson, Troy R. "American Indians, Manifest Destiny, and Indian

Activism." Place and Native American Indian History and Culture. Germany: Peter Lang, International Academic Publishers, 2007: 71 – 92.

Jolivétte, Andrew., ed. Cultural Representation in Native America. UK: Altamira Press, 2006.

Katz, William. Black Indians: A Hidden Heritage. New York: McMillian, 1986.

Kauanui, J. Kehaulani. Hawaiian Blood, Colonialism and the Politics of

Sovereignty and Indigeneity. Durham and London: Duke University Press, 2008.

Keyes, Cheryl L. Rap Music and Street Consciousness. Urbana/Chicago:
University of Illinois Press, 2002.
Kitwana, Bakari. The Hip Hop Generation; Young Blacks and the Crisis in
African-American Culture. New York: Basic Civitas Books, 2002.
Kitwana, Bakari. Why White Kids Love Hip Hop: Wankstas, Wiggers, Wannabes, and the New Reality of Race in America. New York: Basic Civitas Books, 2005.
Kroeber, Karl, ed. American Indian Persistence and Resurgence. Durham
and London: Duke University Press, 1994.
Krims, Adam. Rap music and the poetics of identity. UK: Cambridge University Press, 2000.
Lassiter, Luke E. The Power of Kiowa Song. Tucson: The University of Arizona
Press, 1998.
Lavine, Smadar and Swedengurg, Ted, ed. "Living With Miracles: The

Politics And Poetics Of Writing American Indian Resistance And Identity." Displacement, Diaspora, And Geographies Of Identity. USA/London: Duke University Press, 1996: 26 – 40.

Lawlor, Mary. Public Native America: Tribal Self-representations in

casinos, museums, and powwows. New Brunswick/New Jersey/London: Rutgers University Press, 2006.

Lechusza Aquallo, Alan. The Good, The Bad, The Born at 18 – A Deconstructive View of Native American Identity Through the Song "Born at 18". 2002.
Lippard, Lucy, R. Mixed Blessings: New Art in a Multicultural America. New York: Pantheon Books, 1990.

Lipsitz, George. Dangerous Crossroads; Popular Music, Postmodernism and
    the Poetics of Place. London/New York: Verso, 1994.
Lobo, Susan and Peters, Kurt, ed. American Indians And The Urban
    Experience. London/Oxford: Altamira Press, 2001.
Lobo, Susan and Talbot, Steve, ed. Native American Voices – A Reader.

    USA/England/Canada/Mexico/Australia/Spain/Denmark:
    Addison Wesley Longman, Inc., 1998.

Lornell, Kip and Stephernson, Charles C. Jr. The Beat: Go-Go's Fusion of

    Funk and Hip-Hop. New York: Billboard Books, 2001.
McAfee, Noelle. Julia Kristeva. New York: Routledge, 2004.
McGrath, James and Ballard, Louis. My Music Reaches To The Sky:

    Native American Musical Instruments. Santa Fe/New York: Ford
    Foundation (Center for the Arts of Indian America), 1973.

Mignolo, Walter D. Local Histories/Global Designs, Coloniality,
Subaltern

    Knowledges, and Border Thinking. Princeton: Princeton
    University Press, 2000.

Mihesuah, Devon A. American Indians: Stereotypes & Realities. USA:
    Clarity Press, 1996.
Mihesuah, Devon A. and Whitt, Laurie Anne, ed. "Cultural Imperialism
and the

    Marketing of Native America." Natives And Academics:
    Researching and Writing about American Indians. Nebraska:
    University of Nebraska Press, 1998. 139 – 172.

Mihesuah, Devon A., ed. Repatriation Reader: Who Owns American
Indian

Remains?. USA: University of Nebraska Press, 2000.

Mihesuah, Devon A. and Wilson, Angela Cavender, ed. Indigenizing the

Academy, Transforming Scholarship and Empowering Communities. Lincoln and London: University of Nebraska Press, 2004.

Miles, Tiya. "Uncle Tom Was an Indian, Tracing the Red in Black Slavery."

Confounding the Colorline, The Indian-Black Experience in North American. Lincoln and London: University of Nebraska Press, 2002:137 – 160.

Miller, Paul D. Rhythm Science. Massachusetts: Mediawork/MIT Press, 2004.

Minh-ha, Trinh-T. Woman, Native, Other. Bloomington: University of Indiana

Press, 1989.

Monson, Ingrid. Saying Something, Jazz improvisation and interaction. Chicago and London: University of Chicago Press, 1996.

Moore, MariJo, ed. Genocide of the Mind; New Native American Writing. New York: Thunder's Mouth Press/Nation Books, 2003.

Murray, Albert. Stomping the Blues. New York: Da Cap Press, 1876.

Nagel, Joane. American Indian Ethnic Renewal – Red Power And The

Resurgence Of Identity And Culture. New York/Oxford: Oxford University Press, 1996/1997.

Nagel, Joane. "American Indian Ethnic Renewal: Politics and the

Resurgence of Identity." American Nations: Encounters in Indian Country, 1850 to the Present. New York/London: Routledge, 2001: 330 – 353.

Neils, Elaine M. <u>Reservation to City, Indian Migration and Federal Relocation.</u>
Illinois: University of Chicago, 1971.
Ogg, Alex and Upshal, David. <u>The Hip Hop Years – A History of Rap</u>.
New York: Fromm International, 2001.
Paniccioli, Ernie. <u>Who Shot Ya?, Three Decades of Hip Hop Photography.</u>
New York: Harper Collins, 2002.
Paulitino, Elvira. <u>Toward a Native American Critical Theory</u>. Nebraska: University of Nebraska Press, 2003.
Perdue, Theda. <u>Mixed Blood Indians, Racial Construction in the Early South.</u> Athens and London: University of Georgia Press, 2003.
Perkins, William Eric, ed. <u>Droppin' Science: Critical Essays On Rap Music And Hip Hop Culture.</u> Philadelphia: Temple University Press, 1996.
Perry, Imani. <u>Prophets of the Hood: Politics and Poetics in Hip Hop.</u> Durham and London: Duke University Press, 2004.
Pinder, Kymberly N., ed. <u>Race-ing Art History; Critical Readings in Race and Art History.</u> New York/London: Routledge, 2002.
Ramsey, Jr. Guthrie P. <u>Race Music, Black Cultures from Bebop to Hip-Hop.</u> Berkeley: University of California Press:2003.
Rahn, Janice. <u>Painting Without Permission, Hip-Hop Graffiti Subculture.</u> Connecticut/London: Bergin & Garvey, 2002.
Rhea, Joseph Tilden. "American Indian." <u>Race Pride and the American Identity.</u> Massachusetts: Harvard University Press, 1997. 8-38.
Rivera, Raquel Z. <u>New York Ricans From the Hip Hop Zone.</u> New York: Palgrave Macmillan, 2003.
Rose, Tricia. <u>Black Noise: Rap Music and Black Culture in Contemporary American</u>. Hanover & London: Wesleyan University Press, 1994.

Rushing, W. Jackson, ed. Native American art in the Twentieth Century. New
York/London: Routledge, 1999.

Saavedra, Andrea Avaira. "Mobile Identity: The Mapuche of Santiago,

Chile." Harvey, Graham and Thompson, Charles D. Jr., ed. Indigenous Diaporas and Dislocations. England/Vermont: Ashgate Publishing Company, 2005. 53 – 62.

Schermerhorn, R.A. Comparative Ethnic Relations: A Framework for Theory and Research. New York: Random House, 1970.

Schloss, Joseph Glenn. Making Beats: The Art of Sample Based Hip Hop (Music and Culture). New York: Wesleyan Press, 2004.

Shapiro, Michael J. Methods and Nations: Cultural Governance and the Indigenous Subject. New York/London: Routledge, 2004.

Smith, Linda Tuhiwai. Decolonizing Methodologies; Resarch and Indigenous
Peoples. Dunedin: University of Otago Press, 1999.

Smitherman, Geneva. Talkin and Testifyin, The Language of Black America. Boston: Houghton Mifflin Company, 1977.

Smitherman, Geneva. Talkin That Talk, Language, Culture, and Education in
African America. London/New York: Routledge, 1999.

Snead, James A. "Repetition as a Figure of Black Culture." Robert G. O.Meally, ed. The jazz cadence of American culture. New York:

Columbia Univeristy Press, 1998.

Spencer, Jon Michael. Protest & Praise: Sacred Music of Black Religion. Minneapolis: Fortress Press, 1990.

Spencer, Jon Michael, ed. The Emergency Of Black And The Emergency

Of Rap. Spencer, Jon Michael, ed. Black Sacred Music: A Journal of Theomusicology. 5.1 (Spring 1991), Duke University Press.

Storey, John, ed. <u>Cultural Theory and Popular Culture; A Reader.</u> London/New
York: Prentice Hall, 1998.
Storey, John. <u>Inventing Popular Culture; From Folklore to Globalization.</u>
USA/UK: Blackwell Publishing, 2003.
Sarris, Greg, ed. <u>The Sound of Rattles and Clappers – A Collection of</u>

<u>New California Indian Writings</u>. Tuscon & London: The
University of Arizona Press, 1994.

Scholder, Fritz. <u>Scholder/Indians.</u> Arizona: Northland Press, 1972.
Scholder, Fritz. <u>Indian Kitsch, The Use and Misuse of Indian
Images.</u> Arizona: Northland Press/ The Heard Museum, 1979.
Sounds Of American Records (S.O.A.R.). <u>Product Catalogue</u>.
Albuquerque: New Mexico, 2002.
Stanyek, Jason. "Diasporic Improvisation and the Articulation of
Intercultural Music." Diss. University of California, San Diego, 2004.
Strickland, Reggard. "Beyond the Ethic Umbrella and the Blue Deer:
Some

Thoughts for Collectors of Native Paintings and Sculpture".
<u>Tonto's Revenge: Reflections on American Indian Culture and
Policy</u>. Albuquerque: University of New Mexico Press, 1997. 63 –
77.

Taiwo, Olu. "The Orishas: The Influence of the Yoruba Cultural
Diaspora."

Harvey, Graham and Thompson, Charles D. Jr., ed. <u>Indigenous
Diaporas and Dislocations. </u>England/Vermont: Ashgate
Publishing Company, 2005. 105 – 120.

Taylor, Yuval, ed. <u>The Future of Jazz.</u> Chicago: A Capella Books, 2002.
Teaiwa, Teresia K. "Native Thoughts: A Pacific Studies Take on Cultural

Studies and Diaspora". Harvey, Graham and Thompson, Charles D. Jr., ed <u>Indigenous Diasporas and Dislocations</u>. England/ Vermont: Ashgate Publishing Company, 2005. 15 - 36.

Vander, Judith. <u>Song-Prints: The Musical Experience Of Five Shoshone Women</u>. Urbana/Chicago: University of Illinois Press, 1996.
Vaughn, Alden T. <u>Roots of American Racism, Essays on the Colonial Experience</u>. New York/Oxford: Oxford University Press, 1995.
Vickers, Scott B. <u>Native American Identities; From Stereotype to

Archetype in Art and Literature.</u> Albuquerque: University of New Mexico Press, 1998.

Vizenor, Gerald. <u>Manifest Manners – Narratives on Postindian Survivance</u>.
Lincoln and London: University of Nebraska Press, 1999.
Walker, Thomas. <u>Fort Apache: New York's Most Violent Precinct</u>. New York:
Rooftop Publishing, 1976/2000.
Wade, Edwin, ed. <u>The Arts of the North American Indian: Native

Traditions in Evolution.</u> New York: Philbrook Art Center and Hudson Hill Press, 1986.

Warry, Wayne. <u>Ending Denial, Understanding Aboriginal Issues.</u> Toronto:
Broadview Press, 2007.
Weatherford, Jack. <u>Indian Givers: How The Indians of the Americas Transformed the World.</u> New York: Ballantine Books, 1988.
Wilson, James. <u>The Earth Shall Weep: A History of Native America.</u> New York:
Grove Press, 1998.

<u>ARTICLES</u>

Alvarez, Michelle. *WithOut Rezervation*. <u>News From Native California</u>. 7.4
Fall/Winter (1993/94): 12 – 13.

Aquila, Richard. "Images of the American West in Rock Music." <u>The Western</u>
<u>Historical Quarterly</u> 11.4 (October 1980): 415-432.

Ards, Angela. "Rhyme and Resist: Organizing the Hip-Hop Generation." <u>The</u>
<u>Nation</u> (July 26/August 2, 1999): 11+

Barker, Joanne. "Indian™ U.S. A." <u>Wicazo Sa Review</u> 18.1 (Spring 2003): 25 –
79.

Bartlett, Andrew. "Airshafts, Loudspeakers, and the Hip Hop Sample: Contexts

and African American Musical Aesthetics." <u>African American</u>
<u>Review</u> 28.4 (1994): 639 – 651.

Basu, Dipannita and Pnia Werbner. "Boostrap Capitalism and the Culture

Industries: A Critique of the Invidious Comparisons in the Study
of Ethnic Entrepreneurship." <u>Ethnic and Racial Studies</u> 24.2
(March 2001): 236 – 262.

Beck, David R. M. "Developing a Voice: The Evolution of Self-

Determination in an Urban Indian Community." <u>Wicazo Sa</u>
<u>Review</u> 17.2, Sovereignty and Governance, II (Autume 2002):
117 – 141.

Bell, Wendell and Robinson, Robert V. "European Melody, African

Rhythm, or West Indian Harmony? Changing Cultural Identity
among Leaders in a New State." <u>Social Forces</u> 58.1 (Sept 1979):
249 – 279.

Berlo, Janet Catherine. "Inuit Women and Graphic Arts: Female Creativity and

its Cultural Context." The Canadian Journal of Native Studies 10.2 (1989): 293 – 315.

Black, Jason Edward. "The 'Mascotting' of Native America: Construction,

Commodity, and Assimilation." American Indian Quarterly 26.4 (Autumn 2002): 605 – 622.

Breaker, Shane. "Voices Rising: Native Youth are remixing Hip Hop into an art form all their own." Horizon Zero Issue 08: remix April/May 2003.

Browner, Tara. "Breathing the Indian Spirit": Thoughts on Musical Borrowing

and the "Indianist" Movement in American Music." American Music 15.3 (Autumn 1997): 265 – 284.

Browner, Tara. "Making and Singing Pow-wow songs." Ethnomusicology 44.2 (Spring/Summer 2000): 214.

Cadman, Charles Wakefield. "The "Idealization" of Indian Music." The Musical Quarterly 1.3 (July 1915): 387 – 396.

Capriccioo, Rob. "Regalia traditions meet contemporary innovations." Indian Country Today: Powwow Mar. (2009): 24 – 26.

Charles, Jim. "Songs of the Ponca: 'Helushka.'" Wicazo Sa Review 5.2 (Autumn 1989): 2 – 16.

Chaumont, Kriss. "Rapper Litefoot blazes a cross-country trail with his Reach the Rez tour," The Seattle Times 1 Nov. 2005.

Claphma, John. "Dvorak and the American Indian." The Musical Times

107.1484 (Oct. 1966): 863 – 867.

Coulthard, Glen S. "Subjects of Empire: Indigenous Peoples and the Politics of

Recognition in Colonial Contexts." <u>Canadian Political Science Association</u> (2006): 1 – 22.

D., Davey. '"Missy Is A Bitch.' "<u>FNV Newsletter</u> 21 May 1999.

D., Davey. "'Is Hip Hop Black Culture?' "<u>FNV Newsletter</u> 20 November 1999.

Denson, Andrew. "Muskogee's Indian International Fairs: Tribal Autonomy

and the Indian Image in the Late Nineteenth Century." <u>The Western Historical Quarterly</u> 34.3 (Autumn 2003): 325 – 345.

Deyhle, Donna. "Break Dancing and Breaking out: Anglos, Utes, and Navajos

in a Border Reservation High School." <u>Anthropology & Education Quarterly</u> 17.2 (June 1986): 111 – 127.

de Shane, Nina. "Powwow Dancing and the Warrior Tradition."

<u>Studia Musicologica Academiae Scientiarum Hungaricae</u> 33.1/4 (1991): 375 – 399.

DesJarliat, Robert. "The Contest Powwow versus the Traditional Powwow and

the Role of the Native American Community." <u>Wicazo Sa Review</u> 12.1 (Spring 1997): 115 – 127.

Ellis, Clyde. "Truly Dancing Their Own Way: Modern Revival and Diffusion

of the Gourd Dance." <u>American Indian Quarterly</u> 14.1 (Winter 1990): 19 – 33.

Ellis, Clyde. We Don't Want Your Rations, We Want This Dance: The Changing Use of Song and Dance on the Southern Plains."
Western Historical Quarterly 30.2 (Summer 1999):133 – 154.

Ellis, Clyde. "There Is No Doubt...the Dances Should Be Curtailed: Indian

Dances and Federal Policy on the Southern Plains, 1880 – 1930." The Pacific Historical Review 70.4 (Nov 2001): 543 – 569.

Evelyn, Jamilah. "The Miseducation of Hip-Hop: Are Today's Faculty and

Administrators Simply Out of Touch? Or Has Today's Popular Music Truly Conquered the Minds of A Whole Generation?." Black Issues in Higher Education 17.21 (December 7, 2000): 24+

Fisher, Ian. "Pulling Out of Fort Apache, the Bronx; New 41st Precinct Station

House Leave Behind Symbol of Community's Past Troubles". New York Times, 23 June. 1993final ed.:B+

Fletcher, Alice C. "Indian Songs and Music." The Journal of American Folklore
11.41 (April – June 1898): 85 – 104.

Forbes, Jack D. "The Historian and the Indian: Racial Bias in American History." The Americas 19.4 (Apr 1963): 349 – 362.

Forbes, Jack D. "Mustees, Half-Breeds and Zambos in Anglo North America:

Aspects of Black-Indian Relations." American Indian Quarterly 7.1 (1983): 57- 83.

Forman, Murray. "Represent': Race, Space and Place in Rap Music." Popular
Music 19.1 (2000): 65 – 89.

Frisbie, Charlotte J. "Native American Collected: The Culture of an Art
World." <u>Visual Anthropology Review</u> 17.1 (2001): 86 – 90.

Funk, Brian. "'Jam for Justice' fundraiser celebrates community." <u>CU
Independent Press</u> 29 Sept. 2006.

Grauburn, Nelson H.H. "Nalunaikutanga: Signs and Symbols in
Canadian

Inuit Art and Culture." Department of Anthropology, University
of California, Berkeley. California, 1976.

Graburn, Nelson H.H. "Authentic Inuit Art: Creation and Exclusion in
the

Canadian North." <u>Journal of Material Culture</u> 9.2 (2004): 141-159.

Grossberg, Lawrence. "Putting the Pop back into Postmodernism."
Social

<u>Text, No. 21, Universal Abandon? The Politics of Postmodernism</u>
(1989): 167 – 190.

Hapiuk, William J., Jr. "Of Kitsch and Kachinas: A Critical Analysis of
the

'Indian Arts and Crafts Act of 1990'". <u>Stanford Law Review</u> 53.4
(April 2001): 1009 – 1075.

Harries, Karsten, "In Search of Home, Bauen un Wohnen/Building and
Dwelling. Martin Heidegger's Foundation of a Phenomenology of
Architecture." <u>Wolkenkuckucksheim</u> 3.2 (1998: 2000): 101 – 120.

Heller, Lisa. "Breakin down (stereotypes) with "tribalistic funk"".
<u>Arizona Daily</u>
<u>Wildcat</u> 7 Mar. 1996, 1:15.

Henderson, Errol A. "Black Nationalism and Rap Music." <u>Journal of
Black</u>
<u>Studies</u> 26.3 (January 1996): 308 – 339.

Howard, James H. "The Plains Gourd Dance as a Revitalization
Movement".

American Ethnologist 3. 2 (1976): 243-259.

Howard, James H. "Pan-Indianism in Native American Music and Dance."
Ethnomusicology 27.1 (Jan 1983):71 – 82.

Jackson, W. Rushing. "Critical Issues in Recent Native American Art." Art
Journal 51.3 (Autumn 1992): 6 – 14.

Johnson, Troy R. "Remembering Alcatraz: Twenty-five Years After."

American Indian Culture and Research Journal, UCLA American Indian Studies Center, 18. 4 (1994): 9 – 23.

Kappstatter, Bob. "They Return To Ft. Apache, Police veterans of '70s mayhem hold joyous reunion." New York Daily 20 May 2002, final ed.

Kelly, Lawrence C. "The Indian Reogranization Act: The Drama and the Reality". The Pacific Historical Review 44.3 (August 1975): 291 – 312.

Krouse, Susan Applegate. "Traditional Iroquois Socials: Maintaining

Identity in the City." American Indian Quarterly 25.3 (Summer 2001): 400 – 408.

Lee, Molly. "'How Will I Sew My Baskets?': Women Vendors, Market Art, and

Incipient Political Activism in Anchorage, Alaska." American Indian Quarterly 27.3/4 (Summer – Autumn 2003): 583 – 592.

Levine, Lawrence W. "Jazz and American Culture." The Journal of American
Folklore 102.403 (Jan – Mar 1989): 6 – 22.

Levine, Lindsay Victoria. "Women in Native American Indian Music." Ethnomusicology 38.1 (Winter 1994):175.

Lewis, Rich Davis. "Still Native: The Significance of Native Americans in

the History of the Twentieth-Century American West." The Western Historical Quarterly 24.2 (1993): 203-227.

Lipsitz, George. "Mardi Gras Indians: Carnival and Counter-Narrative in
Black New Orleans." <u>Cultural Critique</u>10 (Autumn 1988): 99-121.
Martinez, Theresa A. "Popular Culture as Oppositional Culture: Rap as
Resistance." <u>Sociological Perspectives</u> 40.2 (1997): 265 – 286.
Matos, Michaelangelo. "All Roads Lead to 'Apache.'" <u>Experience Music
Project</u>
2005. Seattle: Washington, 2005.
McAllester, David P. "New Perspectives in Native American Music."

<u>Perspectives of New Music</u> 20.1/2 (Autumn 1981 – Summer
1982): 433 – 446.

McLeod, Kembrew. "Authenticity Within Hip-Hop and Other Cultures
Threatened with Assimilation." <u>Journal of Communication</u> 49.4
(Autumn 1999): 134 – 149.
Murray, Derek Conrad. "Hip-Hop vs. High Art: Notes on Race as
Spectacle." <u>Art Journal</u> 63.2 (Summer 2004): 4 – 19.
Michael, Mike and Arthur Still. "A Resource for Resistance:
Power-Knowledge
and Affordance." <u>Theory and Society</u> 21.6 (1992): 869-888.
Nagel, Joane. "American Indian Ethnic Renewal: Politics and the

Resurgence of Identity," <u>American Sociological Review</u> 60.6
(1995): 974 – 965.

Nazareth, Errol. "They're on the Worpath." <u>Toronto Sun</u>, 11 Aug. 1995.
Nettl, Bruno. "Stylistic Variety in North American Indian Music."
<u>Journal of the</u>
<u>American Musicological Society</u> 6.2 (Summer 1953): 160 – 168.
Nettl, Bruno. "Polyphony in North American Indian Music." <u>The
Musical</u>
<u>Quarterly</u> 47.3 (July 1961): 354 – 362.
Paniccioli, Ernie. "Interview with Ernie Paniccioli" <u>@ 149st, New York
City</u>

Cyber Bench. 27 Oct. 2001. (http://www.at149st.com/ernie2.html)

Parley, Jon Keith. "Regulations of Counterfeit Indian Arts and Crafts: An

Analysis of the Indian Arts and Crafts Act of 1990." American Indian Law Review 18.2 (1993): 487 – 514.

Patterson, Michelle Wick. "'Real' Indian songs: The Society of American

Indians and the Use of Native American Culture as a Means of Reform." American Indian Quarterly 26.1 (Winter 2002): 44 – 66.

Price, John A. "The Stereotyping of North American Indians in Motion Pictures." Ethnohistory 20.2 (Spring 1973): 153-171.

Reed, T.V., "Old Cowboys, New Indians: Hollywood Frames the American

Indian." Wicazo Sa Review 16. 2 (Autumn 2001): 75-96.

Rickard, Jolene. "Native Networks – Atlatl biennial conference." Afterimage Jan/Feb. 1999.

Rock and Roll Hall of Fame. "Physical Grafitti, The History of Hip Hop Dance." 1999.

Scholder, Fritz. "On the Work of a Contemporary American Indian

Painter." Leonardo, 6.2 (Spring, 1973). Massachusetts: MIT Press:109 – 112.

Schulman, Ken. "Art/Architecture; The Buckskin Ceiling and its Discontents." New York Times 24 Dec. 2000.

Shiner, Larry. "'Primitive Fakes,' 'Tourist Art,' and the Ideology of Authenticity."

The Journal of Aesthetics and Art Criticism 52.2 (Spring 1994): 225 – 234.

Simpson, Jacqueline C. "Segregated by Subject: Racial Differences in the
Factors Influencing Academic Major between European
Americans, Asian Americans, and African, Hispanic, and Native
Americas." The Journal of Higher Education 72.1 (Jan – Feb
2001): 63 – 100.

Sisario, Ben. "Dancing to the hip-hop genre: Smithsonian lauds 'the
rhymes,
the life.'" Herald Tribune 2 Mar. 2006.
Skidmore, Mick. "Plundering the Vaults." Relix Magazine Jan/Feb.
1999:26.

Sluyter, Andrew. "Colonialism and Landscape in the Americas:
Material/Conceptual Transformations and Continuing
Consequences." Annals of the Association of American
Geographers 91.2 (Jun 2001): 410 – 428.

Smith, Michael P. "Behind the Lines: The Black Mardi Gras Indians and
the
New Orleans Second Line." Black Music Research Journal, 14.1
(Spring 1994): 43-73.
Strange, Carolyn and Tina Loo, "Holding the Rock: The "Indianization"
of
Alcatraz Island, 1969–1999." The Public Historian 23.1 (Winter 2001):
55–74.
Strauss, Niel. "THE POP LIFE; Native Genre Takes Pride Of Place at
The
Grammys." New York Times 21 Feb. 2001, late ed.:E1+.
TallBear, Kimberly. "DNA, Blood, and Racializing the Tribe." Wicazo Sa
Review 18.1 (Spring 2003): 81 – 107.
Turino, Thomas. "Are We Global Yet? Globalist Discourse, Cultural

Formations and the Study of Zimbabwean Popular Music." British Journal of Ethnomusicology 12.2 (2003): 51 – 79.

Turner, William C. Jr. "The Musicality of Black preaching: A

Phenomenology", The Journal of Black Sacred Music 2.1 (Spring 1988): 27 – 45.

VanSpanckeren, Kathryn. "The Mardi Gras Indian Song Cycle: A Heroic

Tradition." MELUS 16.4 (Winter, 1989 -1990):41-56.
Verán, Cristina. "Rap, Rage and REDvolution." The Village Voice 4 March

2004.
Walker, Susan. "Pow-wow drum true heartbeat of first nations." The Toronto Star 3 Aug. 1994, final ed.:D1+.
Walser, Robert. "Rhythm, Rhyme and Rhetoric in the Music of Public Enemy."
Ethnomusicology 39.2 (Spring-Summer 1995):193 – 217.

Warminsky, Joe. "Ramp It Up: Skateboard Culture in Native America."

Decider D.C. 15 June 2009 <http://dc.decider.com/articles/ ramp-it-up-skateboard-culture-in-native-america-at,29158/> reviewed 15 June 2009.

ya Salaam, Mtume. "The Aesthetics of Rap." African American Review. 29.2
(Summer 1995): 303 – 315.
Yellow Bird, Michael. "What We Want to Be Called: Indigenous Peoples'

Perspectives on Racial and Ethnic Identity Labels." American Indian Quarterly 23.2 (Spring 1999): 1 – 21.

Zizek, Slavoj. "Multiculturalism, or the Cultural Logic of Multinational Capitalism." <u>New Left Review</u> 225 (1997): 28 – 51.

<u>INTERVIEWS</u>

LaMarr, Chris. Telephone Interview. 4 Dec 2008 – 18 Jan, 15 Mar 2009.

LaMarr, Chris. "Question from Alan Lechusza." May 16 – June 5, 2009.

Lobo, Susan. Telephone Interview. 2 Feb. 2009.

Means, Russell. Personal Interview. 2 Aug 2003.

Nelson, Tracey Lee. Personal Interview. 14 Jun 2009.

Paniccioli, Ernie. "Questions from Alan Lechusza". Dec. 22 - 30, 2008, May 18

– June 8, 2009.

Sainz, Melanie. Personal Interview. 4 Dec. 2008.

Trudell, John. Personal Interview . 4 Dec. 2008, 5 Jun 2009.

<u>DISCOGRAPHY</u>

Allan, Davie and the Arrows. "Apache." <u>Apache '65.</u> Tower, 1965.

Goldie. <u>Inner City Life.</u> FFRR Records, 1994.

Goldie. "Inner City Life." Timeless. <u>FFRR Records</u>, 1995.

Ingmann, Jorgen. "Apache." <u>Jorgen Ingmann and His Guitar</u>, ATCO Records,

1961.

Flash, Grandmaster & Furious Five. <u>The Message.</u> Sugar Hill Records, 1982.

Future Sound of London. "We Have Explosives." <u>Astralwerks</u>, 1996.

Lordon, Jerry. <u>Apache</u>, Columbia, 1960.

Moby, "Machete". <u>Play.</u> Mute, 1999.

Nas. <u>Made You Look (Apache Remix).</u> No Identity, 2002.

Nas. "Made You Look." <u>One Mic</u>. Columbia, 2003.

Nas. "Made You Look." God's Son, Columbia, 2003.

Roots, The. "Thought @ Work." <u>Phrenology.</u> MCA Records, 2002.

Shadows, Cliff Richard and The. "Apache." <u>Apache.</u> Columbia, 1960.

Soul Sonic Force. "Renegades of Funk." <u>Planet Rock.</u> Tommy Boy Music,

1984.

Sugarhill Gang, The. "Apache." _The Sugarhill Gang._ Sugarhill Records, 1981.

Urban Renewal, _Urban Renewal,_ Guidance Records, April 2000.

Ventures, The. "Apache." _Apache_. Dolton/Capitol Records, 1962/63.

Viner, Michael's Incredible Bongo Band. "Apache." _Bongo Rock,_ MGM Records, 1973.

Weedon, Bert. _Apache_. JAR, 1960.

West Street Mob, "Break Dance (Electric Boogie)". _Let Your Mind Be Free._ Disques Vogue/SugarHill Records, 1973 (1983).

WithOut Rezervation, _Are You Ready For War?,_ Canyon Records, 1992/4.

WithOut Rezervation, _World WOR Two,_ WithOut Rez Productions, 1995/9.

WithOut Rezervation. "unreleased singles." WithOut Rez Productions, 2008/09.

X-Ecutioners. _Scratchology: Mixed By The X-Ecutioners._ Nalin & Kane: Andry Nalin, Harry Cane,1997/1998.

<u>WEBSITES</u>

530 Powwow Store. Home page. 17 April 2009

<http://cgi.ebay.com/SEMINOLE-PRINCESS-Native-American-Indian-powwow_tshirt_W0QQitemZ180336084941QQcmdZViewItemQQimsx

1520 Sedgwick. Home Page. 20 Dec 2008 <http://www.1520sedgwick.com/>.
American Indian Movement. Home Page. 2 Jan 2009 <http://www.aimovement.org/index.html>.
Annonymous One. "Are You Ready for W.O.R.?". <u>Youtube</u> 6 Jan. 2008 <http://www.youtube.com/watch?v=fD_jPTHKP-c>.
Bonaparte-Ashman, Collette, ed. Home Page. <u>The Other Side of Hip Hop, The Sixth Element.</u> 5 Dec 2008 <http://hiphopotherside.com/>.
Boucher, Tim. "Carnial Culture 03: The Little Drummer Boy." 17 Dec 2007

<http://www.timboucher.com/journal/2007/12/17/carnival-culture-03-little-drummer-boy/>.

Bryson, Michael. "Ferdinand De Saussure." 2 Feb 2009 <http://www.michaelbryson.net/academic/saussure.html>.
Bureau of Indian Affairs. Home Page. U.S. <u>Department of the Interior</u> 2 Jan 2009<http://www.doi.gov/bia/>.

Canyon Records, "Are You Ready For W.O.R.?" Home Page. Arizona:

U.S. 6 Jan 2008 <http://store.canyonrecords.com/index.php?app=ccp0&ns=prodshow&ref=CR-7035[1]>

Chinook Indian, "Native American Radio Stations and Programs." 5 June 2009

---

1. http://store.canyonrecords.com/index.php?app=ccp0&ns=prodshow&r%20%0def=CR-7035

<http://www.chinookindian.com/greene/chinook_radio.htm>.
Contreras, Felix. "American Indian Composers Go Classical." 1 Jan 2009

<http://www.npr.org/templates/story/
story.php?storyId=98884176&sc=emaf>.

D., Davey. "Hip Hop History 101." <u>Davey D. and eLine Productions</u>. 22 Oct.
2002 <http://www.daveyd.com/daveyhistorylinks2002.html>.
D., Davey. <u>Hip Hop Daily News</u>. eLine Productions. 22 Oct. 2002
<http://www.daveyd.com/>.
Discogs. "Renegades of Funk." 11 Nov 2008
<http://www.discogs.com/viewimages?release=361055>.
DJCDOG. "Renegades of Funk – Africa Bambaataa and the Soul Sonic
Force." <u>Youtube</u>. 16 Jan 2009
<http://www.youtube.com/watch?v=QDdc37P6r3I>.
Doyle, Robert. Home Page. <u>Canyon Records</u> 30 Mar 2002
<http://www.store.canyonrecords.com/>.
Drumhop. Home Page. 11 Nov 2008 <http://drumhop.net/
welcome.htm>.
Duke University News. "The Art of Hip Hop Sampling at Duke
University".

<u>Youtube</u>. 23 April 2007 <http://www.youtube.com/
watch?v=YLg5qwfhHnA>.

Eric (aka DEAL CIA) and SPAR ONE TFP. "History of Graff." <u>Davey
D and</u>
<u>eLine Productions.</u> (1998) 30 Oct. 2002
<http://www.daveyd.com/historyofgraf.html>.
Flavatv98. "The Coup Interview." <u>Youtube.</u> 16 Aug 2007
<http://www.youtube.com/
watch?v=tYUv3QSN3CU&feature=related>.
Flight 808. Home Page. 2 Jan 2009 <www.flight808.com[2]>.

"G-Funk, Gangsta Funk, Mobb Music." <u>Hip Hop Galaxy</u> 7 Feb. 2009
<http://www.hiphopgalaxy.com/g-funk-hip-hop-2090.html>.
GrandMaster Flash. Home Page. 11 Nov 2008
<http://www.grandmasterflash.com/>.
"GrandMaster Flash and the Furious Five." Rock and Roll Hall of Fame.
28 Oct 2007

<http://www.rockhall.com/inductee/grandmaster-flash-and-the-furious-five>.

Head   Quarterz.   Home   Page.   17   Apirl   2009
<http://www.hdqtrz.com/>.
Hernandez, Jesse. Home Page. <u>Immortal Studios</u> 26 Mar 2009
<http://immortalstudios.net>.
Hip Hop Elements. Home Page. 8 Feb. 2009
<http://www.hiphop-elements.com/>.
Hip Hop Network. Home Page. 26 Jan 2004
<http://www.hiphop-network.com>.
Hip Hop Pow. "Hip Hop Powwow" 1July 2008
<http://www.hiphoppow.com/hip-hop-pow-wow.html>.
Hoenisch, Steve. "Saussure's Sign." <u>Criticism</u> 18 Nov 2005
<http://www.criticism.com/md/the_sign.html>.
Inge, Jonathan. "DJ Element." <u>Discreet Alpha</u> 2 Feb 2001
<http://discreetalpha.com/video/djelement.mov>.
International Movie Database. <u>Apache (1954).</u> 14 Jan. 2009
<http://www.imdb.com/title/tt0046719/mediaindex>.
Kellen. "Hip Hop Powwow remix" <u>MySpace Video</u> 4 Nov 2007

<http://vids.myspace.com/
index.cfm?fuseaction=vids.individual&VideoID=21406800>.

Kumeyaay Museums. "Native Indian Gourd Rattles." 20 Feb 2009
<http://www.kumeyaay.info/music/gourdrattles.html>.

Kumeyaay News. "Pala selected for Exhibit on Skateboarding." reviewed 14

June 2009 <http://www.kumeyaay.com/2009/06/pala-selected-for-smithsonian-exhibit-on-native-skateboarding/>.

LaMarr, Chirs. Home page. Home page. 17 April 2009 <http://www.myspace.com/chrislamarr[3]>.
LawziOfItaly. "American Indian Hip Hop." Native Threads 23 Jan 2009 <http://www.nativethreads.com/nativepride/videos-music-hiphop.php>.
Mawer, Sharon. "U.S. Pop Charts: 1961." Official Charts Company 2 Jan.
2009 <http://theofficialcharts.com/album_chart_history_1961.php>.
Miles, Douglas. Home Page. Apache Skateboards 10 Oct 2008 <http://www.apacheskateboards.com/poplife2.php>.
Mitten, Lisa. "Native Music and Arts Organizations." American Indian Library
Association 13 Feb 2009 <www.nativeculturelinks.com/music.html[4]>.
Native Threads. Home Page. 24 Nov 2007 <http://www.nativethreads.com>.
Native American Tube. Home Page. 15 Dec 2008 <http://natube.magnify.net/>.
Nelson, Tracey. Home Page. Fullblood Skates 10 Oct 2008 <http://www.fullbloodskates.com/>.
O.W. "Apache." Soul Sides. 19 April 2005 <http://soul-sides.com/2005/04/all-roads-lead-to-apache.html>.
Powwows. Home Page. 15 Mar 2005 <http://powwows.com/>.
Powwows. "Gourd Dancing." 20 Nov 2006 <http://www.powwows.com/info/?p=3>.
Professor Griff. Home Page. 17 Mar 2009 <http://www.myspace.com/professorgriffofpublicenemy>.

3.　　　http://www.myspace.com/chrislamarr

4.　　　http://www.nativeculturelinks.com/music.html

Public Enemy. Home Page. 16 Mar 2009 <http://publicenemy.com/>.

Redford, Robert. "Incident at Oglala" AOL Video 19 Dec 2008 <http://video.aol.com/video-detail/incident-at-oglala1/ 3673592610>.

Rez Hogs. Home Page. Rez Hogs Records 20 Jan 2009 <http://www.rezhogs.com/>.

Rez Hogs. "Drinkin' Song by Rez Hogs." RezNet 10 Nov 2008

   <http://www.reznetnews.org/multimedia/video/drinkin-song-rezhogs-24480>.

Rock Steady Crew. Home Page. 20 Dec. 2008 <http://www.rocksteadycrew.com/>.

Rwcook. "Tribes." Youtube 30 Mar 2007 <http://www.youtube.com/watch?v=m44_J_Xb4Pc>.

Shadows, The. "Apache (1960)". Youtube 12 Oct. 2007 <http://www.youtube.com/ watch?v=pY-rPDwzM9M&feature=related>.

Shadows, The. "Apache (1964)". Youtube 16 Nov. 2007 <http://www.youtube.com/ watch?v=SLocafpLMi0&feature=related>.

Shadows, The "Apache (1968)". Youtube 24 July 2006 <http://www.youtube.com/ watch?v=1CavdM4lSZU&feature=related>.

Soul Sides. Home Page. 17 April 2009 <http://www.soul-sides.com>.

Shadows, The. Home Page. 5 Dec. 2008 <http://www.btinternet.com/~shadows_archive/shadows/ Default.htm>.

Shadi415. "Native Hip Hop Gathering." Youtube 1 Nov 2008 <http://www.youtube.com/watch?v=t8lFgyu7Mls>.

Simpson, Junior. Native Hip Hop. 12 Aug 2002 <www.nativehiphop.net[5]>.

Sound of American Radio. Home Page. 30 Mar 2002

5.   http://www.nativehiphop.net

<http://www.soundofamerica.com/radio.cfm>.

Snag Magazine. "Beats and Brushstrokes." <u>Weapons of Mass Expression</u> 20 Dec 2007 <http://www.flickr.com/photos/weekendwakeup/page8>.

Snag Magazine. Home Page. 20 Dec 2007 <www.snagmagazine.com[6]>.

Snag Magazine. Home Page. <u>MySpace</u> 20 Dec 2007 <www.myspace.com/snagmagazine[7]>.

Thompson, Gordon. "British Rock and Pop Singles Chart: 1960."

<u>Skidmore College</u> 2 Jan 2009 <http://www.skidmore.edu/~gthompso/britrock/60brchro/60brch60.html#JUN>.

Tribal Gear. Home Page. 24 Nov 2007 <http://www.tribalgear.com/>.

U.S. Department of the Interior. Home Page. 2 Jan 2009 <http://www.doi.gov/>

Vigil, Blue Eagle. "Contents Under Pressure." <u>American Indian Music</u> 19 June 2005 <http://www.tradebit.com/filedetail.php/1540577-the-a-i-m-american-indian-music>.

WithOut Rezervation. Band page.13 April 2009 <http://www.myspace.com/withoutrezervation>.

---

[1] Dead Prez. <u>Let's Get Free.</u> Loud Records, Jan. 14, 2000.

[2] B., Julian. <u>Once Upon A Genocide</u>. New Mexico: SOAR, 1994.

[3] Kautsky, Karl qtd. in Smith, Andrea. <u>Native Americans and the Christian Right, The Gendered Politics of Unlikely Alliances.</u> Durham and London: Duke University Press, 2008 (xvii- xviii).

[4] Andrea Smith discusses the instability of identity in her work building upon Stuart Hall and Foucault as she defines "generative narratology" (xvi – xxviii).

6.   http://www.snagmagazine.com

7.   http://www.myspace.com/snagmagazine

[5] <http://www.daveyd.com/pactributb.html>. Reviewed 20 Nov 2008.

[6] Verán, Cristina. "Rap, Rage and REDvolution." The Village Voice 4 Mar 2004.

[7] ibid. An analysis of Litefoot alongside WOR will be presented in Chapter 1.

[8] Africa Bambaataa offers a "Hiphopography Chronological Listing" in James L. Conyers, Jr. African American Jazz and Rap: Social and Philosophical Examinations of Black Expressive Behavior (182).

[9] S. Craig Watkins does a very nice job of outlining the arrival of aesthetics and journalism in Hip Hop Matters: Politics, Pop Culture and the Struggle for the Soul of a Movement (2005).

[10] It is in this way that Hip Hop functions as a "generative narratology" as defined by Andrea Smith in Native American and the Christian Right, The Gendered Politics of Unlikely Alliances (xxvi).

[11] Robert Warrior in Andrea Smith's Native American and the Christian Right, The Gendered Politics of Unlikely Alliances discusses "intellectual sovereignty" (xxiii – xxiv).

[12] Another insightful review of Native terminology can be found in Michael Yellow Bird, "What We Want to Be Called: Indigenous Peoples' Perspectives on Racial and Ethnic Identity Labels." American Indian Quarterly, 23.2 (Spring 1999), 1 – 21.

[13] Gerald Vizernor viii – xvii; Nagel xi – xii. Vizenor goes one step further noting the use of indian as a constructed simulation of identity which is still under colonialist control. Given this, for Vizenor, there is no post-colonialism for Native people.

[14] Italics in the original.

[15] Chapter 3 of this dissertation develops the terms "Tribal", "Inter-Tribal" and "Multi-Tribal".

[16] The philosophy of signifyin' will be utilized more in Chapter 4 of this dissertation.

[17] WithOut Rezervation, Are You Ready For War?, Canyon Records, 1992/4.

[18] Qtd. in McMaster, Gerald and Clifford E. Trafzer (ed). Native Universe: Voices of Indian America. Washington D.C.: NMAI, Smithsonian, 2004.

[19] In 1789 The U.S. Congress placed the Indian Affairs Office in the Department of War. In 1832 Congress formed a Commissioner of Indian Affairs position. The Office of Indian Affairs was formed on March 11, 1824 and remained in the War Department until

transferred into the Department of the Interior in 1849. The Office was renamed in 1947 The Bureau of Indian Affairs. http://www.doi.gov/ reviewed 26 Jan. 2009

[20] In his chapter on P.L.-280, Donald Fixico goes into depth of how this law affected the eventual termination of the Klamath and Menominee, thereby articulating the actual intent of this, and similar, legislation. The Klamath have since then reacquired their tribal status in 1986 and the Menominee in 1973.

[21] The terms Tribal, Inter-Tribal and Multi-Tribal will be discussed in greater detail in Ch. 3 of this dissertation.

[22] Dr. Troy Johnson is the leading scholar on the Occupation of Alcatraz Island. His work thoroughly documents the history and developments of this important point in Native history.

[23] The terms Tribal, Inter-Tribal and Multi-Tribal will be discussed in further detail in chapter 3 of this Dissertation.

[24] Samples of John Trudell are heard on "Dead Indians", "Born at 18", "Defend the Territory", "Red, White, and Blue". Samples of Nilak Butler are heard on "Are you ready for WOR?". Russell Means is noted by Chris LaMarr as giving "props" for this recording. (phone interview with LaMarr 3 Feb. 2009) WithOut Rezervation, <u>Are You Ready For War?,</u> Canyon Records, 1992/4.

[25] http://www.daveyd.com/historyofgraf.html reviewed 15 Feb 2009.

[26] As these artists have worked to protect their real names I have respected this history by noting them by their artist "tag" name. The exception is Taki 183, who was identified in a New York Times article in 1971 and allowed his first name to be released, and Bom5 who worked with Africa Bambaataa.

[27] It was out of this inspirational time that Ernie Paniciolli became involved with photographing these graffiti art works and documenting the evolution of Hip Hop.

[28] Berlo 309.

[29] These three concepts, Tribal, Inter-Tribal and Multi-Tribal will be discussed in much more detail in Chapter 3 of this dissertation.

[30] Graburn, Nelson H.H. "Authentic Inuit Art: Creation and Exclusion in the Canadian North." <u>Journal of Material Culture</u> 9.2, 2004: 141-159.

[31] Corey Aranaydo is featured on the recording *Are You Ready For W.O.R.?* (1994). Mike Marin is brought back into the group following this recording and Corey Aranaydo no longer performs with the WOR

[32] http://www.nativeamericanmusicawards.com/?mpf=frame& reviewed 13 Feb. 2009.

[33] Seattle Times. Tuesday, 1Nov 2005.

[34] Chris LaMarr did not confirm this point specifically, but the influences to which he speaks certainly outlines the characteristics of Mobb Music. Taking note that Chris LaMarr is very aware of his sonic surroundings and the developments within Hip Hop, he certainly would have been inspired by Mobb Music as a style even if it were indirectly. This may indeed be the case given the timeline for the arrival of Mobb Music, the stylistic characteristics and how these are viewed within WOR and the historical development of their music.

[35] Litefoot. "My Chick." Relentless Pursuit Red Vinyl Records, 2008. http://www.youtube.com/watch?v=P8bLwSZsT-U reviewed 4 April 2009.

[36] Biegenho discusses this point in a similar manner related to Bolivian indigenous music in "Sounding Indigenous: Authenticity I Bolivian Music Performance." 20 – 23.

[37] The use of the lower case "i" and use of Indian in italics is consistent with Vizenor's use.

[38] These identity formations will be discussed in greater detail in Chapter 3 and 4 of this work where they are applied in more detail specifically to WOR.

[39] These three forms of Native identity will be discussed in more detail in Chapter 3 of this work.

[40] Parley, Jon Keith. "Regulations of Counterfeit Indian Arts and Crafts: An Analysis of the Indian Arts and Crafts Act of 1990." American Indian Law Review. 18.2 (1993): 487 – 514.

[41] This legislation proved to define once and for all what and who is a "Indian" artist. The controversy over this law maintains that the understanding of a Native artist must be defined by an outside factor, in this case the US government. The law attempts to read as sympathetic toward Native artists, but the law does not take into consideration the

multiple means by which Native people, and Native artist, are recognized by Indian tribes, bands, and nations. Examples of the legal racism applied through this law are the cases of Jimmy Durham, Bert Seabourn, and Jeanne Walker Rorex all discussed in. Hapiuk, William J. Jr. "Of Kitsch and Kachinas: A Critical Analysis of the 'Indian Arts and Crafts Act of 1990'. <u>Stanford Law Review</u>, 53.4 (April 2001): 1009 – 1075. Some Native artists who have been outspoken about this legislation are Edgar Heap of Birds (see in Berlo) and Jaune Quick-to-See (see in Hapiuk).

[42] Chris LaMarr phone interview December 14, 2008.

[43] WithOut Rezervation, <u>Are You Ready For War?,</u> Canyon Records, 1992/4.

[44] As of today, April/May 2009, the third release by WOR exists in rough tracks that does no have a confirmed scheduled date for edit, mixing or release.

[45] Throughout this listing the spelling and capitalizations will be consistent with WOR's usage on the recording AYRFW.

[46] Chris and Heather LaMarr were also involved with hosting the Lassen College Powwow on the Susanville Indian Rancheria in November 2007 while LaMarr was the Director of American Indian Studies at this College.

[47] Qtd. in Howard, James H. "The Plains Gourd Dance as a Revitalization Movement". <u>American Ethnologist</u>, 3.2 (1976): 243-259.

[48] Capitalization is used here referencing the proper formation of each Element as it is in current use (2009). Raquel Cepeda's <u>And It Don't Stop, The Best American Hip-Hop Journalism of the Last 25 Years</u> discusses this development through research and interviews.

[49] <u><http://www.sil.si.edu/SILpublications/AfricanAmericanIndiansBibliography.pdf</u>>. Reviewed 9 Feb 2009.

[50] Angela Cavender Wilson's article "Reclaiming Our Humanity, Decolonization and the Recovery of Indigenous Knowledge" (69 – 87) defines these oppositional areas as "Indigenous Knowledge" (mental) and the network of "Indigenous nations" (physical landscape).

[51] Miles notes the politics of slavery/Freemen (women), kinship systems and intermarriage between African/African-American and Native people as sites of identity struggle in the southern U.S. states between the 1600 – 1800s.

[6] These characteristics read very close to the three Black Semantic foundations defined by Geneva Smitherman: (1) words derive or have a direct African origin; (2) words entertain a loan-transformation; (3) words result in an inflated vocabulary. Smitherman, Geneva. Talkin and Testifyin, The Language of Black America. Boston: Houghton Mifflin Company, 1977 (43). The application of Smitherman's work will be viewed more in Chapter 4.

[53] Carocci notes reference to the urban center and inner city, i.e. the "ghetto," by urban Natives as the "urban reservations" or "urban rez" (Carocci 263 – 282).

[54] Lornell and Stephenson viii – ix.

[55] Kevin Bruyneel defines that *"postcolonial* refers to the consistencies, contingencies, and fissures in the practices of colonization and decolonization" (xviii). He clarifies that the structures of colonization (economic, cultural, political) are always in place. The "gaps" offer "meaningful expressions of [indigenous] postcolonial resistance" (xviii).

[56] A complete listing with locations that these characteristics are addressed and reads: Characteristics 1 and 2: Introduction (9 – 11) - regarding terminology versus biology and location. Characteristic 3: Chapter 1 (45 – 49). Characteristic 4: Chapter 1 (23, 35 – 53), Chapter 2 (59 – 60, 85, 89 – 90, 99 – 100, 111 – 112), Chapter 3 (142, 147 – 153), Chapter 4 (183 – 185, 201 – 205). Characteristic 5: visible within the overwhelming dominant male representation in Hip Hop (Africa Bambaataa, Cowboy, Pow Wow, et al) and the Native Hip Hop artists discussed herein (Litefoot, WOR). Characteristic 6 and 7: Chapter 4 (200 – 206). Characteristic 8: Chapter 1 (50 – 52), Chapter 3 (109 – 112, 145 – 153) and Chapter 4 (183 – 184, 201 – 206). Characteristic 9: Chapter 4 (166 – 171). Characteristic 10 coincides with characteristic 8: Chapter 1 (50 – 53).

1. Each of these identity formations will be discussed in more depth in Chapter 3.
2. Capitalization in the original.

[57] Hudson's analysis and research of Native rhythm builds upon the ethnomusicological research of Frances Densmore who, in 1943, argued for the origin of call-and-response singing being among the southeastern Native people. "Choctaw Music," in Bureau of American Ethnology, Anthropological Paper 28.136, 1943.

[58] Virginia Giglio's <u>Southern Cheyenne Women's Songs</u> (1994) produces a similar outline. The transformation of traditional songs through religious music "naturally" includes powwow music and contemporary popular music forms such as "marches, rock, disco, latin, country, tango, blues, swing and waltz[es]" (163 - 206).

[59] As noted in the Introduction, this work will focus upon the area within the current established and recognized borders of the United States. Future work of this nature will investigate Native Hip Hop in Canada and other Native indigenous cultures.

[60] Bruyneel, Kevin. <u>The Third Space of Sovereignty, The Postcolonial Politics of U.S.Indigenous Relations.</u> Minneapolis/London: University of Minnesota Press, 2007. The application of Bruyneel's third space of sovereignty will be seen in Chapter 3 of this dissertation.

[61] "Tribal," "Inter-Tribal," and "Multi-Tribal" identities will be discussed in greater detail in Chapter 3.

1. This is specifically with regards to singers and the Drum. This reading is not intended to be gender bias, but rather a transcription of the list provided by Lornell and Stephenson. There are mixed gender and all women drum groups (i.e., Mankiller) now prominent within the contemporary Powwow circuit. For more discussion see Vander, Judith. <u>Song-Prints: The Musical Experience Of Five Shoshone Women</u>. Urbana/Chicago: University of Illinois Press, 1996. and Browner, Tara. <u>Heartbeat of the People – Music and Dance of the Northern Pow-wow</u>. Urbana and Chicago: University of Illinois Press, 2002.

2. The "call and response" has been recognized in socio-linguistic analyses conducted by Smitherman. Smitherman, Geneva. <u>Talkin and Testifyin, The Language of Black America.</u> Boston: Houghton Mifflin Company, 1977. Smitherman's technique will be applied to text in Chapter 4 of this dissertation.

20 More information about Powwow styles can be found in Vander (1996), Lassiter (1998), Browner (2002), Ellis (2003), and Lawlor (2006). A very good discussion of the Gourd and
Rattle tradition of Southern California can be found at <<u>http://www.kumeyaay.info/music/gourdrattles.html</u>>. Reviewed 20 Feb 2009.

[62] The Six Elements of Hip Hop are, in no order: DJ, MC/Rap, breakdancing, graffiti, journalism/media and aesthetics. Each of these Elements are discussed through interviews and articles in, Cepeda, Raquel. <u>And It Don't Stop! The Best American Hip-Hop Journalism of the Last 25 Years.</u> New York: Faber and Faber, Inc., 2004.

[63] Alfred builds his theories upon a strong postcolonial rhetoric that he defines as "the fundamental denial of our freedom to be Indigenous in a meaningful way, and the unjust occupation of the physical, social, and political spaces we need in order to survive as Indigenous peoples" (Alfred 89). Alfred counters the ongoing colonial process through Indigenous intellectualism that he notes in the actions of teaching, doing research and living our lives as Warriors of Truth and/or the Warrior Scholar (Alfred 95 – 96).

25 Bhabha 31 – 39. Chapter 3 discusses the application of Bhabha's "Third Space" in more detail as it relates to the development of Native identity.

[64] There are several Hip Hop artists (Rap, DJ, Break Dance, Graffiti, Aesthetics, Journalism/Writing) who could have been selected for this analysis. For the interest of this work, it was important to focus the range of examples, therefore I have selected these four individuals for their important contributions to the Hip Hop culture both historically and contemporaneously.

[65] The spelling here is consistent with how Robert Darrell Allen uses this stage name.

[66] Soul Sonic Force. <u>Planet Rock</u> Tommy Boy Music, 1984.

[67] <<u>http://www.youtube.com/watch?v=QDdc37P6r3I</u>>. Reviewed 5 Feb 2009.

[68] Sisario, Ben. *"Dancing to the hip-hop genre: Smithsonian lauds 'the rhymes, the life'"* <u>Herald Tribune</u> Thursday 2 March, 2006.

[69] As noted in Chapter 1, Africa Bambaataa is the founder of the Zulu Nation. This leads often to the synonymous exchange of these names.

[70] Barker, Joanne. "Indian™U.S.A." <u>Wicazo Sa Review</u> 18.1 (Spring 2003): 25 – 79.

[71] <<u>http://www.hdqtrz.com/</u>>. Reviewed 5 Feb 2009.

[72] Following the logic of Native identity outlined in Chapter 3, Professor Griff's Native heritage could be understood as a Multi-Tribal identity (African, African American and Blackfoot).

[73] Citations in this section will all come from Welburn, Ron. "A Most Secret Identity: Native America Assimilation and Identity Resistance in African America." (292 – 320) in Brooks,

James F. (ed) <u>Confounding the Color Line, The Indian-Black Experience in North America.</u> Lincoln/London: University of Nebraska Press, 2002. Page numbers will be used for reference.

[74] The socio-literary scholar Geneva Smitherman also discusses each of these cultural aspects in her books <u>Talkin' and Testifyin', The Language of Black America</u>, Boston:

Houghton Mifflin Co, 1977 and <u>Talkin' that Talk,</u> New York/London: Routledge, 1999.

[75] Paniccioli, Ernie. <u>Who Shot Ya?, Three Decades of Hip Hop Photography.</u> New York: Harper Collins, 2002.

[76] In an email interview Paniccioli stated that he references Hip Hop as an "art form" rather than a "culture." Paniccioli also stated that he does not believe in a "singular hip hop history." This references the ongoing evolution that Paniccioli acknowledges of this genre. Email correspondence, 5 June 2009.

[77] In her article "Reclaiming Our Humanity," Wilson substitutes the unspecific term "ways" for "knowledge" which captures the characteristics that are stated here (Wilson 73 – 77).

[78] emphasis in the original.

[79] Cochise was from the Apache nation, not Cree. Paniccioli involves this Native icon as a method of articulating the level of stereotyping and racist mentality to which he was subjected early in his life. The ironic coincidence here, as will be discussed later in this Chapter, is that "Apache" was the title of the work by a non-Native composer that becomes the "National Anthem of Hip Hop" (Africa Bambaataa and Kook Herc).

[80] The second colonization point, in advance, to what Paniccioli will later recognize as a "new enemy" for Native people in <u>Sovereign Bones</u> (2007). Though the names may have changed, the principle remains the same; over-commodification and (mis)representation of Native people within the global mass media.

[81] My emphasis added.

[82] Paniccioli, Ernie. "Interview with Ernie Paniccioli" <u>@ 149st, New York City</u>

Cyber Bench. 27 Oct. 2001 <http://www.at149st.com/ernie2.html>. Reviewed 2 Aug 2003.

[83] My emphasis added.

[84] Bruyneel, Kevin. The Third Space of Sovereignty, The Postcolonial Politics of U.S.Indigenous Relations. Minneapolis/London: University of Minnesota Press, 2007.

[85] Deloria, Philip J. Playing Indian. Yale: Yale University Press, 1994. See also Dunn, Carolyn. "Playing Indian." Jolivétte, Andrew (ed). Cultural Representation in Native America. New York/Toronto/UK: Altamira Press, 2006 (139 – 158).

[86] The artistic areas that Lewis describes for mass media consumption at the dawn of the 20th century are the same for Hip Hop near the close of the 20th century.

[87] GrandMaster Flash <http://www.hiphop-network.com>. Reviewed 6 Feb 2009.

[88] The reversal of placement of these identity markers is specific at this point. From the start of this chapter the focus originated from an Africa-American position with the active integration, involvement, and recognition of Native identity. At this point in the chapter the perspective switches to be from a Native perspective onto an African-American viewpoint as realized through the intercultural connections within Hip Hop. This reading will remain in effect for the remainder of the chapter.

[89] Jerry Lordan, "Apache", Francis Day, and Hunter Ltd./Regent Music Corp., 1960.

[90] Though Bert Weedon recorded his version early in 1960, his tracks were left unreleased until later that same year.

[91] <http://www.skidmore.edu/~gthompso/britrock/60brchro/60brch60.html#JUN>. Reviewed 5 Mar 2007.

[92] <http://www3.sympatico.ca/craig.smith/chum61.htm>. Reviewed 5 Mar 2007.

[93] The (mis)representation brings into the discussion the dual perspective of a representation and the mis-representation. In doing so, the intended and inferred meaning of the example both have an equal location and means of entering the discussion.

[94] See Chapter 1.

[95] Future research will need to be conducted in deconstructing these names and their relation to the development of gang culture for this time. Now it is only suspect that these may be inter-related to the incarceration of Native men/women.

[96] David Lewis qtd. in Clyde Ellis. "We Don't Want Your Rations, We Want This Dance": The Changing Use of Song and Dance on the Southern Plains." The Western Historical Quarterly. 30.2 (Summer 1999):133-154.

[97] WOR, "Skin I'm In." Are You Ready For W.O.R.? Arizona: Canyon Records, 1994.

[98] Qtd. in Gilroy, Wright, The Outsider 129.

[99] As stated in the first chapter, terminology will be consistent with how it is used, defined, and presented by the given scholar whose work is being analyzed. All other accounts will involve 'Native' as the accepted archetypal term.

[100] My emphasis added to this term.

[101] My emphasis added to this term.

[102] The use of lowercase capitalization and italics is consistent for Vizenor.

[103] Joan Nagel offers an insightful tracing and historical realization of the development of the Red Power Movement and how this influenced urban Native identity and culture.

[104] hooks 417 – 424.

[105] Cornell, Stephen. The Return of the Native. New York/Oxford: Oxford University Press, 1990.

[106] My emphasis added here. Cornell uses Indian-White relations to describe the contact between Native and non-Native communities.

[107] Nagel offers important work on ethnic renewal and the emergence of a "new" Native in Nagel, Joan. American Indian Ethnic Renewal – Red Power And The Resurgence Of Identity And Culture. New York/Oxford: Oxford University Press, 1996/1997.

[108] My emphasis added here.

[109] References throughout this section are made to Figure 3.1 offered by Cornell.

[110] Stephen Cornell, The Return of the Native and used extensively by Joan Nagel American Indian Ethnic Renewal.

[111] Pan- defined by Webster's Dictionary (2008) offers three definitions each outlining the general and singular perspective use of this term.

pan- (pan):

1. of, comprising, embracing, or common to all or every *Pan-American*

2. the cooperation, unity, or union of all members of (a specified nationality, race, church, etc.) *Pan-Americanism*

3. Med. whole, general; of all or many parts *panarteritis*.

[112] Other statements are offered by Nagel 234 – 248, Russell Means qtd. in Nagel 244, Fixico a. <u>Termination and Relocation, Federal Indian Policy, 1945 – 1960</u>, Lobo and Peters, <u>American Indians and the Urban Experience.</u>

[113] Susan Lobo phone interview 1 Feb 2009.

[114] Nagel. <u>American Indian Ethnic Renewal: Politics and Resurgence of Identity</u> 338 – 348.

[115] Vizenor, Gerald. <u>Manifest Manners – Narratives on Postindian Survivance.</u> Lincoln and London: University of Nebraska Press, 1999. This work by Vizenor is also discussed in Chapter 2 of this dissertation. Another application of Vizenor's work will be presented later in this chapter.

[116] Paulitino 122 – 123, 126 – 128.

[117] Bhabha, Homi. <u>The Location of Culture.</u> London/New York: Routledge, 1994.

[118] Bhabha qtd. in Rutherford 211.

[119] Jameson, Fredric. <u>Postmodernism Or, The Cultural Logic of Late Capitalism.</u> Durham: Duke University Press, 1991.

[120] Jameson qtd. in Bhabha 218.

[121] Nagel b. 336 – 338.

[122] Nagel b. 330 – 335.

[123] Paulitano offers an insightful reading of this in Paulitino, Elvira. <u>Toward a Native American Critical Theory.</u> 170 – 171.

[124] Vizenor discusses the *postindian* surveillance in each of these areas throughout <u>Mannifest Manners.</u>

[125] Phone interview with Susan Lobo 9 Feb 2009.

[126] Paulitino, Elvira. <u>Toward a Native American Critical Theory</u>. Nebraska: University of Nebraska Press, 2003.

[127] Pulitano, Elvia, Toward a Native American Critical Theory. Nebraska: University of Nebraska Press, 2003.

[128] A very good historical discussion of tribal ethnicity can be seen in Fixico 26 – 42, 43 – 68, 172 - 190 and Nagel 19 – 42.

[129] Pratt in Clifford, James. The Predicament of Culture; Twentiety-Century Ethnography, Literature, and Art. Cambridge/Massachusetts and London: Harvard University Press, 1988.

[130] The philosophy of signifyin' will be utilized more throughout this chapter and chapter 4 of this dissertation.

[131] Emphasis in the original.

[132] Buff 23 – 44, 147 – 163; Nagel 43 – 59; Fixico 56 – 58.

[133] Paniciolli's emphasis to the term "other".

[134] These terms will be discussed more in Chapter 4 of this dissertation.

[135] Gates, Henry Louis. The Signifying Monkey: A Theory of African-American Literary Criticism. New York: Oxford University Press, 1989.

[136] More information on Powwow culture and tradition can be found in; Browner, Tara. Heartbeat of the People – Music and Dance of the Northern Pow- wow. Urbana and Chicago: University of Illinois Press, 2002., Buff, Rachel. Immigration and the Political Economy of Home; West Indian Brooklyn and American Indian Minneapolis, 1945 – 1992. Berkley/Los Angeles/London: University of California Press: 2001., Ellis, Clyde. A Dancing People, Powwow Culture on the Southern Plains. Kansas: University of Kansas, 2003., Fixico, Donald L. The Urban Indian Experience in America. Albuquerque: University of New Mexico Press, 2000., Fletcher, Alice C. "The Relation of Indian Story and Song." Literature of the American Indians: Views and Interpretations. New York: Meridian Books, 1975: 235 - 239., Lassiter, Luke E. The Power of Kiowa Song. Tucson: The University of Arizona Press, 1998., Lawlor, Mary. Public Native America: Tribal Self-representations in casinos, museums, and powwows. New Brunswick/New Jersey/ London: Rutgers University Press, 2006., Lobo, Susan and Peters, Kurt, ed. American Indians And The Urban Experience. London/Oxford: Altamira Press, 2001., Nagel, Joane. "American Indian Ethnic Renewal: Politics and the Resurgence

of Identity." <u>American Nations: Encounters in Indian Country, 1850 to the Present.</u> New York/London: Routledge, 2001: 330 – 353., Nagel, Joane. <u>American Indian Ethnic Renewal – Red Power And The Resurgence Of Identity And Culture.</u> New York/Oxford: Oxford University Press, 1996/1997., Vander, Judith. <u>Song-Prints: The Musical Experience Of Five Shoshone</u>
<u>Women</u>. Urbana/Chicago: University of Illinois Press, 1996.

[137] "TRIBAL SHOUTS." *WOR,* 1994.

[138] A further discussion of signifyin' in this context will be addressed in Chapter 4.

[139] Moore, Trudy S. "How 'The Oprah Winfrey Show' helps people live better lives." <u>Jet</u> April 18, 1994.

[140] "To The Sell Outs." WOR, 1994.

[141] George, Nelson. <u>Hip Hop America.</u> New York: Penguin Books, 1998. and <u>The Death of Rhythm & Blues.</u> New York: Penguin Books, 1988.

[142] James Luna, "James Luna", exhibition catalogue. San Diego: Centro Cultural de la Raza Gallery, 1985.

[143] The use of signifyin' is consistent with the definition, given in the Introduction of this dissertation (11 – 12), by Dr. Henry Louis Gates, Jr. and Samuel Floyd.

[144] All selections in this chapter come from the recording <u>Are You Ready For W.O.R.?</u>, Arizona: Canyon Records, 1994.

[145] Chris LaMarr is noted as being the main creator of the lyrics for WOR. Though the other members of the group contribute their prose, it is LaMarr who often is the creator of the lyrics and text.

[146] Bhabha, Homi K. <u>The Location of Culture</u>. London/New York: Routledge, 1994.

[147] Each of these literary devices can contain many other subgroupings. For the purpose of this documentation, I have elected to illustrate some of the main literary devices and their usage by WOR. Additionally, Alliteration and Assonance are not regularly used literary techniques in the poetry of WOR. Therefore, these poetic devices will not be examined in the following analysis.

[148] See Appendix for the complete lyrics of *Red, White, and Blue.*

[149] The use of capitalizations, spellings and other poetic license will be consistent with how the text is presented by WOR. The line numbers of the text will follow in parenthesis.

[150] Chapter 1 and 2 state some of these legal precedents.

[151] This use of slang is like other Native Hip Hop artists at the time of this writing. Presently there appears to be a form of "Native Hip Hop Vernacular English" (NHHVE) being solidified throughout Indian Country with the assistance of urban/reservation Native intercultural connections and the influence of popular culture, namely Hip Hop. The scholarship of Geneva Smitherman in her socio-linguistic work on Black English as well as the current work of H. Samy Alim investigates these developments and their cultural usage.

[152] The italics to the word "cuz" are added for emphasis.

[153] Other words like, Skinz and Redz also make use of this culturally infused Native literary device. Likewise, where Smitherman notes the "r-lessness" (273 – 274) in African-American Language (AAL), there appears to be the formation of an "z-addition" in Native American Language (NAL) or Native Vernacular English (NVE). Future research into Native linguistics will investigate this hyper-potential and perspective of the letter "z".

[154] Harris, Robert A. <u>Handbook of Rhetorical Devices</u>, VirtualSalt. 11 Oct 2008.

[155] Italics retained from the original.

[156] Glocal and glocalization are defined in Chapter 2.

[157] WithOut Rezervation. <u>Are You Ready For W.O.R.?</u>. Arizona, Canyon Records, 1994.

[158] See Appendix for the complete lyrics of *Born at 18*.

[159] The bracketed numbers here refer to the larger outline of sections that the text represents: 1. Militant/Political/Social views, 2. Despair/Demise/Defeat 3. Optimism/Hope/Empowerment. These sections are each marked by the appropriate number at the beginning and end of each section. The parenthetical numbers refer to smaller sub-sections within the larger sections. The use of the triple-asterisk (***) at the end of a line represents the cadence point of that particular phrase.

[160] A further analysis of the MC names in the section on Sermonizing will come later in this chapter.

[161] Berlo offers a discussion of these different styles of mask/masking techniques that lends itself metaphorically to this discussion. See Berlo 57 – 60.

[162] A much more detailed discussion of the sample will follow later in this chapter.

[163] Further examples of the micro-macro level of development within "Born at 18" will be seen in later portions of this Chapter.

[164] Nagel 335 – 337.

[165] Spencer uses first cites the term "kratophany" used by Mircea Eliade (Spencer: 226) and then associates this with the term "theophany" established by William C. Turner Jr. "The Musicality of Black preaching: A Phenomenology." <u>The Journal of Black Sacred Music</u> 2.1 (Spring 1988), 27 (Spencer 226).

[166] Grandmaster Flash & Furious Five, *The Message*, Sugar Hill Records, 1982.

[167] Future research will serve to discuss the extension, taking/borrowing or giving of a DJ/MC name and the cross-cultural relationship which this process has in 'naming ceremonies' for the different Native communities.

[168] See above discussion of Onomatopoeia.

[169] It is not stated who the Native is with regards to the criminal justice system. In keeping the Native view gender neutral WOR can bridge across a potential gender divide that has already historical worked to separate Native men and women not only from each other but from their culture as well.

[170] All the present and past members of WOR have openly discussed their Tribal affiliations in numerous fashions: interviews, promotions, record covers, etc.

[171] The use of italics and the lower case "i" here is consistent with the application as noted by Vizenor which represents a controlled simulation of Native identity that is subject to and exists within the realm of colonial demands and functionality.

[172] Line 52 from *Born at 18*.

[173] Qtd. in Paulitino, Elvira. <u>Toward a Native American Critical Theory</u>. Nebraska: University of Nebraska Press, 2003: 111.

[174] ibid.

[175] See Appendix. This image may not be available due to the limited reproduction of this initial recording.

[176] Greg Sarris discusses the concept of "Home" and "Autobiography" in Pulitano 122 – 123.

[177] Introduction to *Born at 18*.

[178] A detailed discussion of the Gourd Dance can be found in Lassiter, Luke E. The Power of Kiowa Song. Tuscon: University of Arizona Press, 1998., Ellis, Clyde. A Dancing People, Powwow Culture on the Southern Plains. Kansas: University of Kansas, 2003., Howard, James H. "The Plains Gourd Dance as a Revitalization Movement". American Ethnologist 3.2 (May 1976): 243-259. and Ellis, Clyde. "'We Don't Want Your Rations, We Want This Dance': The Changing Use of Song and Dance on the Southern Plains."
The Western Historical Quarterly 30.2 (Summer, 1999):133-154.

[179] ibid.

[180] Virginia Giglio notes the changes in the Gourd Dance c. 1918, reflecting traditional ceremonial expressions of a veteran's return home from war that included body painting, dancing, socializing and songs. Giglio notes the attention given to the use of red (Giglio 12 – 13).

[181] Berlo 36 – 63.

[182] Scholder, Fritz. Indian Kitsch, The Use and Misuse of Indian Images. Arizona: Northland Press/ The Heard Museum, 1979.

[183] A further discussion of Vizenor's "indian" can be found in Chapter 3.

[184] Introduction to *Born at 18*.

[185] This was discussed at length with Susan Lobo in a personal phone interview 9 Feb 2009.

[186] Alim conducted numerous interviews while constructing his definition of flow.

[187] Rose illustrates how the balance of flow/rupture function together within each of the three classic modes of Hip Hop culture; rap/mc-ing, breakdancing, grafitti (Rose 40 – 61).

[188] WithOut Rezervation. "Skin I'm In". Are You Ready For W.O.R.?, Arizona:Canyon Records, 1994.

[189] The Nativist ideology and its relationship to identity construction is discussed in Chapter 3.

[190] Throughout the numerous email and phone conversations I conducted with Chris LaMarr it became quite evident how aware he and the other members of WOR are to these issues and the national impact which these will have upon Native people. Not only was LaMarr aware of the current cultural and political temperature of Indian Country, but he would also deposit insights and suggest resolutions to the various perplexing situations facing contemporary Native people.

[191] During the interview sessions, LaMarr was always quite cognizant of the impact and importance of the female Native community within his works. We discussed the representation of Native females within popular culture, paying close attention to the images within Hip Hop culture, and why it was that WOR elected to present this work that speaks directly about family issues within the Native community. The layers continued to abound as this selection speaks to/talks back to the stereotypes of the "absent father", young women raising children, and the repeated context and signifier that *Born at 18* has come to represent and re-present for multiple generations of Native people.

[192] Indian Country as a term refers historically to the areas West of the Mississippi River, specifically Oklahoma, where Native people were forced to migrate after 1835 during the adoption and passing of the Indian Removal Act. The phrase "Indian Country' has remained and been reappropriated and transposed by Native people in reference to the multiple conditions (health, welfare, economics, education, et al.) and physical landscape of the U.S.

[193] WithOut Rezervation. *Are You Ready For W.O.R.?*. Arizona, Canyon Records, 1994.

[194] The theoretical concepts of sample/sampling can be viewed in a similar light with regards to all the Six Elements within Hip Hop culture. This discussion intends to not focus on the production or artistry of these techniques, but rather how they are visible within the works of WOR. For other similar discussions about sample/sampling see Schloss 20 - 80, Rose 62 - 99, Keyes 122 - 157 and The Art of Hip Hop Sampling sponsored by Duke University; http://www.youtube.com/watch?v=YLg5qwfhHnA reviewed 1 Feb. 2009.

[195] The term glocal is defined in Chapter 2.

[196] This same point has been articulated by other scholars before LaMarr including; Browner, Tara. Heartbeat of the People – Music and Dance of the Northern Pow-wow. Urbana and Chicago: University of Illinois Press, 2002., Ellis, Clyde. A Dancing People, Powwow Culture on the Southern Plains. Kansas: University of Kansas, 2003., Buff 147 – 170, Fixico 56 – 57, Fixico156 – 157, Nagel 48 – 54, Weibel-Orlando 95 – 114.

[197] Androutsopoulos' three spheres of influence were presented earlier in this chapter (178).

[198] The original Appendix C contained a rhythmic outline of this bass groove. This example has been removed from this updated version.

[199] The placement of the female powwow singers may have a close association to Cheyenne "wolf songs" that later were called "war journey songs" (Giglio 12 – 13). These songs would be the first songs, sung by women, that male veterans would hear upon their return from war. In the modern powwow, these songs have been collected into the category of "veteran's songs."

[200] See Appendix B that contains the selection *Born at 18*.

[201] WOR. "Born at 18." Are You Ready For W.O.R.? Arizona, Canyon Records, 1994.

[202] Qtd. from @149st on-line interview with Ernie Paniccioli (http://www.at149st.com/ernie.html reviewed 4 Jan. 2009)

[203] Deyhle, Donna. "" Break Dancing and Breaking out: Anglos, Utes, and Navajos in a Border Reservation High School." Anthropology & Education Quarterly 17.2 (Jun 1986): 111-127. This article was found after hours of searching various scholarly databases seeking articles focusing on Native Hip Hop. Other non-scholarly articles are much easier to find, but may not be reliable. The earliest book which contained an article about Cree Hip Hop from Canada is Krims, Adam. Rap music and the poetics of identity. UK: Cambridge University Press, 2000.

[204] Toure qtd in Shapiro, Michael J. Methods and Nations, Cultural Governance and the Indigenous Subject. New York and London: Routledge. 2004. (96) and Alim, H. Samy. Roc the Mic Right, The Language of Hip Hop Culture. New York and London:Routledge. 2006.

[205] Alim 12

[206] Paniccioli, Ernie. "A New Enemy." Moore, MariJo, ed. <u>Genocide of the Mind: New Native American Writing.</u> New York: Thunder's Mouth Press/Nation Books, 2003.

[207] Paniccioli in <u>Sovereign Bones</u> 252 – 253.

www.ingramcontent.com/pod-product-compliance
Lightning Source LLC
Chambersburg PA
CBHW070748160726
48004CB00001B/104